SUTTON-WOODS DEBATE

May 29–June 1, 1962

Peoria, Illinois

Carrol Ray Sutton

&

Guy N. Woods

SUTTON-WOODS DEBATE

ISBN: 0-9728625-1-X

Published
By

Thrasher Publications
1705 Sandra Street SW
Decatur, AL 35601-5457

Table of Contents

Foreword

Debates on various aspects of "institutionalism" were conducted between brethren numerous times from 1953 through 1972, but only occasionally in subsequent years. Most frequently, the propositions addressed the issues of congregational contributions to institutional "orphan homes," "sponsoring churches" in evangelism, and who may be the recipients of church benevolence. Brethren Guy N. Woods and Carrol R. Sutton each participated in several of these public discussions. This volume contains the complete text of the Sutton-Woods debate held in the building of the Paris Avenue church of Christ in Peoria, Illinois for four evening sessions (May 29, 30, 31, June 1, 1962).

The proposition for the first two nights was: "It is in harmony with the scriptures for churches of Christ to build and maintain benevolent organizations such as the Tennessee Orphan Home, Boles Homes, Home for the Aged, and other such organizations for the care of the needy." Guy N. Woods affirmed, and Carrol R. Sutton denied.

The proposition for the last two nights was: "It is not in harmony with the scriptures for churches of Christ to build and maintain benevolent organizations such as the Tennessee Orphan Home, Boles Home, Home for the Aged, and other such organizations for the care of the needy." Carrol R. Sutton affirmed, and Guy N. Woods denied.

W. L. Totty served as moderator for brother Woods, and Alvin Holt served in that capacity for brother Sutton. Because of numerous interruptions during brother Sutton's speeches, the reader will note several exchanges that involved the moderators and the debaters. These interruptions were unfortunate in that they probably distracted the audience from the speeches of brother Sutton. To preserve as much as possible the oral presentations as they were originally delivered, this book records the words just as they were transcribed. Although it is common for the speeches of an oral debate to be edited to make reading smoother, that has not been done in this case in the interest of accurately reporting what occurred. Each reader is urged to study carefully what the speakers said, comparing each claim with what the word of God declares. The issues discussed in the debate continue to be a source of division among God's people. The hope is that offering this debate for honest consideration by all will help to resolve the issues by leading brethren back to scriptural practices from which many have departed.

"And ye shall know the truth, and the truth shall make you free" (John 8:32).

—Thomas N. Thrasher

Guy N. Woods

Carrol Ray Sutton

Biographical Sketch of Guy N. Woods

Guy Napoleon Woods was born September 26, 1908, in Vardeman, Mississippi, the oldest of three children born to George Emmett and Eula Estelle Stokes Woods. He was baptized by J.W. Grant on August 24, 1926, and the following month he preached his first sermon at Holladay, Tennessee. He attended Freed-Hardeman College in Henderson, Tennessee, and was later admitted to the bar, although he never practiced law.

Through the years Woods preached for several congregations on a regular basis; however, beginning in 1945 he devoted himself to gospel meeting work throughout the country. By the early 1950s Woods had participated in more than 100 formal debates. Among those published in book form were the *Woods-Nunnery Debate* (1946), *Woods-Porter Debate* (1956), *Griffin-Woods Debate* (1957), *Woods-Cogdill Debate* (1957), *Woods-Franklin Debate* (1974), *Britnell-Woods Debate* (1977), and *Indwelling of the Holy Spirit: A Debate between Guy N. Woods and Given O. Blakely* (1985). The Sutton-Woods Debate was Woods' eighth formal debate on issues of institutionalism.

Besides his published debates, brother Woods was the author of many other books, including *John*; *James*; *First and Second Peter, First, Second and Third John, Jude*; *How To Read The Greek New Testament*; *How To Study The New Testament Effectively*; *Shall We Know One Another In Heaven?*; *Questions and Answers Open Forum*; and *Questions and Answers Open Forum Volume II* He was a staff writer, and later editor, of the *Gospel Advocate*.

Guy N. Woods passed away in Nashville, Tennessee, on December 8, 1993, and his body is buried in Holladay, Tennessee.

Biographical Sketch of Carrol Ray Sutton

Carrol Ray Sutton was born on April 13, 1932 to Thomas and Irene Sutton in Limestone County, Alabama. He was one of six children (four brothers and one sister). At age 19 he married Mamie Cook, his loving companion for 65 years. They had five children, 18 grandchildren, and several great grandchildren, whom they adored.

Brother Sutton dedicated his life to preaching the gospel of Christ. He preached his first sermon at the age of 14 and the last at the age of 84, two days before his tragic death in an automobile accident near Winchester, Tennessee. During his 70 years of preaching, he worked full-time with local churches in Tennessee, Kentucky, Illinois, and Alabama. He spent the last 53 years laboring with the East Albertville church of Christ in Albertville, Alabama, with which he also served as an elder from 1991 until his death on December 20, 2016.

Brother Sutton preached regularly on the radio in Albertville and frequently in gospel meetings in several states. He held at least 34 formal debates on various religious topics. He was valiant for the truth, yet he strove to be fair, compassionate, charitable, and amiable even with those who disagreed.

For 53 years he edited *The Instructor*, a monthly bulletin of the East Albertville church, covering a wide array of Bible topics. He is the author of several tracts. His book, ***Must We Keep the Sabbath Today?***, is a thorough exposure of Sabbatarian error.

Carrol Sutton lived to glorify God, and to that end his life touched numerous lives. Many were forever changed through the gospel that he shared so boldly.

First Session

May 29, 1962
7:30 p.m.

W. L. Totty's Preliminary Remarks

Ladies and gentlemen:

We appreciate the opportunity that is afforded us this evening to discuss these propositions before you people. We commend the brethren of this city for the open-minded attitude that they have in order that these things may be discussed. There isn't anything that brings the truth to the attention of the people any more than a discussion, whether it be religious matters or otherwise and so, again this evening, we are glad that this opportunity has been afforded. I shall read now the proposition that is to be affirmed by brother Guy N. Woods and also the arrangement or the rules to govern the debate. The proposition reads as follows:

"It is in harmony with the scriptures for churches of Christ to build and maintain benevolent organizations such as the Tennessee Orphan Home, Boles Homes, Home for the Aged, and other such organizations for the care of the needy." Brother Guy N. Woods will affirm, and brother Carrol R. Sutton will deny that.

The rules for this debate, or the rules to govern it, are: 1. The discussion shall be conducted at a time and place acceptable to all parties participating. Rule 2. It shall continue for four evenings. The speakers shall divide time equally and each shall make three 20-minute speeches each evening. 3. Each speaker shall be permitted to submit five written questions to his opponent and the answers shall be in writing. The questions shall be submitted early enough for the answers to be written before the session begins each evening. I would like to repeat that the questions shall be submitted early enough for the answers to be written before the sessions begins each evening. Each speaker may submit five questions each evening of the debate. 4. The speakers agree to conduct themselves as Christians. That's signed by Carrol R. Sutton and Guy N. Woods.

Would you like to have something to say, brother Holt? At this time, it gives me great pleasure to introduce to you brother Guy N. Woods, who will affirm this proposition.

Guy N. Woods' First Affirmative Speech

Brethren moderators, brother Sutton, and ladies and gentlemen:

It is a matter of regret to me that there is such an occasion as this necessary, but in light of the fact that such does exist, I am glad that I am here. If I know my heart, I have no other purpose in mind in coming to these parts save to defend what I believe the Bible teaches. I have been preaching for more than a quarter of a century, and I have engaged in many religious discussions. My sole purpose is, and has always been, to defend the truth as I conceive it to be set out upon the sacred page of God's Word, and such is our aim and our design on this occasion.

It is proper for me, as the affirmant in this discussion tonight, to define briefly the terms of the proposition, and yet I regard this as largely a formality in view of the fact that the terms are simple and the issue very clear. "It is in harmony with the scriptures for churches of Christ to build and maintain benevolent organizations such as the Tennessee Orphan Home, Boles Home, Home for the Aged, and other such organizations for the care of the needy." By 'in harmony with the scriptures,' I mean, of course, according to the Bible. By 'churches of Christ,' I mean congregations of the Lord's people. 'To build and maintain,' to support and establish and to cause to operate. That does not mean, of course, that the church itself literally and actually builds. The church builds a meeting house, but it sometimes uses an

10

organization, an incorporation. We'd say that the church does it. Yet notwithstanding the fact that the church builds it, it simply supplies the money and it's done by an organization. By 'benevolent organizations,' we mean, of course, organizations that are benevolent in character. The word 'benevolent' means *good*. And so, a benevolent organization is a good organization, and they're specified in the proposition, "such as The Tennessee Orphan Home, Boles Home, Home for the Aged, and other such organizations for the care of the needy."

I would like to say in the outset, and before I offer my affirmative proof, that I believe that the church is an all-sufficient organization to accomplish every work that God gave to it; matters that the church cannot delegate its authority or its work to any other organization, either human or divine; that the church must perform its functions that God ordained, and that it cannot designate any other organization to perform such. We're not here to impeach God's wisdom with reference to the design characteristic of His organizations. But we also believe in the all-sufficiency of the family. That it's just as wrong for the church to usurp the functions of the family as it is for the family to usurp the functions of the church.

I need not remind you, if you have even a smattering knowledge of the teaching of the Bible, that there are three organizations existing by divine right. I will designate them as follows: the first is the family. It is indeed the oldest of all God's organizations. I have not the least idea that brother Sutton will allege that the family is a human institution as opposed to the divine. There is a second institution that's almost as old as the family and that's the State. It is necessary in any civilized land to have civil government, and the Bible so ordains it. Romans chapter 13 sets out in detail that fact. Then there's also the divine organization, the church, and it, too, is an institution existing by divine right. That's the youngest of the three. It is itself 2,000 years old. Its establishment will be found in Acts the second chapter. God ordained the family and founded it Himself. That's a matter which is found in the earlier chapters of the book of Genesis. Now, we believe that these institutions exist by divine right, that one cannot usurp the functions of the other, that it's wrong so to do. Get this please. The Catholics teach that when the State breaks down that the church can take over and operate in the realm of the State as the church organization. That's the union of church and State. That's the Catholic doctrine of supreme domination over the State. We oppose that because we believe that that's making the State subservient to the church in those realms where God ordained that the State should perform its peculiar functions. We think that the State has duties that the church must not perform, just as the church has duties that the State must not perform. Hitler sought to reverse the order. Hitler attempted to take over the church—that is, what he called the church, at least religious activity, and operate it as part of the State, thus making the church subservient to the State. We're against that. We say, 'Let the church be the church; let the State be the State.' Tonight, brother Sutton will stand before you in the unenviable position of advocating, in principle, a doctrine that is as dangerous and as foreign to the truth as that of the union of church and State or State and church. For he'll tell you that when the family breaks down that the church may take over and operate this family as a part of the church organization. I deny that. I say that's dangerous doctrine. I say that that's as dangerous, in principle, as the Catholic doctrine of church and State united, or the doctrine of Hitlerism that the State can take over the church. But if the position that brother Sutton tonight holds is correct, if this divine institution, when it fails, can be taken over by the church, then why gag at the idea of the church taking over the State and operating it? If I accepted his position, I'd not stumble at the other. I say they're both wrong. Let the church be the church; let the State be the State; let the family be the family. Now, that, friends, will suggest to you the distinction that we hold tonight.

Now, let's look at it a little closer. Every child, when it comes into the world, has or is entitled to have and be a part of a family. Sometimes that family falls into need. And when such is the case, it's proper and right that the church should come to its assistance. For example, if the family needs food, then that which the family lacks is supplied, supplied by the church, but it still remains a family relationship. Just because the church makes a donation to the family doesn't mean that the family becomes a part of the church. It's still a family. It's simply receiving assistance from the church. It's still a divine institution existing by right and supported by the church. I'm not

12

going to allow brother Sutton to quibble over whether the contribution is to the family organization. Let it be to the members of the family, that's alright with me. That's what it is actually. It still remains, that one organization, the church, is making a donation to members of another organization, the family, and this family administers these funds.

For example, in Acts 6 we have an account of the daily ministration. Funds raised by the church, turned over to the Seven, who administered these funds for the needy. But now, get it, friends. They didn't turn that money over to a Board to operate as a part of the church. They gave the money to the family and the family spent it. There's one institution, the church, coming to the aid of another, the family. One organization helping another. Now, sometimes instead of food or, in addition to food, it's clothing, and it's shelter, and in the case of children, it's discipline and supervision, and so on. But the church doesn't take over and operate in the realm of the family. It can't. It mustn't. The very idea. I'm talking about elders, as elders, running two divine institutions. Elders over a family? Might as well put parents over a church or civil servants over a church or elders over the State. All of those ideas are wrong.

What is the church? It's a spiritual institution. What's the State? It's a civil institution. What's the family? It's a domestic institution. Each one has its own respective sphere and operates in it. Now, then, sometimes, through no fault of the children who are members of the family, that family becomes dissolved. There may be many reasons why that happens: death on the part of the parents, desertion, divorce, delinquency. There are many reasons, and the child is without a family relationship. Then it happens. Sometimes they're people, with sufficient of the milk of human kindness in their veins, who decide to restore the family relationship and provide these children, who lost their family relationship, another. If the church had an obligation to the family when it was together, it has an obligation when that relationship is restored. But it had an obligation here; therefore, it has one here. If a child had a right to this relationship to begin life with, it has a right to that relationship to end life with or to end his childhood with. What then are we defending tonight? The right of the child to have a family relationship. He'll tell you that that is a benevolent society. There'll not be a word of truth in it. He'll shout it long and loud that I'm defending a benevolent society just like the missionary society. There won't be a word of truth in it. He'll use the expression "benevolent society" repeatedly for the purpose of trying to create prejudice on your part just like a Baptist preacher, when I meet one, calls me a Campbellite. There won't be any more truth in one than there will be in the other. You remember that now.

What I'm defending here is a family relationship. That's my position tonight. Now, let's see if the church sustains an obligation to it. He doesn't think it does. I'm willing to point this out to you in my very first speech. If there should be a tornado rip through Peoria, and there were a thousand dollars in the treasury of this congregation and every home in the congregation, every group in the congregation, suffered damage and your property destroyed, your food, your clothing gone, this man would not agree for you to take one penny out of the church treasury for the purpose of feeding your children. Now, I charge that. I just challenge him to deny it. Not one penny would he take, allow to be taken, out of the church treasury. He'll feed himself with the money from the treasury. He'll feed his own children from the treasury, but he won't let you feed yours. Now, that's either so or it's not. One or the other. I'm telling the truth or I'm not. One or the other. It's up to Sutton to tell us whether I'm telling the truth or not about it. I want you people to get the truth. He's misrepresented it enough through this section of country. We intend for you to know the truth by the time this debate's over. Now, let's see if the church does have an obligation.

Now, brother Sutton, I would suggest to you, listen to what I have to say if you intend to answer these matters. May I suggest you do that? This debate's been pending a long time. You've had a lot of time to make preparation. Just listen to what I'm saying, 'cause I expect you to answer it.

Now, let's see if the church has an obligation. We read in James the first chapter and verse 27 that "Pure religion and undefiled before God and the Father is this, to visit the fatherless and widows in their affliction, and to keep oneself unspotted from the world." That sets out an obligation to somebody to care for two classes: 'the fatherless and the widows.' Incidentally, those terms are plural. "Fatherless" in the Greek is plural; and "widows," even both Greek and English, the word is in plural form. Now, somebody is expected to perform those duties. James 1:27 sets out that obligation. That says what is to be done. What is it? 'Visit the fatherless and the widows.' Now, turn with me to first Timothy chapter five [TOTTY: Three minutes.] and verse 16 (Thank you.), where Paul sets out the duty of the daughter to provide for her mother, "that the church be not charged." Now, if that were all, if the Bible said no more than that, then let me call your attention to this fact that would indicate that the church is not obligated. But that's not all it says. It goes on to say, "that it." The antecedent of "it," is the church. "That *it*" may care for them that are widows indeed. "*It*," what? The church. The church may do what? May care for the widows. But get it now. The same passage of scripture that designates "widows," designates "fatherless."

Now, the next question is: Where is the church to do that? Turn with me to Psalms 68, verses five and six. This is the crowning part to my argument in this first speech. God is the "father of the fatherless and a judge of widows." Now, get the next statement. "God putteth the solitary in families." In what? What are we defending? Families. God puts the solitary in *families*. That's what I've been saying all along. Now, God doesn't pick them up by miracle and set them down there, but God does it! Now, how does He do it? Does it through His people. Who are His people? The church. Where does the church put them? Puts them in families! But you've got to adhere to the law. For example, in the state of Kentucky, you've got to have seven men, at least seven men, one of which is or has been the president of a PTA, another is a doctor, another a lawyer, to serve as a group of foster parents for these people in this family.

Now, what have we seen? We've seen the difference between the family, the State, and the church. We've seen the obligation of each. We've seen the church's duty in that obligation. We've seen where the needy is to be put. In families! We've seen that they're to be supported there. We've seen that the church is one thing and the family another. He can just shout long and loud about a Benevolent Society and an

15

organization parallel to the Missionary Society and so on, but while he's doing that, you just remember that we've established: Number 1. The distinction between the church and the family, and the obligation of the church to the family. I thank you.

Carrol R. Sutton's First Negative Speech

Gentlemen moderators, brother Woods, ladies and gentlemen:

I'm glad to appear before you for this speech of the evening, my part in this discussion, and the very fact that you're here shows that you're interested in these matters being discussed. Now, certainly when such interest is manifested, as you're manifesting here tonight by your presence, that shows that we ought to engage in such discussions as these. The fact that brethren have been and are being alienated and churches have been and are being divided over these matters are sufficient evidence of the fact that we need to give a very serious and fearful study to these issues. And certainly tonight, brother Woods and I have a very fearful responsibility upon us as we discuss these matters. Now, if I know my heart tonight, I'm here in the interest of truth and that alone. Truth is important. Our Lord said on one occasion in John 8 and verse 32: "And ye shall know the truth, and the truth shall make you free." In John 18 and verse 38, Pilate asked Jesus saying, "What is truth?" On another occasion in John 17:17 Jesus said, "Sanctify them through thy truth: thy word is truth."

Now, I'm not here tonight to please any man or group of men. Now, I'm not here to defend any paper, school, or human institution. I'm not here to defend the practice of those who claim to be Christians. If I know my heart, I'm not here to win a personal victory over brother Woods, but I'm here that I might win a victory for truth, that you might see truth in contrast with error. I'm here to please God who made us, Galatians 1 and verse 10. I'm here to defend a divine organization, the church of Jesus Christ, as being all-sufficient in organization to do all the work that God requires of His people in an

16

organized capacity. I'm here to oppose human organizations such as Tennessee Orphan Home, Boles Home, Childhaven, etc., being set up to do the work of the church. I'm here to defend and "contend for the faith which was once delivered unto the saints," Jude 3.

Now, let us read the proposition that brother Woods is supposed to be affirming. "It is in harmony with the scriptures for churches of Christ to build and maintain benevolent organizations such as the Tennessee Orphan Home, Boles Home, Home for the Aged, and other such organizations for the care of the needy."

Now, before considering the arguments that brother Woods has offered in defense of the proposition, let's consider just a few things that I believe will help us clarify the issue that we're discussing. Now, back in the 1800's when the question and the problem of the missionary societies arose among the people of God, there were many who failed to understand the truth involved because they did not know what the issue or question of difference really was. The issue back then was not: Should the gospel of Jesus Christ be preached? It was not: Is the church obligated to preach the gospel? It was not: Could a place be maintained for gospel preaching? It was not a matter of systematic arrangement. It was not a matter of how, with respect to means, modes, or methods. The issue back then was: Could churches of Christ scripturally build and maintain missionary societies through which to do their work of evangelism?

The issue tonight is not: Should the needy be cared for? Brother Woods and I agree that the needy ought to be cared for. It's not a matter: Is the church obligated to care for those whom God has charged it with? We believe that. It's not a question of whether or not a home can be maintained in which the needy are cared for. It's not a matter of systematic arrangement. It's not a question of how with respect to means, modes, or methods. But our issue of difference tonight is … now, I keep this before you, God being my helper tonight: Can churches of Christ, according to the scriptures, build and maintain—not families, as brother Woods has tried to leave the impression—but as he signed his name to the proposition, can churches of Christ build and maintain benevolent organizations such as those that are mentioned in the proposition, that they in turn might do works of benevolence? Now, since brother Woods is affirming that it is in harmony with the scriptures, then he is obligated to show authority from the scriptures. Now, you've listened for 20 minutes tonight, brethren, neighbors, and friends, but you haven't heard one passage of scripture given or one cited that remotely refers in any form, shape, or fashion to benevolent organizations such as those mentioned in the proposition that he signed his name to affirm. Brother Woods, I want the scripture for it. I'm not asking for a scripture for the family. I'm not asking for a scripture for the church. I want a scripture that you cite to show that the scriptures teach that churches of Christ may build and maintain benevolent organizations. Now, if you didn't intend to show the scripture that it's in harmony with the scriptures to so do, you ought not to have signed the proposition. Brethren, neighbors, and friends, you keep this point in mind. He talked for 20 minutes, but he did not cite one passage of scripture that even refers in any way, shape, form, or fashion to a benevolent organization such as Boles Orphan Home, Tennessee Orphan Home, etc., which are caring for the needy. Brother Woods, I'm asking for the scripture that justifies the benevolent organizations.

Now, brother Woods had quite a bit to say about what he meant by 'build and maintain.' He simply meant, he said, to support and establish or, of course, to establish and support. He said, "Now, the church doesn't actually build these things." So, brother Woods, you don't believe churches may establish them, do you? Brother Woods does not believe that churches can establish these things. He believes that all the church can do is simply send funds to them after they are established. Is that right, brother Woods? Now, his proposition says, 'build and maintain.' That means to establish and support. Two things involved in it. Brother Woods, you signed your name to affirm that churches 'may build and maintain' these benevolent organizations, and yet he turned around and said, before he was through, that churches supply the money and then something else over here spends the money. Brother Woods, that hasn't shown anything about building benevolent organizations. That's what your proposition says. I intend to hold you to it, too, the Lord willing.

And then he said, "Now, the church builds a church building, but it doesn't mean it actually builds it, but it supplies the money for the building of it." That's right, brother Woods, but it not only supplies the money for the building of it, but it has oversight of it, too, doesn't it? Does the church have oversight of the establishing or building of these benevolent organizations, brother Woods? See if he answers.

And then he said, "The church is all-sufficient to do its work." He says, "We believe in the sufficiency of the church, but we likewise believe in the sufficiency of the family." And before he got through, we found out what he meant by 'sufficiency.' He believes that the church is sufficient to raise money and then donate money, and then the family is sufficient to spend it. Isn't that right, brother Woods? Isn't that your conception of the matter? Now, isn't that some 'sufficiency'? He believes the church is sufficient to send the money and the family is sufficient to spend it. That doesn't take much efficiency or sufficiency to spend it, does it, brother Woods? Now, that is exactly what he's contending for. That's his argument.

And then we notice also that if the church and the family is sufficient like brother Woods said, then why on earth, friends, did brother Woods sign the proposition that says churches 'may build and maintain benevolent organizations'? Brother Woods, if you believe in the sufficiency of the family, why are you defending benevolent organizations? Have you thought about that, friends? He says the church is sufficient and the family is sufficient. But, friends, he has a benevolent organization in his proposition that he's defending. And incidentally, brother Woods, is that benevolent organization a family? What about that Board of Directors, nine men, for example, in different parts of the state. Do they serve as a family? Now, brother Woods knows better than that. He knows this Board of Directors, this benevolent organization, is not a family and yet he says he's defending the family. Well, you signed your name to defend a proposition that says that churches 'may build and maintain benevolent organizations.' He thinks I'm opposing the family. That's far from it, brother Woods. I believe in the family. I believe in the State as God ordained. I believe in the church as God set it up. But where is the scripture for this benevolent organization that his proposition says? Things are rather amusing sometimes, aren't they?

And he says there are three organizations existing by divine right: the family, the State, he says, and the church. Well, where's your benevolent organization, brother Woods? That's what your proposition says.

And then he had quite a bit to say about when the State breaks down. He says, "The Catholics say the church can take over, and brother Sutton believes that when the family breaks down, that the church can take over. And he's just as bad as the Catholics." Well, brother Woods, if I did believe that, that still wouldn't have anything to do with benevolent organizations, would it? That's what you're defending. He's defending benevolent organizations that's neither family, it's not the State, and it's not a church. He says, "Mention that!" I have, brother Woods. Now, where's your benevolent organization up here? What brother Woods believes is that the church, when the family breaks down, may build and maintain a benevolent organization here. That in turn, this benevolent organization can restore the family. That's what he believes. He doesn't believe that God's divine organization can do it, but a human organization can restore that thing when it breaks down. Brother Woods, do you believe that when the State breaks down, the church can build and maintain an organization to restore the State? If not, why not? That's your position. Now, when the State breaks down, why don't you take the Catholic position as you do in the case of the family? Why don't you build and maintain an organization here that in turn might restore the State? And he talks about somebody else trying to confuse the church and the State, and the church and the home, or the family, as he said, rather.

We notice also that brother Woods says if a family needs food, the church supplies the food. Brother Woods doesn't believe that the church can actually supply the food, because he went on to say the church simply sends money to the family and then let the family, in turn, spend the money for food. Suppose they buy liquor with it, brother Woods? Has the church fulfilled its obligation? It sent the money. If it has no control over that, that's the work of the home or the family, as he says, to spend the money, can they spend it like they want to? If not, why not, if that's their work? And incidentally, brother Woods believes also, if he hasn't changed, that the church may

20

dispense food, not only supply money. But, brother Woods, can the church dispense food as those Seven did in Acts 6:1-6 to those widows in the daily ministration?

And then he's had quite a bit to say about Acts 6:1-6; that the Seven gave money to the family, and the family spent it. Brother Woods, where in the text do you find that? Where do you find anything about, in Acts 6, the spending of money by the Seven? The sending of the money by the Seven and the family spending the money? That simply says they "served tables" and there's a lot of difference in serving tables and simply sending money. Brother Woods used to believe in 1946 that these Seven dispensed food. Do you now, believe that, brother Woods? You did in 1946, but now, he says all the church can do is simply send the money. Have you changed, brother Woods?

And then further he says that the church supports the family. Incidentally, where is the passage of scripture that shows that the church ever supported a family as an organization? I know the Bible shows the church helped needy saints. But where does the Bible show that the church sent to a needy family as a group or as an organization? That's what you're contending for. Show the passage of scripture for it.

And then brother Woods says, "Well, I'm defending a family relationship, not a benevolent society." The proposition says, and he affirms, that: "that it is in harmony with the scriptures for churches of Christ to build and maintain families?" No. "To build and maintain benevolent organizations such as Tennessee Orphan Home, Boles Home," and so forth.

And then, we might mention this, too. Let me ask you again, brother Woods: Does the Board of Directors serve as a family? That's what you're defending in the proposition. But now, where's the Board of Directors involved here in this thing that he says he believes is all-sufficient? If this thing's all-sufficient, brother Woods, the family is, why do you continue contending for a benevolent organization, then, that the church is to build and maintain that it in turn might restore the family. We're asking for the passage of scripture.

He says, "James 1:27 shows an obligation to the fatherless and widows, and then 1 Timothy 5:16 shows who's to do that. James 1:27

shows what's to be done and 1 Timothy 5:16 shows who's to do it." Brother Woods, James 1:27 says that "Pure religion and undefiled before God and the Father is this, To visit the fatherless and widows in their affliction, and to keep himself (or oneself) unspotted from the world." That shows what is to be done and who is to do it, doesn't it? "Oneself": *Individual* obligation, brother Woods.

And then 1 Timothy 5:16 shows that "it," the church, might "relieve them that are widows indeed." That shows obligation to relieve destitute widows and then shows who is to do that, the church. But he's defending a benevolent organization doing what God said for the church to do. I maintain that 1 Timothy 5:16 shows what is to be done and who's to do it. James 1:27 shows what is to be done and who's to do it. Brother Woods doesn't believe that. He doesn't believe James 1:27 and 1 Timothy 5:16, friends. That is, if what he said here were so.

And then we notice also that he said, "Psalm 68:5-6, and this is my main point," he said. He showed how that "God setteth the solitary in families." He said, "This is the main point of the evening." Did you really mean it, brother Woods? Did you really mean that was the main point of the evening? Yet friends, he stood up here and read the proposition that said that it's "scriptural for churches of Christ to build and maintain benevolent organizations." Then he turned right around and said that God puts the solitary in families. Brother Woods, why are you defending these benevolent organizations then, if God puts them in families? Why on earth, friends, would a man like brother Woods defend these benevolent organizations, churches building and maintaining benevolent organization, when God sets the solitary in families, not in benevolent organizations like he's defending? Brother Woods, do you really believe that passage? Is that your main point? Friends, all I'm doing this evening is following brother Woods; just showing that what he says doesn't prove his proposition. The last two evenings I'll show, beyond a shadow of a doubt, that it is not in harmony with the scriptures for these things to be built and maintained by churches of Christ.

Now, brother Woods, we want you to notice again Psalm 68:5-6. If God puts them in families, why do you try to put them in the institutional orphanages and the institutional homes for the aged? Isn't that strange, friends, that he'd put them somewhere that God doesn't put them, that God doesn't want them, but he wants them there anyway; yet says he believes what God says. That's the main point of the evening. That's my passage, brother Woods. That's exactly what I advocate. I advocate what God advocates. I believe that takes his speech up item by item and statement by statement. How much time? [HOLT: Three minutes.]

We want to notice just a little bit further; we have over here a chart that's entitled COMMANDS—GENERIC OR SPECIFIC. I have in one column the "Command," the next column "Generic" terms, and then another column "Specific" terms. *[NOTE: Charts are provided in the Appendix beginning on page 234. This chart may be found on page 237.]*

We notice in Genesis 6:14 that God gave the command to build the ark. God did not give a generic term: 'wood.' God gave a specific term: 'gopher wood.' And so, when God said, 'gopher wood,' that ruled out other kinds of wood. In 2 Kings 5, God's servant told Naaman to go wash seven times in Jordan. God did not simply have his servant say, 'in water,' but he said, 'in Jordan.' That meant 'in Jordan,' not some other body of water. In Leviticus 14, we notice that God said, "Offer a lamb." Had God simply said, 'Offer an animal,' any animal would have been sufficient. But God specified the lamb; ruling out all other kinds of animals. We notice in John 9, verse 7, that Jesus said, "Go wash in the pool of Siloam." That would rule out other bodies of water. We notice now, with respect to the work of the church, Ephesians 3:10 and 1 Thessalonians 1, showing how the church is to preach the gospel. It is to evangelize. Had God simply said, 'organizations,' friends, we could not rule out the missionary society, but God specified 'the church,' the local congregation being God's organization for his people to work in organized capacity. That rules out other organizations. The same thing is so with respect to edifying. In Ephesians 4, we notice that God says that "it," the church, might edify itself in love. Had God simply said 'organizations,' then an organization would have been sufficient. But God specified the church, that is, the local congregation, then, that's to do that, ruling out other organizations. In 1 Timothy 5:16 we notice that Paul says that "it," the church, might "relieve them that are widows indeed." Acts 6 shows how the church did relieve some widows. If God had simply said 'organizations,' then his benevolent organizations might have been alright, but God didn't say that. God specified the church, the congregation; therefore, that rules out his benevolent organization. There's no authority for them, friends. When God specifies a thing, others are eliminated. And so, we see that God specified the church in evangelism, the church in edification, and the church in benevolence. So, I'm defending the divine organization, the one God pitched and not men. Brother Woods is defending human organizations; those that men have pitched and not God. Thank you.

Guy N. Woods' Second Affirmative Speech

Brethren moderators, brother Sutton, and ladies and gentlemen:

We have here a splendid demonstration of the value of the debate. Brother Sutton is unhappy because he can't make the definitions. Now, I told you that I was defending the right of churches of Christ to support children in another organization, the family, besides the church. That is, that the church has a right so to do. But brother Sutton has so long shouted 'benevolent societies' that he wants to saddle off on me something that I do not believe, never did believe, and am not defending tonight. He said, "Why, if you're defending the right of the church to support families, why did you sign your name to a proposition that mentions benevolent organizations?" Because the word 'family' is a synonym for benevolent organizations. That's what I mean by benevolent organizations! Exactly! Now, that's it. I defined it to begin with. I knew he wouldn't like it. But he won't like it till he gets back on the truth. Now, he's so obsessed with the idea of some other organization, that he's unwilling for me to define my proposition. Brother Sutton, by 'benevolent organizations' I mean a legal family. I'm going to show you what that legal family has to be before we get through.

Now, he started off by calling attention to some passages, John 8:32 and 18:28 and 17:17, that mention the truth. Well, no issue there. That's what I'm up here to defend, the truth, for I told you that in the outset. He said he wasn't here to defend any paper or school. He was not here to gain a victory and so on. I'll tell you what he's here for. He's here to fight the work of one of God's divine institutions. That's what he's here for. I'm here for the purpose of defending all three of them! Not just two of them. He would repeatedly say to me, "Brother Woods, if they ought to be put in families, why do you insist on putting them in these other institutions?" Well, I wasn't the one who said they were to be put in families, the Bible says that. Does he question that? He says, "I think they ought to be put in families." Now, friends, I'm going to tell you, respectfully, that he doesn't believe anything of the kind. He doesn't believe anything of the kind, because he said that the church was all-sufficient to do everything that is expected of the Lord's people in organized capacity. Now, he must say that the family is disorganized or else his statement is not so; one or the other. Now, which is it? Right here's proof of it on his chart. Now, we may just dismiss this from here up because I believe that, and I was preaching that before he was dry behind the ears and have for many, many years. No need to bring in matters here that we all agree on.

Now, let's start right down here. The church is commanded to preach. The organization is the church and we agree that the church is the organization that God ordained to preach the gospel. But now, let me come down here to the matter of relieving. As far as edifying, we agree on that. But now, let's take this right here. The church is the only organization that can relieve. Alright then, the family can't do it, can they? If the church is the only one, the family can't do it unless the family's the church. Now, one of two things is true: either his statement here is wrong or else the family and the church are the same thing. I told you that's what he made out of them. He wants to turn a family into a church. Ladies and gentlemen, this position right here means that the church can't spend a dime or send a dime to a family relationship. I told you he believed that. What'd he say about it? He knew I could prove it. He knew I could put a tape on one of these machines and prove where he's made statements that are comparable to that. He knew that. He didn't deny it. It wasn't any use to. It wouldn't do him any good to deny it. I'd just prove it, that's all, so he just passed it by. Now, I'll tell you, candidly, I'd rather be among a bunch of heathens because they would feed me, and he wouldn't if I were a child. That is, he wouldn't let it come out of the church treasury. Now, brother Sutton, that's the truth of the business so you're here fighting the Lord's divine organization. The church may do all the work of the Lord's people in organized capacity. Alright then, the church can't donate a penny that is to be spent in a family. Now, brother Sutton, just write it down here and tell me: Can the church turn money over to the family and let the family spend it? Put it down there. Write it down there. You're not going to answer it! Write it down there. That's the issue here tonight, friends, and I want us to get on with it. That's the real issue. Can the church do it? I say that he teaches it can't. Oh, he said, "Now, we found out what the church can do. It can raise the money and the home can spend it." Said, "That's what he means by an all-sufficient home." Well now, he doesn't miss that very far. The church raises the money and he spends what the church gives him. He does the same thing. He's a preacher. Why can't the needy do the same thing?

Then he sends us to the 1800's. That hasn't a thing on earth to do with this; not one single, solitary thing for this reason. Back in that day the very men that fought the missionary society defended and supported the orphan homes. So, the men who were opposed to missionary societies saw a difference between the missionary society and the orphan home. The orphan home is as old, or older, than the missionary society, that is, as far as the restoration plea is concerned. So, there isn't any point in bringing that up. Now, I do remember, he went over it again, "The church is the only organization that can perform in an organized capacity—functions for the needy." Therefore, the family can't do it. Well, I answered him about the family.

He said here that according to my position that when the State breaks down, that if I teach that the church can restore the family relationship, why don't I teach that the church can restore the State relationship? Well now, brother Sutton's position is that when the family breaks down that it becomes a part of the church. I don't teach that. I teach that the church sustains an obligation to the State to pay taxes if the State asks it, but it can't take it over and operate it. The church sustains an obligation to the family to support it, but it can't take it over and operate it as a part of the church. What did he say about putting elders over a church's elders? What did he say about putting parents over the church's parents? What did he say about putting civil authorities over a home as civil authorities running the home? Not a thing. That's a silly and absurd position anyway. God never put elders over two divine institutions. Let the church be the church and the home and the family, the family. Let it be, brother Sutton.

Then of all things, he denied that the money, that money, was turned over to families in the case of the Seven. They took that fund that was laid at the apostles' feet and dispersed it to every man as he had need. Did what? They dispersed it. Dispersed what? The fund that was raised. And then he said, "Why according to you, why, they could even take the money and buy liquor with it. What's to keep them from doing that?" Well, not anything but when we found out that they were buying liquor with it, we'd quit sending money. That's what we'd do. Now, you get this, friends. He has taken the position that you can't send money even to a family because they might take it and buy liquor with it. If his argument has any merit at all, that's it. And anybody, what? He argues that because I say that the church can take money from its treasury and give it to a family, that therefore they might take it and buy liquor with it. Alright, according to him then you can't take money and give it to a family because they might buy liquor with it. Doesn't that follow? Of course, it does. Anybody that can see through a barrel with both ends knocked out could see that.

Now, he's taken a position the church can't give any money to a family. Oh yes, now, James 1:27. He said, "I'm going to show you that this has reference only to individuals because it says, 'let a man examine himself,' or in this particular instance, in this passage, in James 1:27: 'Pure religion and undefiled before God and the Father is this, To visit the fatherless and widows in their affliction and keep oneself," "oneself unspotted from the world.'" He said, "Now, that can't mean the church because it has reference to 'oneself.'" Alright, let's see a parallel. Over in 1 Corinthians chapter 11 where Paul makes mention of the Lord's institution of the supper, he said, "Let a man examine himself"—himself. "Let a man examine himself, and so let him eat of this bread and drink of this cup." Is that individual, exclusive individual action, brother Sutton? That's the Lord's supper. At least now, you'll agree that that's church activity, surely. "Himself" means an individual, he says. It can't mean the church. Alright, I've found where the Lord's supper is spoken of in that capacity. I wonder if he thinks that the Lord's supper is exclusive individual action? Now, he won't do anything to that because he can't. Now, I've covered his speech. How much time do I have? [TOTTY: Eight minutes.]

Alright now, let's take my question. Now, remember this, friends, we have an agreement to ask each other five questions and in writing and the answers to be given. I sent them ahead because I wanted him to have plenty of time. Now, I can't write out his answers and listen to his speech, so I can't answer his questions in writing. I didn't get them in time. The mails operate to Memphis the same as they do from Memphis to Peoria and I'll have them answered and written out tomorrow night. So that's a part of our agreement, just so we'll have it down on paper because these brethren have a way of forgetting that they make certain statements here.

Now, number one: May every need of an orphan child be met by the church without the child being a part of the family arrangement or relationship, and if no, is this relationship a family, a church, neither, or both? State which.

Now, it looks like it's getting it down to where he could answer one way or the other, but do you think he did? You listen to this double talk. Answer: a) "assuming that the orphan child you have in mind is a subject for church relief, it would depend upon the particular child and his needs." Well, that answers my question, doesn't it? It 'depends'! I said, "Is it a family relationship, a church relationship, neither, or both?" That looks like it would get one or the other, doesn't it? It does look like he could have said one or the other. Well, it 'depends.' "The church would supply only what the child needed. In some cases, the child would need to be a part of a family arrangement

28

or relationship. In other cases, such would not be required. In case where a child may be part of a relationship, the relationship would be neither a family nor a church, but a relationship." Well, that's very dear, isn't it? Now, that's answering our question, I tell you. Brother Sutton, I'd be ashamed of that. I literally would be ashamed to come up with a thing of that type. I would, if I couldn't answer a question without talking all the way around it and saying nothing. He said when I said, "What is the relationship," he says, "It's a relationship." Well, that's wonderful as far as we know.

Now, you know why he didn't answer that? Simply because he can't and stay in this debate, that's the reason. If he says it's the church, then he's got a child in the church. If he says it's the family, he surrenders his position because that's the very thing I am contending for. So, what'd he do? He just talked around it, that's all. Take more than a silly grin to answer it, too, wouldn't it, Sutton?

Number 2: When the church engages in child care in meeting the needs of destitute orphan children, is this child care church work, family work, neither, or both? "Any work the church engages in would be church work. If the church is engaging in child care, then the work of child care would be church work." Alright now, what have we found? We found that it's church work to provide the actual needs of a child. Well now, let's see what some of those needs are. One of them is recreation. Now, then, he says it's church work for the church to supply the needs of children. One of the needs of the children is recreation. Then the church can engage in recreation according to brother Sutton. Well, he either can or he can't! Now, if he can't, then he can't engage in church work or else that's not church work. I say it's not church work. It's family work. Anybody else who thinks will know that is what it is. One of the needs of a child is a spanking once in a while. Now, brother Sutton, who is it to do the spanking: the elders or the deacons. Which one do you delegate and give us chapter and verse for it now.

Let me tell you this, ladies and gentlemen. These people try to parallel this with a Bible study but let me tell you this. If you were to lay a hand on a child in a Bible class, in this congregation or any other, the parents could have you arrested. There isn't any parallel between the two and anybody ought to know it. Could you give a child in a Bible study your pig to raise? Don't forget to put that down. Let me know when I have three minutes, please.

May every need of destitute orphan children be met by the local congregation without the use of any other organization and is it a sin for the church to make a contribution to be used for the care of orphans by any other organization except the church? Answer: "If by 'the use of any other organization' you mean without buying the products of or the services of another organization, the answer is no." Now, he admits here that the church can buy services of another organization. An all-sufficient church can turn around and send its money to another organization to do that which the church itself was set up to do. That's what it amounts to. Now, then, if it can, if it can buy one product, why can't it buy another? Could it buy preaching the gospel from a missionary society? He won't answer that. "If by 'contribution' you mean a donation by any other organization, you mean any other association, society, corporation, or institution, yes, it would be sinful for a church to make contributions to such. Any other organization but a family is another organization; therefore, it would be a sin for a church to make a donation to a family for the family to spend." Now, do you think we believe such stuff as that? [TOTTY: Three minutes.]

Thank you. Well, oh yes, I have time for one more here. May the church in its organized capacity operate a kitchen and provide meals for needy saints with money out of its treasury? "If they operate a kitchen, 'provide meals for needy saints,' you mean provide the necessary facilities and dispense food for hungry saints for whom the church is responsible, yes." Yes, the church can operate a kitchen, he says. Well, the elders have got to oversee everything they do, so the elders can oversee this kitchen. Could you have it in the basement or would it have to be outside the building? Now, don't forget to put that down. Where's it going to be, in the basement or out here? Now, which is it? Now, Sutton, I intend for you to answer that question. Put it down. Alright.

Now, then, as to the identity of the organizations which I'm defending with the family. I told you tonight that a church may contribute to a needy family. That God put the solitary in families. That these families are legal organizations. That they must meet certain legal requirements. Now, here is a statement based upon the Code of Alabama, Title 49, Section 78. Look, this makes it a criminal offense for any person to take custody of any child under the age of 16 years unless the person taking custody is related to that child within the second degree without obtaining either a license as a state agency or a court custody order from a court having jurisdiction. "Any person or organization obtaining a license from the Department of Pensions and Security from Alabama, commonly known as the Welfare Department, would become an agency of the State, by definition, in Article 2 of the Code of Alabama from 1940, Title 49." An agency is an organization acting as an agent. Now, listen here to what it is in Kentucky. "a. Each institution shall have an organized Board of Directors with at least five members who live in Kentucky within commuting distance of the institution. The names and addresses of the Board members shall be forwarded to the Department of Economic Security. Board meetings shall be held regularly. The board shall include at least five members who are or have served in one of the following positions: County Judge, School Superintendent, banker, merchant, president of the PTA, a minister, a priest, county health nurse or a physician." Now, Sutton, suppose there are five children abandoned on the steps of a meeting house in Kentucky. Just using this as an illustration here, how do you think we're going to go about getting the money out of the church treasury to those children? You tell me without following an arrangement of this kind. That, ladies and gentlemen, is what these institutions are that I'm defending tonight and they're as true as they can be. Sutton will fight against it in vain because you can't oppose the truth. Now, he hasn't got any plan. He doesn't support any family arrangement of that type. He doesn't have any intention of starting one. If he were to start one, the arguments he made would weigh against his just as much as against these existing. That's the reason why he's not going to start one. I tell you tonight, he's fighting a losing battle and I'm glad that we're having this discussion here so that you folks can see the truth. So, you can learn that all of this stuff about benevolent societies is just so much hogwash. That's all there is to it and I intend for you to see it.

Now, brother Sutton, don't you forget that kitchen question. You said the elders could oversee a kitchen. Now, have they got to have it outside the building or in it? Can they have it in the basement or upstairs or in the attic? We'll be expecting that.

Carrol R. Sutton's Second Negative Speech

Gentlemen moderators, brother Woods, ladies and gentlemen:

I'm glad to appear before you for the next twenty minutes in defense of the truth as revealed in the book of God. It's always a pleasure to have the opportunity of talking to those who are concerned about truth and knowing what truth is.

I would like to make mention of the fact that the proposition that we're discussing, or at least what we're supposed to be discussing, says: "It is in harmony with the scriptures for churches of Christ to build and maintain benevolent organizations such as Tennessee Orphan Home, Boles Home, Home for the Aged and other such organizations for the care of the needy." Now, brother Woods signed his name to affirm that proposition, but brethren, neighbors, and friends, have you heard one passage of scripture cited that, in the very remotest sense, even refers to such a benevolent organization? Brother Woods, where is that passage? I believe that I've mentioned every passage that he's brought up. I believe that I've noticed, that is, in his first speech, but I believe I've noticed all of those passages. But even if I haven't, yet have you heard one word about a benevolent organization? Brother Woods, that's what you signed your name to affirm and all that you might say about other matters will not prove that it's in harmony with the scriptures for churches of Christ to build and maintain these human organizations, and incidentally, brother Woods, if you believe they're divine organizations, please give the passage of scripture for that. He may talk about it, friends, but he won't cite the passage of scripture. When brethren, a long time ago, tried to defend the missionary societies, they'd talk about this thing and that thing, but they never did produce the passage of scripture that showed authority for those human organizations. Now, brother Woods, we won't let you side track it by saying, "Now, here's the family and God ordained the family." What you signed to affirm was these benevolent organizations. Incidentally, brother Woods said that, "It's just a matter that brother Sutton doesn't know the definition of terms." Brother Woods, I may not know much about the definition of terms, but I believe that I know enough about it that I know the difference between a family and this benevolent organization that you're trying to defend. That is, a group of men that live in various parts of the state, sometimes different states, and you never did tell me whether or not that board, those men that constitute that benevolent organization, serve as a family.

Now, neighbors and friends, here's the set up. Here's a group of men, in some cases nine in number, they in turn come from different parts of the country. They form a human organization. It's not a family, friends. It's chartered under the laws of the State as a human organization, as a benevolent society in the State of Alabama, brother Woods. In the case of Childhaven, it is a benevolent society. The State so recognizes it as being such, now, if that's what he's defending. But the State does not recognize this family relationship as being a benevolent organization.

Incidentally, friends, everybody in this audience knows the difference, too. When you filled out your income tax papers, every contribution that you made to a charitable organization of any kind, you could deduct on your income tax, couldn't you? What if you made a donation to what he calls a family? Could you do that? What about it? If you did, you might have a visit from Internal Revenue men. Brother Woods would not try to deduct anything that he gave to brother Totty or brother Totty's family or anybody else. He knows that he can't deduct that. That even the State, the United States, recognizes a difference between these benevolent societies, their charitable organizations, and simply a family where there's parents and children involved. Brother Woods, let's stay with the proposition. Let's show authority for these benevolent organizations.

He says, "Brother Sutton shouts about benevolent societies," he says, "I'm not defending such." Well, I've been shouting about benevolent organizations, and that's what you signed to defend. Why don't you defend them? That's what he signed to defend, didn't he? And incidentally, he said, "Well now, a family is a benevolent organization and a benevolent organization is a family." Brother Woods, why did you write 'family' here? Why didn't you just write 'benevolent organizations'? Is this divine institution and then the State and the church? Why didn't you do that if they're the same? Why don't you do that yet? Brother Woods knows the difference, friends, but didn't want you to see the difference. He knows the difference in it.

Incidentally, I'd like to know this. He talks about my not answering questions. Well, I did answer everyone that he wrote me. He said quite a bit about my not answering. Of course, the truth about it is, I didn't answer them like he wanted me to. Well, I knew that. I wasn't trying to answer them like he wanted me to. And he said, "I'd be ashamed if I was him." Well, I would too if I was in your position. Yes sir, if I was in your position, then answered it like I answered it, I would be ashamed of it. But since I've got the truth, I'm not ashamed of the truth, friends. I'm proud of the truth.

Then I asked brother Woods: Is the board a family? Is this Childhaven organization, Boles Orphan Home organization, Tennessee Orphan Home organization a family? Did he answer? But he chides me for not answering although I do answer.

He kept talking about his family and so forth and I asked him where the passage of scripture was that showed the church ever supported or sent a contribution to a family as an organization. Did he give it? He said, "Brother Sutton doesn't believe that the church can give a donation to a family out here." You give the passage and I'll believe it, brother Woods. You didn't produce the passage, did you? Do you expect me to accept what you assert without the passage of scripture? I'll accept it, friends, when he gives it.

We notice also that he, on Psalms 66 verse 5 and 6 that says God sets the solitary in families, he said, "Well, oh, that's what I believe about it." Brother Woods, why are you defending benevolent organizations then? Why are you defending these organizations that the State of Alabama recognizes as benevolent societies? Incidentally,

34

while we're talking about these benevolent societies and the fact that the State recognizes these things as benevolent organizations, I'd like to notice chart number 22, that we might see just a few things about Childhaven being a benevolent organization, a benevolent society. I maintain, friends, that THE STATE OF ALABAMA RECOGNIZES CHILDHAVEN AS A BENEVOLENT SOCIETY. Proof of it: Title 10, Chapter 7, Article 3, Section 124 of 1940 Code of Alabama, under which Childhaven is incorporated, provides for the "incorporation of churches and educational or benevolent societies." Note, brother Woods, since Childhaven is not a church, or educational society, it must be a benevolent society. Yes, my opponent is defending benevolent societies, and according to the State of Alabama even, and he introduced something from Kentucky as legal proof. Do you accept this, brother Woods, as legal proof? Now, brother Woods, does the State of Alabama recognize a family, as you're talking about, as a benevolent society? Does it? Friends, don't let him get you away from what he signed his name to affirm. You know, the Apostle Peter said in 2 Peter 2 that there would be those who'd deny the truth, and said in verse two and three, "that many shall follow their pernicious ways by reason of whom the way of truth shall be evil spoken of, and through covetousness, shall they with feigned words make merchandise of you." You know, it doesn't take a Solomon to understand these simple passages. Psalms 119 verse 130 shows how the entrance of God's word gives light. It gives understanding to the simple. So, just anybody can use feigned words and try to make you think that when James 1:27 says, "Keep himself unspotted from the world," that's talking about the church. Friends, if you're just simple minded like I am, you can understand that. You know what it's talking about if it says 'himself.' It's not talking about the church; it's talking about an individual. Verse 26 says, "If a man," talking about an individual. "If any man among you seem to be religious...." It's talking about a man, not a church. And Psalms 68, verse 5 and 6, says, "God sets the solitary in families." You understand that, friends. The footnote says, "in a house," doesn't it, brother Woods? Not in an institution. So, it's not using families in the sense of an institution such as Tennessee Orphans Home, Boles Home, etc.

We notice also that brother Woods had quite a bit to say about the chart over here, and he said, "Now, all of this over here, all this up here I agree with." Brother Woods, I had scriptures down here showing this, too. Why didn't you agree with that, too? He just implied that he didn't agree with the scripture down here. That's what he implied.

WOODS: I resent that. That doesn't follow at all. I said nothing about denying the scripture, and I see no point in him making such allegations. Now, keep it on a high plane, Sutton.

SUTTON: Hold my time. I'll let you be the judge in it. You heard what he said. Let everyone of you be the judge in it. It doesn't take a Solomon to understand what he said. He said, "I agree with all this up here." That left the implication that he did not agree with this down here, in my way of thinking. What about yours? You be the judge.

Now, let's notice. He says, now, with respect to the church being an organization to preach, "I agree with that." Now, brother Woods, the same book that told the church to preach told the church to relieve. Why don't you agree with that, too? 1 Timothy 5 verse 16 says, "If any man or woman that believeth have widows, let him relieve them, and let not the church be charged; that it..."--'it' what? The church, "might relieve them that are widows indeed." Acts 6 shows how the church did that by selecting seven men. That these seven men might serve tables, and in 1946 brother Woods said that they dispensed food. Now, he says they gave money. Which time did you tell the truth, brother Woods? Just for fear that someone might think he didn't say that in 1946, here is the *Annual Lesson Commentary* on page 100. It has this to say, and brother Woods is the author of it. "Stephen was one of the seven selected to dispense food for the Grecian widows who were being neglected in the daily ministration." But now, he says they can't dispense food. It's got to simply be money. Now, brother Woods, when did you tell the truth about it?

WOODS: I never said that they couldn't dispense food.

SUTTON: Can they dispense food today?

WOODS: They can dispense both of them.

SUTTON: They can give something besides money, then, can't they?

WOODS: Well, I ...

SUTTON: They can give food then, can't they?

WOODS: Are you addressing me, and do you want an answer now,?

SUTTON: You can suit yourself about it.

WOODS: Alright. Here I said that they dispensed money. I also said they dispensed food. I think they can do both. You don't think they can do either.

SUTTON: Alright, it is the work of the church then to dispense something besides money, isn't it? And yet, he said a while ago, in his first speech, that it's the work of the church to supply the money and the work of the home to spend the money. You heard him say it, didn't you? Brother Woods, did you mean it? Do you want to take it back? Would you like to take it back, brother Woods? That's what he said. Now, if he didn't mean it in 1946, then we'll just drop the matter. But unless he apologizes for it in 1946, or denies it one, we'll have to say that he has admitted tonight that the church may do something besides supply money. It may dispense food. Alright, brother Woods, maybe you'll agree with me that the church might operate a kitchen, then. How would he dispense food without a kitchen of some kind or some kind of facilities?

Well, we notice also, he said concerning this chart further, that "Brother Sutton ought to know better" and so forth. and he had quite a bit to say about. "Why, I was preaching before brother Sutton was dry behind the ears." Well, brother Woods, surely then you ought to know better than what you said about it. If you've been preaching that long, surely then you ought not to deny that the church is the organization that God specified to do their relieving. I believe anybody in this audience can see that. If the church is the organization to do the preaching because the Bible says so, why isn't the church the organization to do the relieving because the Bible said so? He says, "Well, if that's the case, then that rules out the family." Alright, brother Woods, does it rule out the family in the case of preaching the gospel? And if it doesn't, and if the church can preach the gospel through another organization that you call the family, why can't it then preach through an organization that's known as a missionary organization, since you say that organizations and families are one and the same thing? If not, why not?

Then he pressed me about, "Can a church support a family?" And he said, "Write it down." Well, I did, brother Woods, and I told you a while ago, if you'd give me the scripture that showed it, I'd accept it. You show it.

Then he says, "Brother Sutton spends money the church gives him, but he doesn't think that there can be any money taken out to feed your children." Now, brother Woods, I don't know about you. The church may give you money, but it doesn't give me mine. Now, I don't know, maybe they do give it to him, but I understand in 2 Corinthians 11 and verse 8 that Paul said he received "wages." If I understand what I'm doing, I receive wages. All you brethren that work at Caterpillar: Is Caterpillar giving you your money or are you earning wages? Brother Woods, maybe the church does give you yours, but I think I earn mine. Now, maybe you're right about them giving it to you, but don't accuse them of giving it to me. Now, it may be some time that I may be a charity case, and if I am a destitute saint, then the church may relieve me just like any needy saint. Any of you brethren, it could relieve. It could relieve you, if you become a charity case. Then me and you would be in the same category in that respect.

Then he said the orphan home is older than the missionary society. Brother Woods, I'm not too much concerned about that. Although I'd like the proof that churches of Christ have been supporting benevolent organizations, such as these you've mentioned, back before this missionary society was started. I'm talking about loyal churches of Christ, brother Woods. I'm talking about those who oppose the missionary societies. I'd like to have proof of it, but even if he proves that, friends, what he needs to do is go back nearly 2000 years ago and find it in the book of God. That's what we're discussing. Does the "scriptures" teach it? Not what brethren have practiced. You know the scribes and Pharisees, in their day, thought because they practiced things, that was right. But Matthew 15 and Mark 7 show how that Jesus says they made void God's word by their traditions which they had delivered.

Then we notice also that he said, "Well now," talking about this on the board, "and he keeps talking about it." Brother Woods, I still want to know that since you say that when the family breaks down, that the church may support the family, and since you say that the State is a divine institution, when it breaks down, why can't the church support the State? You say it's a divine institution. Why can't it or why can't it build and maintain an organization here that in turn will restore the State. That's your position. That's not mine. That's his position, friends.

Then he says, "Well, you can't put elders over families." But you know, back in 1939 brother Woods said that the elders were over the benevolent work of the church and was over the Tipton Orphan Home. Yet, he says the orphan homes are families. So, he said in '39 that you can put elders over families, if they're the same, and if they're not, he said you put them over orphan homes. Brother Woods, you're the one that said that, and yet he's trying to say you can't do it. Have you changed your mind about it, brother Woods? And then he said, "You can't put parents over a church." Well, brother Woods, didn't you know that the very qualification of an elder, before a man can ever become an overseer of the Lord's church, he must be a parent. Didn't brother Woods know that? In 1 Timothy 3 and Titus 1 there's got to be. I don't believe a bachelor can serve as an elder, do you, brother Woods? I believe he's got to be a parent, got to have faithful children! Yet you can't put parents over the church. I'll tell you what you can do, though. You can put men who are parents over the church, and if a man hasn't become a parent, he can't be put over the church. That's one thing about it, according to God's book. Now, don't you come back and say, 'Well, they're serving because they are parents though, aren't they?' One of the qualifications: If they weren't parents, they couldn't serve.

Then he said Acts 6 and 1 through 6 shows that the family spent the money and so forth. Brother Woods, you know you better back up in what you said in your first speech tonight. You said in your first speech on Acts 6, the Seven gave the money and the family spent it. Yet, a while ago, you admitted that when you said in 1946 that the Seven dispensed food, that they did dispense food; they can do both of them. So, that gives up his argument on Acts 6 in his first speech, and all of you can understand that, too, friends. That's simple. You can

39

understand that. That's why I understand it, because it's simple.

Then he said, "Since he said James 1:27 says about 'himself' or 'oneself,' well," he said, "according to brother Sutton, then what about over in 1 Corinthians 11, it says, 'let a man examine himself.' Does that mean an individual or a church?" I'd like to ask you that one. That's what I wanted to ask you. Yep, that's what I wanted to ask you, brother Woods. Is the church the one that does the examining or is the individual doing it? "Let a man examine himself." I maintain it's a man doing it. What do you maintain, brother Woods? "Let a man examine himself," and so here's individual action, self-examination that's being done, and then he eats the Lord's Supper in the assembly of the saints. Now, you find the assembly in James 1:27, and you'll have a parallel to it. You find this activity done in James 1:27 as being done in the assembly, and you'll have a parallel to it, brother Woods.

Then he said quite a bit about my questions, but I'll just skip that because he's ashamed of my questions, and then he talked about recreation is one of the needs of children. He said, "Can the church engage in recreation? According to brother Sutton, it can." Now, brother Woods, now, if you read all my questions, you'll know that I said differently. So, we agree on that, evidently.

Then he said, "If a child needs spanking, then who does it, an elder or a deacon? Well, brother Woods, I'll just let you answer that one. In this Board of Directors that you have, who does the spanking when a child needs a spanking? Is it the president, vice-president, or secretary-treasurer? Who is it that does the spanking, brother Woods? Is it the president? He lives in a different part of the state! Is it the vice-president? He's across the other part of it! Is it the secretary or treasurer? Who spanks them? Brother Woods didn't have any difficulty in that. No, they provide somebody else to do the spanking, so I suppose upon the same basis the church could provide somebody to do the spanking then, couldn't they?

Then he said concerning the kitchen, "Is it in the basement?" Well, brother Woods, let me ask you where it was in Acts 6? Let me ask you where it was in Acts 6, since you said they dispensed food. Was it in the basement? God didn't specify the place for the facilities, so I don't specify them. Do you, brother Woods? And so, I believe we can see that. Thank you.

Guy N. Woods' Third Affirmative Speech

Brethren moderators, brother Sutton, ladies and gentlemen:

We found out where we could put the kitchen, didn't we? He told us all about it, didn't he? Now, I tell you, friends, before I'll dodge and quibble and evade and shrink away from an effort of that type, I'd give up what he's trying to defend. I can't understand how good people can support a man who will deliberately avoid and evade like he's doing. Now, brother Sutton, it doesn't make any difference if I think that it ought to be in the attic or in the basement or out on the front lawn or anywhere else. I asked you where you thought it ought to be. Can you tell us? I don't think there's anything wrong in having a kitchen in the basement any more than I do his house. I answered his question. Now, why won't he answer mine? I'll give you a minute of my time to get up and answer it right now. Sutton, stand up there and answer the question now. Is it scriptural to have it in the basement or does it have to be out in the yard? No, I wouldn't let him answer it either. Now, he's allowed, he's allowing my last opportunity tonight to pass without answering the question though it's been asked him repeatedly. Why doesn't he answer it? I'm not mad at him. I'm just sorry for him, and I'm not going to allow him to escape the issue here. I'm going to press it until this debate's over. That's what I'm up here for, and I'm going to do it in a nice way, but I intend for you to see that this is what these men resort to when we finally get them into debate. Now, that–that's the real issue here. We still don't know if it can be in the basement. Brother Sutton, I'll still give you a half minute of my time if you'll just say can it be, or can't it be? Answer one or the other. Nod or shake or do something. Can it be or not? I tell you, friends, he's on the hot spot. I'll tell you he is.

Alright now, he said, "Ah, you proved something by the law of Kentucky." I didn't do anything of the kind, brother Sutton. I didn't introduce that to prove. I just introduced that to show what the law of Kentucky requires before you could take care of orphan children up there, and I can prove that you've got to go by the law, too. I can prove you get in trouble if you don't. Yeah, that I can. I can prove that. I'm just showing what the law requires along that line.

He said, "Cite scripture for your human institution." Why, if I were defending a human institution in the sense of being opposed to the divine, that's what I ought to do, but I'm not doing that. I'm defending a divine institution, and that's what I'm up here for the purpose of doing. Not my obligation to cite scripture for a human institution. That which I'm defending is no more a human institution than the church is. The church is made up of human beings, but it's a divine institution. The family is a divine institution, but, when you restore the family relationship, you've got to go by the law and the law requires you to have men that stand in the place of parents. You couldn't possibly have an orphan home any other way except that. That's right, that's the truth! Can't do it any other way. Not anybody knows that any better than you fellows do, and that's the reason why you haven't got any home of that type, because you have to do what we're telling you we're doing in order to do it. We're at least making an effort in that respect.

Now, he says, "If the family and the benevolent organization are the same, why don't you put it up there?" Well, because brother Sutton wants to turn around and tell me what I mean by benevolent organizations. He won't let me define my terms. He wants then to change it into a benevolent society parallel to a missionary society. I'm not defending that. I'm defending the right of a child to be in a family relationship, and that we ought to go by the law of the land in arranging it. That's we've got to do. That's what I'm defending.

"Oh," he says, "how does the Board of Directors constitute a part of a family?" It's a part of the legal family. Yeah, it's a part of the legal family. He says, "Well, they don't live in the same place, they even live in different states." Now, how far do you have to live away from a domicile in order to be a part of the family? Used to be that down in Tennessee, in the rural area where I grew up, that they used to be that they'd build a house and part of it over on this side and there'd be part of it over here, and there'd be a hall in between there, and the parents would live on one side and the children sometimes in the other. Now, according to this fellow, they weren't any part of their family because they didn't live under the same roof. Sometimes they'd even have a room back out here that wasn't even tied to it. Now, he wants to know how could they be a part of the family if they don't live at the same place? "Why," he says, "they even live in different states." He thinks because somebody lives in another part of the state they're no part of the family. God's family is all over the world. Now, if you're going to limit the family, how far apart have they got to be, Sutton? That's just a quibble, but that's the best you can do. If you had anything better, you'd do it.

He says, "The State of Alabama says that these organizations are benevolent societies." The State of Alabama says it's legal to sell whiskey. Now, does that prove it's legal to sell whiskey? The State of Alabama says that it's proper to get a divorce on grounds aside from what the New Testament teaches. I don't believe either one of them. That is, either one of the things the State claims about liquor or divorce. I don't cite this as authority. He cites the State of Alabama because he can't prove it, my position, wrong by the Bible. He proves it by the State of Alabama. Well, he can do a better job by the State of Alabama than he can the Bible, I'll tell you that.

"Why," he says, "now, you charge me with believing that the church can't send a donation to a needy family." Alright, I charge him with that. I said that's what he believes, and he won't come up here and say it. I know that's what he believes. He won't come up here and say it. He said, "Well, you produce the passage of scripture showing where the church ever gave any money to a family." Now, I'm just about to do that, but that's still not doing what I asked you to do. I'm just going to do that, and while I'm doing it, I'm gonna kill two birds with one stone.

Turn over with me to Acts the fourth chapter and begin to read at the thirty-fourth verse: "Neither was there any among them that lacked: for as many as were possessors of lands or houses sold them, and brought the prices of the things that were sold," prices, mind you, of the things sold, now, that's money, "and laid them down at the apostles' feet: and distribution was made unto every man according as he had need." Now, turn on over. This is that same matter that created a problem in the church a little later. Acts 6, "And in those days, when the number of the disciples was multiplied, there arose a murmuring of the Grecians against the Hebrews, because their widows were neglected in the daily ministration. Then the twelve called the multitude of disciples unto them, and said, It is not reason that we should leave the word of God and serve tables. Wherefore, brethren, look ye out among you seven men of honest report, full of the Holy Ghost and wisdom, whom we may appoint over this business." What business? The business of making distribution to those in need. Now, they either gave it to a church or they gave it to members of the family, one or the other! Did they give it to a church or, he said, "Show where they ever gave it to a family." I said in my first speech, "I'm not going to quibble with you over where they gave it to the organization or the members of it." I said, in the very first speech, I was willing to accept the premise that they gave it to the individuals, but they gave it to the individuals in another organization, and that other organization supervised its spending! And that's exactly what we're contending for here with reference to the home or the families that we're defending here. Now, there's his scripture. Why don't you answer as I do? Now, he misrepresents me on this. In the first place, brother Sutton draws a deduction. He said that I took the position these scriptures weren't true over here. Well, I do nothing of the kind. I believe those scriptures, but I don't believe Sutton's use of them. In the first place, I maintain that the church relieves. There isn't any question about whether the church relieves. The only question is whether or not it's the function of the church to serve as a child care agency; whether the church can take over the business of the family and operate the family as a part of the church? That's the only question.

He cites us to 2 Peter 2 about some who with feigned words would make merchandise of the gospel. He sounded a whole lot to me like he was the fellow that was doing it. He said he was paid. I don't think you can pay a man to preach the gospel. I wouldn't know how much you'd have to pay him in order to pay him to preach. Who's going to decide how much it's worth? Now, that's a misuse of Paul's

44

statement in 2 Corinthians 11:8. The word "*opsōnion*" there actually is trans—is a term that was used to apply to the support of soldiers in the army, and that wasn't on the basis of wage. If you ask any soldier if he thinks that he's paid in harmony with his activity there, I think you'll get a little different answer. Now, he just doesn't know what he is talking about when he brings that up. I'd say this, brother Sutton. If they're paying you to preach, whatever they're paying you, they're paying you too much. Unless you change your doctrine, I'll guarantee you that. I don't think you pay a preacher to preach. I think you support him so that he can live and preach the gospel. That's the truth of the business.

Now, then, on James 1:27 brother Sutton is having a time with this. He wants to make this exclusively individual, which means, of course, that the church can't practice pure and undefiled religion. He makes this individual, which means, that you can't obey James 1:27 without having two children, two orphan children, and two widows in your home. You've got to have two of each. Can't have one of each because the terms are plural. So, according to Sutton this is the only way you can obey James 1:27 is as an individual. That as an individual you have to have two of each because the terms are plural. Now, he hasn't got two of each in home, that is, two orphan children and two widows. Therefore, he's not practicing it. But he says, "Now, that still means an individual 'keep oneself unspotted from the world.' Well, I cited him 1 Corinthians 11: "Let a man examine himself." "Well," he said, "who is it that's to do the examining? Is it the man or the church?" Well, it's the man, but it's the man that eats, because the next statement is: "Let a man examine himself and so let him eat." Is that exclusively individual or is that church activity? Well, I won't insult your intelligence by ask—by drawing the conclusion for you. "Ah," he says, "Now, that's in the assembly." He said, "Find the assembly in James 1:27." Now, you remember this, friends, that when James was written that the chapter divisions were not inserted. The divisions were inserted long years after the book was written. The chapter divisions in about 1215 by Catholic priests ... A.D. 1215. And the verse divisions by a man by the name of Stephen Langdon, who was on a horseback ride from Paris to Lyon, France, and amused himself by inserting those divisions. Now, you remember that there's not any divisions in this context in which James wrote it. He said, "Find the assembly here." I'm glad to do so. Let's just read it like James wrote it. "But whoso looketh into the perfect law of liberty, and continueth therein, he being not a forgetful hearer, but a doer of the work, this man shall be blessed in his deeds. If any man among you seem to be religious, and bridleth not his tongue, but deceiveth his own heart, this man's religion is vain. Pure religion and undefiled before God and the Father is this, To visit the fatherless and widows in their afflictions, and to keep himself unspotted from the world. My brethren, have not the faith of our Lord Jesus Christ, the Lord of glory, with respect of persons. For if there come unto your assembly a man with a gold ring," and so on. There it is in context. Well, I just do it because I could. Yes, it's the church that relieves. The church relieves by supplying the funds. The church supports his family, but the church doesn't run it. The church gives them the money so to do, and that's exactly what we are defending here.

"Oh," he said, "you took the position at one time that they could dispense food, and you took the position another time they could dispense money." I think they could dispense either or both. Actually, that's what we all do. We send a donation from the church treasury, and sometimes they take money out of the treasury and buy a lot of food to send down there. Sometimes they have it in baskets out in front. Of course, we do that what—we've always done that—both food and money. I don't see his point there.

Well, he said if the church can relieve and send the money, can the family preach? Why, of course, they, the family, can preach. Many a boy has learned to preach from his father; got outlines from his father. Why, is this man taking the position that the family, as such, cannot teach or preach the gospel? That would be the implication. He said, "Show where," said, "evidently you think that the family can preach." Why, I think I can, too. Of course, I do.

Then, friends, of all things, these brethren never cease to amaze me with some of the things that they come up with. He said, "I'm going to prove to you that you can put parents over a church," and here's how he went about it. Now, then, before you can be an elder you must be a parent. Therefore, all elders are parents, but when you put elders over a church, you've got parents over the church. Now, that's marvelous logic, isn't it? Isn't that wonderful? Let me call your attention to this fact, friends. One man may be the head of his house, the president of a bank, an elder in the church, and a foster parent of an orphan home, but he's not any one of those because he's any of the others. Those are individual and distinctive relationships and responsibilities. Now, this, though, takes the cake right there. That's the–that's one of the most ridiculous things that I've heard in many a day.

Now, one other matter. He said, when I asked him the question: Who does the spanking, the elders or the deacons, he answered that question, didn't he? He said, "I'll answer it by asking you: Who spanks in the organization, the Board of Directors, or the vice president, or the treasurer, or who?" Well, actually, those who have the qualifications do the spanking. Now, then if, according to him, it's the duty and the function of the eldership to do it, where are the qualifications for the spankers in the church? It's a remarkable fact, friends, that for every legitimate function in the church there's a functioner, and his qualifications are given. We've got to have elders; therefore, the elders are given, and their duties pointed out. We've got to have deacons. The deacons are given, and their duties are pointed out. Teachers, preachers, evangelists, local workers; we have all of these, and their duties are pointed out, but where are the qualifications of the spankers? Friends, it seems to me sometimes, it seems to me just a little ridiculous for me to have to draw out these conclusions, to point out to you that the church can't serve as a family; the family as a church. You just can't do it. You just can't confuse the three. Now, that's covered his speech item by item, and how much time? Three minutes, alright.

Now, then, friends, let me summarize what I pointed out to you tonight. I have shown you that there are three institutions existing by divine right: the family, the State, and the church. I've shown you that the church sustains an obligation, and I want to do this again, just in order that it may be very clear to you in the three minutes remaining. I have shown you that every child is entitled to the relationship of a family; a family relationship. That the church sustains an obligation to that family in its need. That when that family loses its basic structure, when it breaks down, that this may be re-established or restored. And then the church sustains an obligation to the restored family. That's exactly what we're defending tonight. But this family has to meet certain legal requirements. You can't have seven children not related to you by blood without going through a court relationship. And when you go, when you get them under court jurisdiction, get them in the custody of the court, then this institution falls under State law.

Let me tell you briefly about this. Over in Ft. Smith, Arkansas, the Southern Christian Home started by the elders of a congregation asking a family there, who had a large house, to take three or four children and provide for them. They took them. The church gave them the money to support them in this family relationship. A few days later, or few weeks later, I don't know how long it was, they had other children that needed a home. They gave them a home there. They were operating out there with more than seven children. One day the sheriff went out there and arrested that man and woman for operating an unlicensed home because they were violating the law. They hadn't obtained a State license. The church was supporting them in a family relationship, and it didn't make any difference whether there were seven or seventy or seven hundred. Expediency might enter into it, but you've still got to go by the law. The church still has an obligation to them. It's not in conflict with the church because it's not performing the work of a church; it's performing the family relationship. It's not in conflict with the family which it replaces because that family's gone. What is the orphan home? It is the family relationship that the child has lost, and it's been restored, and the church is supporting it then. That's our position. It will stand because it's the truth, and this man or no set of men will ever shake it. And I hope that you'll not allow yourselves to be deceived or deluded by men who are doing it.

He cited us 2 Peter 2, 'men who make merchandise of the gospel.' That passage also says that some forsake the right way and go astray. I was talking to one of his teachers a few days ago, was associated with him in a meeting, and he said back in the days when Sutton was in school down there, why he believed like all of us do on these matters. So, he's the fellow that's forsaken the right way and gone astray. I hope he'll come back to the truth. Thank you. Now, don't forget to tell us; is that kitchen in the basement or out of it?

Carrol R. Sutton's Third Negative Speech

Gentlemen moderators, brother Woods, ladies and gentlemen:

I'm certainly glad to appear before you again for my final twenty minutes of the evening in defense of the truth of God as revealed in the scriptures. I'd like to call your attention again to what brother Woods is affirming, I mean, what he's suppose to be affirming. "It is in harmony with the scriptures for churches of Christ to build and maintain families such as..." Wait a minute. "It is in harmony with the scriptures for churches of Christ to build and maintain benevolent organizations such as the Tennessee Orphan Home, Boles Home, Home for the Aged, and other such organizations for the care of the needy." Has brother Woods cited the passage of scripture yet, friends? He talks about my fighting a losing cause. I'll let you be the judge. I'll let you be the judge, based on scriptural authority, as to whether or not the truth is being made known tonight relative to these benevolent organizations.

I've read to you, friends, where God specified the church in 1 Timothy 5:16 as the organization to relieve destitute widows. He hasn't shown a passage of scripture that shows that a human organization such as he's defending, I mean, what he's supposed to be defending. He keeps talking about: "Well, I'm defending the family." Brother Woods, I still say that your proposition says, 'such organizations as.' It doesn't say private families, either. "Such organizations as the Tennessee Orphan Home, Boles Home, Home for the Aged, etc." Now, that's the kind of organizations that brother Woods is supposed to be affirming. I'm going to show you, neighbors and friends, now, he's defending the Tennessee Orphan Home which is an organization. It's not a family.

Now, let's notice, for way of illustration, that we have here a

Board of Directors, which are nine in number, it was at one time, that has formed a corporation under law of the State of Tennessee. Now, this corporation receives funds from churches in various parts of the country. This is a humanly formed board under State law. This board in turn provides a home, necessaries, and personnel for orphans at Spring Hill, Tennessee. Now, this organization here is not the church. It's not the home that's provided. It's not the family. This organization here may provide or may establish branches in any county in the State. We could read from the Charter of Incorporation, for example, and notice that it has this to say: "The corporation may establish branches in any other county in the State." Now, here's a corporation that has established one branch in Spring Hill, Tennessee. This board is no part of this family relationship at Spring Hill, Tennessee, if you might call it such. It's no part of the place. It's no part of the necessities. It's no part of the personnel, and the personnel, which includes superintendent, the matrons, etc., are no part of the corporation. They are hirelings of the corporation. The superintendents of these benevolent organizations are no part of organizations, are they brother Woods? Are they, brother Woods?

WOODS: Do you want me to answer now,?

SUTTON: You can suit yourself about it. I'm not meaning for you to, but you can if you want to.

WOODS: Let me say this. I don't want you to come over here and ask me questions if you don't want me to get up and answer them. In fact, that's out of order anyway, unless you want a fellow to answer. Now, I wanted you to answer. I would suggest that you talk to the crowd, not me. Isn't that correct now? I appeal to your moderator to answer that.

SUTTON: I'll say this. That when I ask brother Woods questions...

WOODS: May I say this, one other question, one other statement...

SUTTON: Hold my time.

WOODS: I'll be glad to answer your questions.

SUTTON: When I ask brother Woods questions, I'm asking for emphasis. But if he wants to jump up and answer, that's perfectly alright with me. Now, when he asks me questions from the floor, I intend to keep my seat till I get up and then answer, but, now, if he wants to answer, he can. You can suit yourself about that, brother Woods.

WOODS: Alright, I will.

SUTTON: I'm not asking you for a specific answer, but if you want to answer you feel free to answer as far as I'm concerned.

WOODS: Alright, ask your question and I'll answer it.

SUTTON: Alright. Is the superintendent and the matrons down at Spring Hill, Tennessee any part of the Board of Directors that's known as Tennessee Orphan Home?

WOODS: Well, of course, they're not a part of the Board of Directors, any more than the Bible school teachers are part of the eldership, but that doesn't mean they're not a part of the organization.

SUTTON: Alright. He says they're no part of the Board of Directors, but yet the Board of Directors is the corporation, so then this thing is no part of that. But his proposition says that it's scriptural to build and maintain that, and yet he's contending on the board for this. Thank you, brother Woods. No, they're no part of it, friends, but let me ask you, let me point this out to you. He says they're no more a part of that organization than teachers are part of the elders. The teachers of the classes, brother Woods, are part of the church though, isn't it? Aren't they? Sure, they are! The elders are an incorporation separate and apart from the teachers, aren't they? I know. He doesn't have a parallel at all, because the elders do not form a corporation that's separate and apart from the class teachers. He'd have to have that to have his parallel. I thank you again, brother Woods.

Then, of course, he had something to say about: "Can the church give a pig to a child in a Bible class?" Brother Woods, would that be relieving one of his needs? Does a child need a pig? Now, brother Woods doesn't believe that. Of course, I don't either, brother Woods. I don't believe that the church can give a child a pig in the Bible class, but he does believe that the church can send money to this human organization that's known as Tennessee Orphan Home and let them, in turn, buy a pig for the child. Don't you, brother Woods?

WOODS: I certainly do.

SUTTON: He said he certainly does. Well, I certainly don't.

And then he also said, "All that brother Sutton says about the benevolent societies is hogwash." Well, why are you defending them then, brother Woods? If they're hogwash, why are you defending them? I certainly wouldn't defend a thing that fell in that category if I were you.

Then he said he finally got him in a debate. Well, that's good. I'm glad of it. What about you, brother Woods? You ready for another one? Want to extend this one four more nights after these four nights? If so, just say so.

He said, "He didn't prove anything about Kentucky." But he said, "I just simply showed what the law required." Alright, brother Woods, does the law require churches to incorporate in the State of Kentucky before the church can provide the needs of the destitute for whom it's responsible, or does it require the churches to form a separate organization that it might thus do that, or may churches function as churches and thus supply the needs of those who are in need? You tell us about that.

Then, of course, he mentioned this and said, of course, he could put benevolent organization right here. He sure could, but he couldn't find the scripture for it. His proposition says, 'benevolent organizations such as Tennessee Orphan Home.' Now, notice here. Brother Woods says Tennessee Orphan Home Corporation is one thing, and he says the personnel, the superintendent, and matrons are no part of that Board. And yet, he says over here that this family is a benevolent organization. He's got them separate over there. He spoke from his seat and said so, but he's trying to say there that they're the same thing! Which time did he tell the truth? You be the judge. Is it a losing cause, friends?

He says a Board is a part of a family. What part, brother Woods, parents? I believe brother Woods says that the Board are parents. I believe he refers to the Board as being parents. Yet he says they don't spank the children. Why don't they if they're the parents of them, brother Woods? Why don't your Board spank children if they're the parents of the children? You say they stand in place of the parents, so they are legal parents. Why don't they spank children, then? They're

52

not very good parents if they don't spank children when they need spanking, and you said they needed spanking.

I know something else, too. 1 Timothy 5:8 says, "If any provide not for his own, and especially they of his own house, he has denied the faith and is worse than an infidel." Brother Woods, I'd like to know: Is the Board of Directors, known as Tennessee Orphan Home, destitute saints and, if not, upon what basis could the churches send funds to this corporation that is a group of men who are not destitute saints. And if they don't provide for their own children, and you say they're parents, then Paul says they're worse than infidels. He's trying to saddle off upon the church something that Paul tells the parents to do, and if they're parents, brother Woods, and don't provide for their own children, they're worse than infidels. And in many cases, friends, the Board of Directors are men who have quite a bit of means, materially speaking. In many cases they don't contribute one dime to these benevolent organizations either, for the upkeep of their children. But they beg churches, and they hire men that these men might go all over the country and beg funds from churches, that they in turn might supply the needs and let this corporation thrive and prosper, in many cases, until they have material assets over a million dollars, maybe, in some cases. Two thousand acres of land, $706,000—$706,000—two thousand acres of land—begging all the time! Benevolent organizations.

He said now, with respect to this here, that the State of Alabama says it's legal to sell whiskey but said, "Is it right?" Why no, brother Woods. This here isn't either. And the State of Alabama says this is a benevolent organization, but this benevolent organization isn't right when built and maintained by churches of Christ. Just because the State legalizes it–and last night he said that doesn't make it right. Why no, I'm not contending that's right. It's wrong. That's right, it's wrong. Well, let me tell you this. He said now, "If the State says it's legal to sell whiskey, is it right?" No, but I'll tell you one thing. If the State licenses a group or corporation as a liquor store, you can mark it down, it's a liquor store. And if the State licenses a corporation as a benevolent society, you can mark it down, it's a benevolent society. Right or wrong, it's one. And I say it's wrong. Thank you, brother

53

Woods.

Then he said concerning Acts 4 and Acts 6, he said the same matter. They either gave it to the church or family. Which? Well, Acts 6, brother Woods, says for the "widows." Acts 6 shows how this daily ministration was for "widows" who were neglected. He said, "Was it to the church or families?" Well, Acts 6 says "widows," brother Woods. Is a widow a family or is she a church? He implied that it was one of the two, but it said "widows." That's all I know about it. "Widows," brother Woods, and Acts 6:1-6 says so. And, of course, he said in Acts 6 all we have is the home. No, we don't, brother Woods. That's not all we have. We have destitute widows there, the church helping them. And if we did just have a home, and a church helping a home, that still isn't what you're defending. You're defending a benevolent organization which you say is, that this superintendent so forth, is no part of that and yet here's the family as you'd say.

Then he also said, in respect to 2 Corinthians 11 and verse 8, he said the support of soldiers, you know, wages. Well, brother Woods, you can call it anything you want to. Paul said he received wages from churches, and that's what I receive. If I know what I'm receiving, it's wages. It's what Paul said. Now, was Paul a hireling? He received wages. Were they given to him or paid him? He said they weren't paid him; you didn't pay a preacher. Well, I'd just as soon somebody give me wages as pay me wages. It doesn't make me any difference. What about you?

Then he said, "James 1:27, according to Sutton, would require that he take two of each in his home." No, it doesn't, brother Woods. No, it doesn't. Friends, here's what James 1:27 says. It says, "… to visit the fatherless and widows in their affliction." It doesn't even say anything about taking them in a home necessarily. Why, I can visit fatherless and widows and never take them into my home. In fact, all James 1:27 says is to visit them in their affliction. "Visit" them and do that in their "affliction." Suppose, brother Woods, here's a widow and she has some fatherless children, and they need food. They're in the straits of want. Can I take food to them? Just visit them and give them some food? Encourage them if they're down and out and go back home? Have I visited the fatherless and widows? Can I do two families like that? Why sure, friends. Surely, we can all see better than that. He just requires us to visit the fatherless and widows, and do that in their affliction, but yet he's maintaining benevolent organizations. Even if he were right about me, and if I were wrong, he still hasn't shown the scripture for this benevolent organization that's between the church and the home for the children. And if this is not a benevolent society, friends, here in the case of Tennessee Orphan Home, if the same thing was set up down here, and instead of doing the work of benevolence, it did the work of evangelism, would that be a missionary organization, brother Woods?

Then he said, "Of course, in James 2, I can show the assembly in the context." With respect to James 1:27 he says, "Brother Sutton said it showed the assembly in James 2." Yeah, brother Woods, you can show the assembly in James 2, but you don't have it on the same subject, do you? He doesn't have the assembly on the subject of doing relief work, of visiting the fatherless and widows in their affliction. And that's what we're talking about, brother Woods. Let's notice what we have in James 2. It says in verse 2, "For if there come unto your assembly a man with a gold ring, in goodly apparel, and there come in also a poor man in vile raiment; And ye have respect to him...." Why, brother Woods, do you know what that's saying? That's on a different subject. It's not relieving people anyway to begin with, and then James 2 refers to the assembly, right, but individual action in the assembly. Does the whole church speak out at one time and tell this fellow, 'You come over here and sit here, there, or somewhere else,' or are they individuals that do that? Individual action is being done in the assembly, and James condemns it because individuals are showing respect of persons. Now, if you want a parallel to it, you find in James 1 and verse 27 the assembly in the work of visiting the fatherless and widows. He doesn't have it.

Then he said, "The church can dispense food and money." Alright, brother Woods. We're coming along nicely, friends. To start with, he said it just supplied the money, sufficient to do that and the church sufficient—I mean the *home* sufficient, the *family* sufficient to spend it. But now, he says the church can also spend the money for food and then dispense the food. Well, I think we made a lot of progress tonight.

In fact, we've just made a considerable amount of progress. Now, brother Woods, can the church supply a building in which the needy can be cared for in? It can dispense the food. Can it supply a building when such is necessary? And then, brother Woods, can it supply the personnel? If so, if it supplies it, it dispenses it, is it church work or home work? It's church work to dispense food. Why isn't it church work to provide a building and personnel? Just like 1 Timothy 5:16 says, "… that the church may relieve them that are widows indeed." Item by item, statement by statement.

Then he says concerning … Can a family preach? He says, "Of course, they can." Alright, can both the family and the church, brother Woods, relieve? If so, why are you contending for this benevolent organization? Just let them do it. And if you can get another organization besides the family, and you say this organization here is different from the superintendent, matrons, so forth, why can't you have the same thing in evangelism? Show the principle that condemns it.

Then he says a man's a member of his own family and also a member of the orphan home and so forth, but it's just one man serving. Here's an elder serving as an elder and he's serving as a Board member and something else and so forth. Well, brother Woods said that was rather absurd, or something to that effect. I don't remember, but it doesn't make too much difference. What does that prove about benevolent organizations? Where does that show the scripture for his benevolent organizations such as this one that he says that these things are not a part of that corporation? But he says something about them being a part of the organization. What's the difference in the organization and the corporation as referred to there, brother Woods? Tell us. And incidentally, when you've got a man a member of this benevolent organization known as Tennessee Orphan Home and you've got a man a member of his own family, is he in two divine institutions? He says that thing is a divine institution and he says his family is a divine institution, is he in two of them, brother Woods? Is he? Is he?

WOODS: What about the church and his own home?
SUTTON: The what?

56

WOODS: What about the church and his own home. Is he in two divine institutions?

SUTTON: The church in his own home?

WOODS: The church and his own home.

SUTTON: The church and his (the church's) own home? Is that what you're talking about?

WOODS: No!

SUTTON: What are you talking about? The church in whose home?

WOODS: You were ridiculing the idea of a person being in two divine institutions. What about a person who's a member of the church and a member of his own home? How many is that?

SUTTON: I got you now.

WOODS: Does that add up to two?

SUTTON: I got you now. Alright, he says, "What about a member of the church and a member of his own family?" You're going to have him in three institutions. You're going to have him in the family, the church, and his benevolent corporation that's no part of his family. So, you've got him in three; and if he happens to be a member of the State, he'd be in four according to you. And yet you say there are only three divine organizations. Thank you again, brother Woods. [HOLT: One minute.]

Of course, he wants to know about the qualifications of elders to spank, so forth. Well, you say the Board is parents, and yet you say they don't spank, so I suppose elders could do the work of relief and get somebody to spank like the board would, don't you? If not, why not? And of course, brother Woods said you can't put elders over the home, and yet in 1939, friends, he contended that was the only setup that was right, when you put elders over the home such as Tipton Home. You can read it over there on the wall if you want to; his direct quotation. That's what he contended for in 1939, but he says it can't be done, then he says it was done, and any other method was sinful. Read it anytime you get ready. We'll leave it there every night if you want to.

Then he had quite a bit to say about the restored home. He talks about here's the family destroyed and restored. My time is gone. Thank you very much. Brother Totty.

TOTTY: We want to express our appreciation to every one of you for your attention tonight and presence and invite you back tomorrow evening at 7:30. They will be discussing the same proposition and the same order tomorrow evening that they have tonight. That is, brother Woods would be in the affirmative and brother Sutton in the negative. We hope that all of you will be back and that even they'll be more. Shall be have a song at the close or just dismiss? Which one do you want to have? Just dismiss. Would you like to say something, brother Holt?

HOLT: I'd like to make about two or three brief statements. I, too, would like to express appreciation for the wonderful attention and the good order during the discussion. Certainly, we expected that knowing the people here and that is very commendable. This kind of discussion will always help all of us and we invite you back tomorrow evening at 7:30. But also in the morning at 10:00, remember the two speakers with about thirty-minute speeches each, bring the lessons, and you're invited to be in the building at that time.

TOTTY: What will be the subject tomorrow morning at 10:00, brother Holt?

HOLT: There are no certain subjects that have been selected. Who are the two men in the morning? [Someone in the audience: Brother Hollingsworth and Roy Fudge.]

Maybe some in the back didn't hear that: Brother Hollingsworth and Roy Fudge will be bringing a lesson on any subject they may select here at the building in the morning at 10:00.

TOTTY: It's usually a custom at debates like this that they have an open forum, but I don't suppose that will be the condition tomorrow since—it will not, will it brother Holt? There will not be an open forum. We just want to get this matter straight, so we'll know what to expect.

Second Session
May 30, 1962
7:30 p.m.

W. L. Totty's Preliminary Remarks

There is just a little explanation I'd like to make before we enter into the discussion tonight. It is customary in debates that the affirmative always open the service. I have seen many debates, I've attended many, and been in quite a number myself. I've never seen that custom broken by anybody until last night. I've debated with Holiness, Baptist, Methodist, and just about everything. I asked brother Sutton, tonight, if that were an oversight and he said no, that it was agreed by this congregation that we cannot lead a song in this house. I just don't feel like this congregation agreed to that. I feel like maybe it's brother Sutton and two or three others. Now, the point that I want to make is that they have cried all over the country that we "quarantine" them; that we're drawing a line of fellowship, but I've never seen that before in any church, not even Baptist or Methodist. I'd just like to call attention to that tonight, that who is drawing the line of fellowship when you refuse to let a person lead a song or lead a prayer in your building, and he said, "This building belongs to us, and you can't do it." Garfield Heights, where I preach, has furnished a building for three debates for these brethren. They always have equal rights. I've just come from one in Clearwater, Florida in January where we furnished the building there, and we had the equal rights. Now, we want to be respected and we intend to respect everybody, but we have to have our rights, and that's the reason I'm making this statement. All of us are not amateurs in this, and if everything goes off and each side shows the due respect, we won't have any trouble with it. Otherwise, we might. So, we just want the congregation to know that is the way it stands tonight. You are the ones whom the blame is laid upon, that you have agreed. Now, I don't know whether you did or not. That's between you and brother Sutton.

The propositions for tonight, I shall read it now,: "It is in harmony with the scriptures for churches of Christ to build and maintain benevolent organizations such as Tennessee Orphan Home, Boles Home, Home for the Aged, and other such organizations for the care of the needy." Brother Guy N. Woods will affirm that tonight and brother Carrol R. Sutton will deny it.

Another statement is that it's against the rules of honorable debate for the negative to introduce any new material in his last negative. I would like to insist that brother Sutton has, tonight, to introduce any chart or anything new in the way of new material will have to be introduced before his last speech if it's allowed to go in this debate. Brother Woods will now ...

HOLT: I want to say something, brother Totty.

TOTTY: Alright. Pardon me.

HOLT: Before brother Woods brings the first speech, I did want to say this. I know that you're not here for confusion that might arise over and result in a wrangle. It was the decision of the congregation, as the men have told me, to come to the decision that was mentioned by brother Sutton and, of course, they know it. But some are here visiting, and we appreciate your presence, that doesn't know it. Whatever reflection was cast on him, I'd just like to suggest it was the decision. But they have consented, since they do want the discussion to go on so badly, to go ahead with what has been gone through with tonight. At this time, you can hear brother Woods.

TOTTY: Just another statement, too. They insisted when we told them we would do it if the debate continued, and if they had thought it was a sin for us to lead a song or lead a prayer on this debate, they have consented to sin in order for it to go on. The point I want to make is it was merely a personal matter with them, and they

60

didn't think it was a sin in the beginning, and they didn't dare say they did. If they do, then they're guilty of condoning sin in order to have the discussion. I don't think brother Sutton's ready to say that. It isn't any matter of ours who's responsible for it. We're just standing for our rights. Now, brother, do you want to say something else?

WOODS: Now, you folks just sit down, and we may continue this for an hour.

HOLT: One more statement I'd like to make. The congregation here has not consented to what happened. In other words, without one brother here saying it could go different than what the congregation decided, the song was led and the prayer. But we want the discussion to go on and, hence, have allowed it for that reason.

TOTTY: Yes. I'd just like to emphasize, too, that he doesn't believe it's a sin. It was a personal matter in the beginning. If he'd thought it was a sin, they would not have allowed it to go on. I just want that to go into your minds. It was purely a personal matter. If they had believed it was a sin for us to lead a song in this building, they would have rescinded their decision, and I don't think they'll say they would. Brother Woods will now ...

WOODS: Now, brother Totty, before my time begins, I want a word or two along that line, too. Now, will you fellows please sit down and let us proceed.

SUTTON: Alright, just a minute, brother Woods. I'm having a little difficulty with my recorder.

WOODS: Just wait until he gets his recorder fixed.

Now, before my time begins, just a word or two, friends. We are by no means aroused about this matter. I am really surprised. I have been engaging in debates for about 35 years. I have met Holiness and Baptist and Catholics and Methodist and almost every type and kind of representative. I've met many of them in their meeting houses. For the first time, here tonight, we were asked not to take part in the affirmative preliminary matters. That's the first time I ever heard of that happening. We didn't ask it as a favor, we demanded it as a right. When we are in the affirmative, it's our place to have charge of the preliminaries, and we simply said either we'd do that or the debate would not proceed. We did not ask that as a favor, we insisted upon it as a right, and the fact that these people have decided that we're not to do that is unheard of and unparalleled by people who claim to deal fairly with another. Now, we ought to be, we ought to act like Christians. We ought to conduct ourselves in the way that Christian people are expected to do so, and it is ridiculous and regrettable that brothers can become so obsessed in their malice against others that they would act in a fashion worse than denominational people.

Another thing, brother Sutton last night repeatedly walked over here and asked me questions. Now, anytime anybody asks me a question that I think deserves an answer, I feel like giving him an answer, and I shall rise up on my feet and answer each question he asks on those under those circumstances, if I feel that it's a matter that deserves an answer at the time. Now, he can remember that, and when I walk over here and ask him to answer, I mean for him to answer right then. Anytime I ask him a question, I'd like an answer right then, and he can use his judgment about whether he does or not. I just explained that.

A third thing. These brethren, usually along toward the end of the debate, distribute a lot of mimeographed material in an effort to try to patch up what they can't answer in preaching. If that's done here, either before or after the session begins and outside the time of it, I'm going to take up such material and reply to it. Now, I just served notice that there may be no misunderstanding regarding it. There's nobody disturbed or aroused or mad, but we do intend to conduct our part of the debate as it should be. Now, my time may begin.

Guy N. Woods' Fourth Affirmative Speech

The proposition that I'm affirming tonight is this: "It is in harmony with the scriptures for churches of Christ to build and maintain benevolent organizations such as the Tennessee Orphan

Home, Boles Home, Home for the Aged, and other such organizations for the care of the needy." I went into detail last night and defined the terms of that proposition. I do not think it is necessary to consume valuable time repeating those matters. The issue is clear.

It's my obligation to show from the scriptures that it's scriptural for congregations to make donations from their treasuries to the organizations named. I'd like to emphasize briefly the argument that I made last night which brother Sutton didn't touch top, side, edge, or bottom of. I could sit down now, and my part of this debate has been established, but in order that you may see how clearly and how strong the truth is, let me call your attention to this fact. We pointed out to you that every child has, or is entitled to have, a family relationship. The word 'home' on this chart simply suggests that relationship. I am not referring to the building. I defined the word by the word 'family.' I used the word 'family' as a synonym for it, and in any instance where brother Sutton is confused regarding the significance of the word, let him substitute the word 'family' for the word 'home' and you'll have my usage of it here. Every child then, has a right to that relationship. Sometimes, through no fault of the child, that relationship is lost, and then there are those who re-establish that family relationship. It's proper and right for the church to donate to the needy family so long as the structure is obtained. That when the structure is gone, it's proper and right for it to be re-established and the church to contribute to this re-established family relationship, and last night we established that beyond controversy.

Now, brother Sutton comes back with this contention. He said last night that what we have here is a corporation. The churches contribute to the corporation and the corporation in turn provides a home and necessities and personnel. He maintains that there is some sort of organization between the church that contributes and the family relationship. Now, if he's right about it, he's just as wrong in his practice as we are. Now, get this please. They have here, or have had in the past, an incorporation that operates a church building. At least, that is organized for that purpose. The church donated funds to this corporation. Now, if Sutton is correct in his argument, what that corporation did was to take the money that the church gave it and, with

63

the money, provide what he calls a house. He means by the word 'home,' a house. Now, if what he says is right about the orphan home, you have had here and, perhaps still have, exactly what he opposes. If the corporation that we refer to as a part of the orphan home, if it is distinct from and independent of it, then you've got exactly what he opposes right here. I ask you, Sutton, is the corporation the church? Is it another organization? If it is, then you've got what you oppose. If it's not, then your objection is invalid. The truth of the business is that the corporation is itself an integral part of the home, and the money is simply sent to the home. The only reason that there is a corporation is in order to meet the requirements of good business practice, and the only reason that it's a lasting institution is because you have to have such in order to be legal. Now, that argument is utterly without validity. I just insist that he tell us where the corporation that provided this building is in relation to this drawing. Now, Sutton, don't forget that when you get up here. That will suffice for the speech that he made last evening. That was the only point that he made that had any significance whatsoever.

Now, friends, since I am in the affirmative, I wish to proceed with some affirmative material. But I'd like to know when I have about five minutes left.

I have called your attention to the fact that every child is, or should have, a part in a family relationship. Paul establishes this in Ephesians 6:1-6; establishing, if you will, the parent-child relationship there. In Galatians chapter four and verses one and two, the apostle chose the legality of a parent, or of a child being placed in a guardian or steward relationship, and that to be maintained in harmony by law. A child needs and must have food and shelter and clothing and supervision.

Now, let's turn this chart around right here. Now, you may see the need of an orphan child. In Galatians chapter two and verse ten, Paul said they were admonished to remember the poor, which also they did. Now, for the orphans, there is the requirement of a place and food and clothing and education and supervision and medical care. Those are not functions of the church as such. It is not the function of the church to serve as a child care agency nor to administer discipline or recreation. These are responsibilities of the home or the family and, hence, the church cannot operate properly in that realm, but it can support a needy family and enable the family to operate.

Now, our second part here is: Is the church obligated to supply the funds with which to provide these needs? In James 1:27, James tells us that we're "to visit the fatherless and widows in their affliction." That's not exclusively individual. If it is, you couldn't obey it without providing for at least two children and two widows because the word "fatherless" is plural in the Greek text and so also is the word "widows." In 1 Timothy chapter five and verse sixteen, Paul makes obligatory, for the church, the care of the widows. That since James mentions the fatherless in connection with the widows, it would follow that the obligation is equal and, hence, it's a church relationship. Now, friends, one of two things is true. Either the New Testament designates clearly how that obligation is set out or it doesn't. If it designates the obligation, then all we need to do is turn to the text, find what it says, and put it into practice, and we'll have it. But there's not a person present who knows anything about this matter but that knows that there's not the remotest hint as to the details by which to carry out this obligation right here. Now, when God gives a law and, in connection with that law, specifies the mode of procedure, then it becomes a part of the law. But when He doesn't, then it falls into the area of expediency. Now, get this. In 1 Timothy chapter four verse 1, Paul said that, "The Spirit speaketh expressly," that is plainly and clearly, "that in the latter times some shall depart from the faith, giving heed to seducing spirits and doctrines of demons." Now, look. "Forbidding to marry and commanding to abstain from meats." Paul said that a token of the apostasy would be that men would forbid to marry and command to abstain from meats.

In 1 Corinthians 7, Paul discusses the subject of marriage at length and points out that it was a matter of choice. That it was not wrong if a person, assuming there were no scriptural barriers, whether he got married or not. If he did, he was not violating God's law or if he didn't. It was a matter of choice. But Paul says if somebody says you can't, that's the doctrine of demons. There was nothing wrong in eating meat that was sold in the market place providing, of course, it didn't cause a weak brother to stumble. It wasn't wrong to eat it, it wasn't wrong if one didn't eat it. One could exercise the choice, but if somebody came along and says you can't, Paul says that's the doctrine of the devil.

Now, you get this, friends. There is the base of every division that has originated in the church of Christ. It's over an effort on the part of brethren to make laws where God made none. For example, we're commanded to teach, and we're told what to teach. But the anti-Sunday School fellow comes along and says that you've got to teach in one way or you can't teach another way. What does he do? He makes a law where God made none. Take the one cup advocate who substitutes the container for the content. He makes a law where God made none. What about the anti-preacher position advocated by some? That's exactly the same thing. What about those who oppose meeting houses? Same principle.

Now, the Bible commands us to visit. It does not designate how that obligation is to be carried out by the church. It necessitates church activity, but it doesn't designate whether it will be in a private home, in a foster home, in an adoption home, or in a legal home. When Sutton comes along and specifies how it can't be, he's making laws where God made none. Paul says that's the doctrine of the devil. You've seen the bitter fruits of it in this area. Now, that, friends, is what we're arguing here tonight. Get this please. The orphan home isn't in conflict with the church because they're not performing the work of the church. They're performing the work of the family. Because it's not family work, they're engaged in church work. They're engaged in the actual participation here. It's up to the church to administer the funds. It's the obligation of the family to take the money and spend it.

I've asked this man repeatedly to tell us whether or not the church can engage in recreation. He answered a question last evening in which he said that, "No. The church couldn't buy toys for an orphan child." That is, he said that it wasn't necessary to do it. Now, he thinks it's necessary to buy toys for his children. By what right does he think that an orphan child ought to be denied what he grants his? I'm perfectly willing for his children to have them, but I'm not willing for him to say that the church can't provide the same thing for those who call upon the church for assistance. Now, that, friends, is the matter.

Now, to his question before. Or to the answers to his—to my questions—answers I say. [TOTTY: Five minutes.] Answers, mind you. You decide whether they're answers. I asked last night—I asked him repeatedly, "Brother Sutton, could the church operate a kitchen in the basement of this building"? Now, you may wonder why I asked that question. Here's the reason. He has said that there's no need for any other organization except the church to provide for the needs of the needy. One of the needs of the needy is food. I say, according to your proposition, the church could supervise a kitchen, operate a kitchen. I said, "Brother Sutton, could you put a kitchen in the basement of this building"? I pressed that point repeatedly. Did he answer it? No. Now, do you think these fellows intend to reply to what I'm saying? Do you? They're paying no attention whatever to what I'm saying. Did they evidence to you any desire to answer this? Now, Sutton, I intend for you to answer this. I intend for you to answer this, or these people will leave here tonight knowing that you won't do it. And I asked him the question. Here's what he said, "The scriptures that authorizes the church to provide such when and if necessary are 1 Corinthians 16:1-4; 2 Corinthians 8 and 9; Acts 6:1-6. God hasn't bound a method; hence, the church would have a choice in the method it uses." I never asked him anything about a method. I asked him if you could have a kitchen in the basement of this building. What has that to do with methods used? Now, Sutton, can the church operate a kitchen in the basement of this building?

I asked him secondly, in order to pinpoint it, "Suppose a cyclone should strike through this area and should destroy every private home in this congregation and the only building left standing was the meeting house. If that were to happen, would it be scriptural for the church to set up a soup kitchen and have a bread line to feed the people? I asked him to specify who could be assisted. Listen to at least a part of what he said here. He just rambles on and on. You could write and say, use more words and say less than anybody I've heard in a long time. He said if that were to happen the congregation would decide on the method of administering the relief it would assist. The congregation would decide. I never asked him that. I never asked him about anybody deciding anything. I asked him if it would be scriptural for it to happen in a basement here. Why doesn't this fellow answer these questions? And you heard him preaching around here. You see?

Then I asked him next, now, this is a gem here, I said, "Brother Sutton, does the scriptures, in your opinion, make any provisions for the care, by the church, of a retarded child?" You'll listen to this gem of an answer. "In some cases, possibly. In most cases, no." Now, that's really answering my question, isn't it? That's saying yes and no at the same time. I just asked him this simple question: "Can the church, with its own organization, provide for a retarded child"? Well, in some cases, possibly. In most cases, no. Now, would that retarded child be a part of the congregation or would it be in another congregation?" Now, friends, he hasn't answered the question, and you know he hasn't, and Sutton knows he hasn't. But the reason he won't answer it is that he's afraid to make a statement that he knows he can't justify in harmony with his position.

Now, also, he has up here, on these charts, statements which he alleges are in conflict with my position tonight. There is not a word of truth in it. I endorse every statement that's on the top. These quotations from me, he takes them out of context. I was fighting the missionary society before anybody ever thought about opposing the orphan home, and I believe every one of them, but what I believed or didn't believe in 1939 has nothing to do with this matter tonight. I'm not opposed to him using it, but I'm just serving notice on him that one more reference to that and I'm going to proceed to show the ugly trail of divided churches that's in his path. Now, Sutton, just drop it. Just go right on and that's what will happen, thank you.

Carrol R. Sutton's Fourth Negative Speech

Gentlemen moderators, brother Woods, ladies and gentlemen:
I'm certainly thankful for this occasion on which we have here

assembled for the purpose of discussing things that are taught in God's book. The very fact that you're here evidences your interest in such matters. I trust and pray that, as we study together a number of things that we find in God's book tonight, all of us will be impressed with the simplicity of the word of God and how the word of God will show that which isn't right will certainly fall. The very fact that you're here shows that you're concerned about truth, and we trust and pray that all of us will be interested only in that which is right.

Truth is important. Our Lord on one occasion said, "And ye shall know the truth and the truth shall make you free," John 8 verse 32. In John 17 and verse 17, Jesus said, "Thy word is truth." We find in John 12 verse 48 that Jesus shows we'll be judged by His words in the last day. In view of the fact that we'll be judged by the words of Christ on the last day, we ought to be more concerned about discussing what the word of God says. I trust and pray that all of us are here for that purpose. I believe that we are. At least, most of us.

If I know my heart, I'm not here to please men but God, as Galatians 1:10 shows. I'm not here to defend human organizations, but I'm here to defend a divine organization, the church of the living God, as being an all-sufficient organization to do all that God requires of His people in organized capacity. I'm here to oppose human organizations such as Tennessee Orphan Home, Boles Home, etc. being set up to do the work of the church. Now, brother Woods says that these organizations are not set up to do the work of the church but the work of the family, yet he says that churches may build and maintain such. Therefore, brother Woods is saying that churches may build and maintain organizations to do a work which is not the work of the church. Now, brother Woods, why are you defending churches of Christ building and maintaining benevolent organizations to do a work which you say is not the work of the church? He says that's the work of the family and that he's going to build and maintain, by churches of Christ, those organizations to do some work which he says is not the work of the church, but he failed to produce any scripture.

Now, let's read the proposition that brother Woods is supposed to be affirming: "It is in harmony with the Scriptures for churches of Christ to build and maintain benevolent organizations such as the Tennessee Orphan Home, Boles Home, Home for the Aged, and other such organizations for the care of the needy." Now, brother Woods signed his name to that proposition. He spoke for one hour last evening, but he failed to produce one passage of scripture that remotely hints at such a benevolent organization as the Tennessee Orphan Home. Brother Woods spent one third of his time this evening and still hasn't given that passage of scripture that authorizes that human organization. Now, brother Woods, you signed your name to give the passage of scripture. I'm asking for the scripture, brother Woods. You only have two more speeches, twenty minutes each, and then you'll be out of the affirmative. Why don't you give me that passage of scripture tonight? I'm asking you, brother Woods.

WOODS: Brother Sutton.

SUTTON: Give me the passage of scripture that...

WOODS: Alright.

SUTTON: ...authorizes churches of Christ to build and maintain benevolent organizations such as Tennessee Orphan Home, Boles Home, etc.

WOODS: Alright.

SUTTON: Hold my time, brother Holt.

WOODS: No, don't hold his time. He asked me to do this. James 1:27 and 1 Timothy 5:16, Mark 14:7, Acts 20:35. That ought to be enough for you to start on. Work on those awhile.

SUTTON: Brethren and neighbors and friends, not one of the passages of scripture that he gave even remotely hints to a benevolent organization. I referred to those passages last evening. James 1:27 doesn't, Galatians 2:10 doesn't, 1 Timothy 5:16 doesn't, and so, brother Woods, I'm still looking for the passage of scripture that gives authority for the benevolent organization. Will you give it to me? I'm asking you, brother Woods. Please give me the passage of scripture...

WOODS: I defined benevolent organizations.

SUTTON: Hold my time, brother Holt.

WOODS: Don't hold his time. He's asking me.

SUTTON: Hold my time.

WOODS: I didn't ask you to hold my time.

TOTTY: Point of order. Now, if he wants these questions

answered, they'll be answered on his time. If he doesn't want them answered on his time, then don't ask them.

WOODS: Brother Sutton, here's what I said. I said by the word 'benevolent organization,' I simply meant the family legally determined, and I gave as my passage that God wants it done that way. Psalms 68:5 and 6, "God's the father of the fatherless and a judge of widows. God puts the solitary in families." That was my authority for the family and I defined the family as a benevolent organization, and then other passages show the obligation of the church to it.

SUTTON: Alright, start my time, brother Holt.

WOODS: You take up those passages.

SUTTON: Neighbors and friends, he still hasn't given one passage of scripture that mentions benevolent organizations.

TOTTY: That's a point of order.

SUTTON: Hold my time, brother Holt.

TOTTY: Yeah, hold his time this time because I'm talking. You take those passages of scripture and prove they don't mean that. It's not enough to say they don't mean that. We don't know whether you know that much or not, but you take them up and prove they don't mean that. Tell us what they do mean. Now, you can start his time.

HOLT: Uh, I'd like to suggest this. It seems that some, for some reason, are a little bit bothered. I'm going to repeat, first of all, that brother Sutton, since it seems to be bothering brother Woods, just address the audience. And number two: the people who were here last night realize that brother Sutton took those verses up, one by one, and so if you were here, you heard, and you know they were dealt with in a way that all could see.

TOTTY: When brother Holt says he took them up last night he admits that brother Woods gave them last night. Brother Sutton said he didn't get any. Now, we want your exegesis on those verses before you just passed them by and say that's not so. You tell us what they mean.

SUTTON: Are you through?

TOTTY: For the time being, yes.

SUTTON: Start my time, brother Holt. Brethren, neighbors, and friends, I still suggest to you that not one passage of scripture that he's given remotely refers, in any sense, shape, or fashion, to a

71

benevolent organization such as the Tennessee Orphan Home. Here's a thing that's chartered under laws of the State of Tennessee. Here's a Board of Directors. Here's a human organization. Now, brother Woods can talk about a family all he wants to, but this human organization is not a family. This human organization is chartered under the laws of the State of Tennessee that in turn provides a home, necessaries, and personnel.

Last evening, brother Woods said that the personnel, that is the superintendent and the matrons, were no part of this Board of Directors. So, he admitted last evening that this Board of Directors then is one thing and the superintendent and the matrons, which comprise the family with the children, is something else. So, I maintain, brethren, neighbors, and friends, that he still hasn't shown any passage of scripture. Let me say this. When I address questions to brother Woods, I'm doing that for emphasis. I explained that last evening. Now, when he addresses questions to me, I know enough to keep my mouth shut till I get up on the platform, and brother Woods used to know enough, too. I don't know what's the matter tonight, but anyway, he said over at Newborn that when a man popped up from his seat, his seat was getting hot. I don't know what's wrong tonight, so you be the judge. But anyway, I will say this: that I'm asking questions for emphasis, and I'm asking brother Woods to answer those questions when he gets on the platform. Will you do that, brother Woods?

WOODS: I will answer every question asked me at the time you ask it. Now ...

SUTTON: When you get on the platform.

WOODS: Now, you're out of order when you ask me a question from the platform if you don't want it answered. If you're debating with the congregation—if you don't want it answered from me.

SUTTON: Stop my time, brother Holt. I suppose brother Woods wishes I were debating with you, but for some reason you haven't signed your name to this proposition, have you? Now, brother Woods signed his name to affirm that 'it is in harmony with the scriptures for churches of Christ to build and maintain benevolent organizations'! Now, that's what he signed to affirm. Now, brother

72

Woods should give a passage of scripture. You can ask Baptist preachers for the passage of scripture which shows salvation by faith only and, oh, they give a lot of passages of scripture, but not one of them shows salvation by faith only. I can ask brother Woods for the passage of scripture that shows his benevolent organization, and not one of them even mentions such benevolent organizations as those in the proposition. You be the judge.

Now, we're not discussing the question of should the needy be cared for, is the church obligated, can a home be provided when necessary, systematic arrangement, or matter of how or method. We're discussing: "Is it scriptural for churches of Christ to build and maintain benevolent organizations." Brother Woods says that churches of Christ may do that, but he hasn't shown the scripture for it. He says, "by build and maintain" he means support and establish, but yet he's contended that the church can supply the money only. That's all it's authorized to do. Now, where does the establishing or building come in? If he says they can build and maintain them, he says they can build and maintain that over which the church has no control whatsoever. Deal with it, brother Woods, when you come to the platform. Now, since brother Woods is affirming that these benevolent organizations are scriptural, then we're asking for the passage of scripture that mentions benevolent organizations in principle. Anyway you get it in. He hasn't got it in yet brethren, neighbors, and friends. I believe all of you can see that.

Now, let's notice here, for example, brother Woods' chart on the church and the home move entirely aligned. Brother Woods, where's the passage of scripture on that chart. You said, "It's in harmony with the scriptures." Where is the passage of scripture, neighbors and friends, that shows such to be 'in harmony with the scriptures' as his proposition says? Now, just grant everything on the chart to be so as far as there being a home, a family, to begin with; that thing broken and then that thing restored. Where is his benevolent organization? That's what his proposition said. Now, where is it? It's not even on the chart, is it? And if it were, he wouldn't have any scripture for it.

Alright, let's notice this other chart he has here. He says, "Remember the poor, Galatians 2:10." He says this requires for the orphan a place, food, clothing, and so forth. And he says, "Now, this is family work and it's the work of the church to furnish money." Last evening, he said it was the work of the church to dispense food, didn't he? Is the church getting involved in family work when it dispenses food? And incidentally, brother Woods, I'd like for you to show us, when you come to the platform, your benevolent organization on here. Where is his benevolent organization, friends? Galatians 2:10 says, "remember the poor." That's what I advocate. Remember the poor but where is his benevolent organization? Where is it? Has anybody seen it? Can anybody find it in that passage? That's what he's offered as proof. He says, "There it is," but his benevolent organization is not on the chart. But now, these things here, he says, are means for the orphans and these things over here are means for the aged are simply supplied by his benevolent organization which isn't on the chart and not authorized. Incidentally, brother Woods said back in 1946 that those seven men in Acts 6 had the supervision. Were they engaged in family work or church work when they supervised the serving of the tables? We're still asking for the passage of scripture, neighbors and friends, and that's the very thing that brother Woods hasn't shown and he won't show because it's not to be found in God's book.

I might mention here also, too, in respect to what's been suggested about the last negative speech of the evening and new material being presented in it. There hasn't been any rules, as far as I know, in any way, shape, form, or fashion signed to that effect. Now, if they want to enforce a rule that isn't a rule at all then they can feel free to do so, but there's not a rule signed to that effect whatsoever. I accept every rule that we signed, and so they can do as they see fit about that.

We might notice chart number 3 here again. That here is the Tennessee Orphan Home, a benevolent organization, to which churches send their funds that it, in turn, might provide the home, necessary, and personnel for the care of the orphans at Springhill, Tennessee. That charter of incorporation says it may establish branches in any county of the State. That means that it might provide at least 94 other orphanages or orphan homes for those who are needy. One institution, one Board of Directors oversee, if they want to, a number of homes.

We notice also another chart that entitled: "Is Boles Orphan Home a Benevolent Society?" We have here a situation which the Board of Directors calls Boles Orphan Home and this Board of Directors supervises Boles Home at Quinlan, Texas. It also supervises the Sherwood-Myrtle Foster Home at Steubenville, Texas. There's a place, facilities, necessaries, and personnel at both of these different places. They're 150 miles apart. Both of them have managers over them but here's one board. Here's one organization that operating two orphanages, if you please. Here's one institution that is overseeing Boles Home; yet this institution overseeing the Sherwood-Myrtle Foster Home. There are two Homes being operated by this one Board of Directors and, so then, we see a distinct difference between the Boles Orphan Home Corporation, this Board of Directors, and the Homes that they supervise and oversee. Now, brother Woods is supposed to be defending this organization that's between the churches and the Homes provided by the corporation. I'm not asking for scripture for the churches. I'm not asking for scriptures for the homes or families. I'm asking for the scripture for Boles Orphan Home Board of Directors. That's the thing that brother Woods hasn't shown yet. That's what I'm asking for, brother Woods. Would you please give it when you come to the platform? Would you give me that passage of scripture when you come to the platform, please? I want you to, brother Woods. You feel free to do that. In fact, write it on the board for me.

Then brother Woods said the obligation is set forth in James 1:27. That doesn't give the how.

Then with respect to 1 Timothy 4, verses 1-4, about some forbidding to marry, men abstaining from meats, and he says, "doctrines of devils and when somebody tells, like brother Sutton does, that you ought not to live this way, that's a doctrine of the devil." Now, with respect to the means, modes, or methods, that I'm not doing that, and brother Woods knows it. I'm not binding a "how," but I am showing that God has bound in 1 Timothy 5 and verse 16 the church. The apostle Paul says that "it," talking about the church, "that it may relieve them that are widows indeed." That's what Paul bound by divine authority. That's the organization that God said ought to do that work of relief that the church is responsible for. That's what I'm contending for, brethren.

Then he talked about the no-class people, the one-cup people, the anti-preacher people, and so forth, and he says they're making laws where God hasn't made one. But, neighbors and friends, think about this. When it comes to the church relieving, I'm not making a law where God hasn't made one because I've read the passage of scripture that says that the church is to do that. That's what I'm contending for. [HOLT: Five minutes.]

But when brother Woods will step outside of the bounds of divine authority and then take hold of the human organization, then he tries to bring that over and tie that on to the church, then you have an addition to the word of God. If he could produce the passage of scripture, he would have done so. I believe that he would. I'm asking him to, when he comes to the platform, tell the passage of scripture, brother Woods. That's what your proposition says. Incidentally, when he talked about it being a doctrine of the devil to tell how not to do it, it just happens on page 238 of the *Porter-Woods Debate* that brother Woods described a situation that would be sinful; that would be wrong for churches to engage in: in sending money to an organization that in turn would establish orphanages. Now, he showed that it's wrong to do it like that. I wonder if brother Woods is teaching a doctrine of the devil? He said it was a doctrine of the devil to do that. He said it was a doctrine of the devil to do that. He said Sutton is teaching the doctrine of the devil when he says it's wrong to do it like this over here. Brother Woods comes up here and says though, in the *Porter-Woods Debate* on page 238, that it is wrong for churches to send to an organization that in turn establishes orphanages. He's teaching the doctrine of the devil according to his own writing, isn't he? He says that's wrong; that's the wrong way to do that thing. Well, thank you, brother Woods. Thank you very much.

Then, of course, brother Woods read my questions and he said, "Now, brother Sutton doesn't intend to answer them." Said, "Look at him. He doesn't intend to." Did you know at the very time he said that, I don't know whether he was rattled or not, but he had the answers

76

written out to his questions on the sheet he had in his hand? And he said, "Brother Sutton doesn't intend to answer." Why, I had already answered them, handed them to him, in writing! That's what the rules were, and that's what I did. And he said, "Now, look here. He doesn't intend to answer them." I'd already done that, brethren. I wonder sometimes. Do you ever wonder?

Notice also that brother Woods had quite a bit to say about the church furnishing money, and he says that's church work. Families should try to relieve by family work, and yet last evening he said that the Seven in Acts 6 dispensed food; that the church may dispense both money and food. Is it getting involved in family work when it does? What about it, brethren? I maintain that the church can relieve. That's what the apostle Paul said, "That *it*," the church, "might relieve them that are widows indeed." Now, brother Woods has two more speeches tonight in the affirmative. I'm encouraging him to come before this audience and produce the passage of scripture that authorizes, not the church, not the family, but this benevolent organization that he signed 'is in harmony with the Scriptures for the churches to build and maintain.'

He used last evening a statement or two concerning the family and benevolent organizations being synonyms. I deny. I demand the proof of it. I deny that the word 'family' and the word 'benevolent organization' are synonyms. I demand the proof of it. There's a vast difference, neighbors and friends, between a family and a benevolent organization such as Boles Orphan Home. You keep this in mind. It doesn't matter what may be said. The point that we're discussing is: 'Is it scriptural for churches of Christ to build and maintain such organizations as Boles Home.' That's the proposition. It's not whether or not churches of Christ may relieve the needy. It's not whether or not churches of Christ may provide a place, facilities, necessaries, and personnel, but it's whether or not churches of Christ may build and maintain benevolent organizations such as Boles Orphan Home that is operating two homes. I'm asking for the scripture. Brother Woods, I want you to bring the scripture when you come before us. All that he may say about it won't change what the word of God says in the least. I'm asking for the scripture. Not the scripture for the church, not the scripture for the family, but the scripture for these benevolent organizations—these human institutions that stand between the church and the work that's being done. Now, I believe if there is any such scripture, surely, brother Woods will produce it in his next speech. Thank you.

Guy N. Woods' Fifth Affirmative Speech

Brethren moderators, brother Sutton, ladies and gentlemen:

One of the rules that we signed was that we'd divide time equally. Now, this moderator of his gave him three minutes extra tonight, so we claim that in order that we may divide time equally, I have—just sit down now. That's what we're going to do, just sit down. You're out of order.

HOLT: I'd like to suggest since he says brother Sutton used three minutes extra, the clock is now 20 till, brother Woods is welcome to three minutes—23 minutes.

WOODS: Thank you, sir. Well, that's very generous of you to give us what is rightfully ours. Much obliged, sir.

Now, friends, we're all in good spirits, and nobody is disturbed. We're just arguing these points, and we're enabling you to see some matters that you'd never hear from this pulpit, unless some of us come in here and taught you this, because Sutton's not going to teach you. He cited here in the outset John 8:32, John 17:17, and 12:48 — references to the truth. They're totally out of his category. A man that's fighting the truth like he is should have no interest in such passages. I'm contending for the truth tonight. All of us ought to be. You'll decide who has it, and all this stuff about who has the truth and who hasn't is certainly beside the point because it's a question for you to decide. I'm perfectly willing to leave it up to you.

Now, brother Sutton says that I'm using the phrase benevolent organization, in the sense of family, improperly. There's a quick way to settle that. Brother Sutton, is your family a benevolent organization?

78

Now, it either is or it isn't. If it is a benevolent organization, then he admits that the family is a benevolent organization. If he says it's not, then he denies the very argument that he's making that some of these obligations are individual obligations. Now, Sutton, I don't have the least idea you'll answer that, but I'd like to know if you think your family is a benevolent organization. I'd just be glad to know what that fellow thinks about that, and you see he can't see one inch ahead of his nose. He just plunges headlong into difficulty, one after another. Every time I meet one of these fellows, I think each one of them gets worse. I don't see how a fellow could blunder as badly as he does on some of these things. Come up here and say the family is not a benevolent organization. Well, it either is or isn't. If it's not, then he's shown us how that even the individual can't practice benevolence. Why, he just told us that James 1:27 was exclusively individual and was to be done by individuals, but he tells us now, that the family is not a benevolent organization; therefore, the family can't perform benevolence. I wonder how long you fellows are going to swallow this stuff. I just wonder how long intelligent people can swallow this stuff. The family not a benevolent organization.

Incidentally, you fellows start writing up this debate in your bulletins now. You be sure, now, and remember some of these little things happening around here. You start telling us about how Sutton wound Woods up. You remember about the kitchen deal, too. We'll have a little more to say about that later.

Ah, he says that Woods is defending human organizations and he's up here defending a divine organization. I say he's up here attacking a divine organization. I maintain that the church is all-sufficient for the work which God gave the church to do, and that's all I say in these statements. But God never gave to the church the work of being a family. Now, it just seems to me like an insult to your intelligence to go over and over and over that. Now, anybody ought to know there's a difference between a family and church! That the family has obligations that are not church obligations. That the church can't perform in the field of the family. Looks like anybody ought to see that.

"Now," he says, "give us proof where a church can build and maintain." I showed you there were more ways by which to build than take a hammer. The church doesn't go out and take a hammer and build a church building. The church supplies the funds, and what do you say about that organization here you've got to build the church building here? What do you say now, brother Sutton? You just grinned, didn't you? That's all. Now, if we've got a Board—let's turn that back over here and we'll have this later. If what he says about us is so, he's practicing the same thing. Many of these instances, they've got the same thing in reference to the preacher's home, his house, where the preacher lives. They have a corporation that provides a home for the preacher. Now, a lot of you fellows live in an arrangement of that kind. They don't object to it. It's alright for a Board of Trustees to furnish them a house, but they think it's wrong for the church to send money to a Board to conform to legal requirements in order to furnish a home for orphan children.

He said I failed to produce one scripture. Now, friends, he keeps calling for scripture. I produce passage after passage. I'm going to put some up here on the board. Now, it takes a lot more than Sutton's saying that these passages don't prove what I say they do. You want to know what the passage said. Now, here's my proof. In Matthew 16:18 we have the Lord's promise to build His church. We have in 1 Timothy chapter 3 and verses 13 and 14 that the church is the family of God, the household of God. We have in 1 Timothy chapter 5 and verse 16, we'll just put it down there, we have the church's obligation to widows. We have in James 1:27, we have the obligation to visit the fatherless and the widows. We showed from Galatians chapter 2 and verse 6 that the churches have an obligation to the poor. We've shown that the obligation necessitates clothes, food, clothing, shelter, recreation, discipline, education, and so on. We've shown that that's the function of the family. Now, the only question is: Where does God want these people that need this assistance that the church can provide? Where are they? Is it done in a church or is it done in a family? Will you let the Bible answer it? Now, get this. Psalms 68 verses 5 and 6: "God is the father of the fatherless and a judge of widows." Now, listen, "God setteth the solitary in families." Now, God says that it's in families! That's what I say. Sutton says it's in a church organization. Now, you can't just get out here and start a family of people who are not kin to you. You can't do it anywhere. You've got to have a license from the state. You'd get arrested if you tried to. It's right to conform to state law. When you conform to state law, this thing then becomes a benevolent organization, legally accepted, and it's complied with the law. Now, get this argument, please: All total situations, the scriptural characteristics of which can be established, are total situations which are scriptural. Every point of my proposition I've shown to be scriptural. Therefore, my argument here involves a total situation which is a scriptural situation. Now, that's the argument that these fellows have made so much fun about but never have answered. And which even Cogdill used on his last debate. Now, make fun of it. That's the argument how we prove items of worship that way. Look at it. You find in no passage all the scriptural items of worship: teaching, singing, contribution, Lord's Supper, and such. But if we know each one of these to be scriptural, then we have a 100% scriptural situation, and when we put them all together, we have a total situation which is scriptural. We prove the items of salvation that way: faith, repentance, confession, baptism. Not all of them mentioned in any one passage, and yet each one is scriptural, properly related. Then when they're all put together, they all constitute a one hundred percent scriptural situation. I proved each item in my proposition to be scriptural. Since each item is scriptural, then when you put them all together they make a scriptural situation. That's the argument, and nobody this side of torment are entered tonight.

"Now," he says, "write them on the board." Well, I've written on the board. I'd give a lot more, but I don't have time to write all these, but then that will do for him to work on for a while. I'll affirm that these fellows have no objections to the church providing a home by using a board of trustees. They have no objection to a board of trustees providing a church building. Now, I'd like to know if it's all right for the church to give money to their incorporation in order to provide a preacher's home. Why is it wrong for the same thing in connection with the orphan's home? Now, Sutton, answer that. We've asked you that two or three times; now, answer it.

Then he says, "Where's the scripture up here?" But it so happens that this is the G. C. Brewer chart that I've used in every debate. Brother Brewer prepared this chart. He wanted to know where the scripture is on it. The purpose of this is just to show that the church and the home move on parallel lines. One couldn't put on the chart all the scriptures that he proposes to use. The fact that there's not one written out on it is not significant. We've given passage after passage. That was the weakest, silliest quibble that an intelligent man could come up with.

He said, "Brother Woods has contradicted himself." I once said that the church could dispense money, and then I said it could dispense food. Why, of course, it can. It can dispense food just as well as it can money. But then when it dispenses food, it doesn't take over the family and tell the members of the family what they can have for breakfast, lunch, and dinner. It doesn't do that. It still lets the family run its business. One divine institution can't usurp the functions of another and operate like this fellow says.

He said if I want to enforce the rule of the no affirmative material in the last negative, well, I could just do it, but he hadn't signed any proposition. He didn't know any rule that established that. He didn't sign anything like that in the propositions—the rule. Well, that's very true because that's a universal rule of honesty and fairness. That shows how little regard that he has for fairness in this debate. Suppose that I'd wait until the last night, happens that in this particular debate I have the last speech. Suppose that I waited until that speech to bring in new material which I knew he wouldn't have any chance to answer. What would you think about me on that? Well, that would be dishonest; of course, it would. It's a fair rule that's been accepted by debaters in order that the opponent might have a chance to reply. That's all. Nothing but common honesty. Now, he can introduce it if he wants to tonight, but we'll stop him when he does.

He says that Boles Home is operating two or three different ones. Let's have the other chart over now, if we may, please. How much time is left? [TOTTY: Two minutes.]

Now, he says here that Boles Home is operating a home over here at Quinlan, and here's another one down at Stephenville, Texas. Now, brother Sutton, you're using the word home in two different senses, aren't you? You're using it in two different senses. You've got what you call the Board of Directors' home. You may say, "Oh, well, I got it in quotation marks." Now, I want to know if you actually think this is Boles Home here. If it is, then when you said that Boles Home is operating two other homes, then you were not telling the truth. If you think this is not a home here, then you ought not to say it is! The truth of the business is, friends, that he'd be just as truthful if he said Boles Home was operating thirteen homes because, listen, it so happens that they have the cottage system down at Boles Home. That is, instead of having one large building, as we represented here, they have a whole bunch of cottages over a large campus with people supervising over the children in these different cottages maintaining as close, as much as they can, a family relationship. Now, it would be just as truthful if he'd say there are thirteen homes. Well, he might say, "Yes, but one of them is way off down there 150 miles." He says they've got two different homes then. He has the idea that a person cannot live in the same family without living under the same roof. That's his argument. Now, get this, please. According to him, some man sends his son and daughter off to college, he's operating two families because he's got one of them, part of his family off in college and he's got another one, part of it, at home. If not, why not! Just because part of Boles Home is in one place and part is in another that means there are two different families. In that sense, then he's got two different families when part of the children are off at school. How many families can a fellow scripturally have, Sutton? Now, do you think he'll answer that when he gets back up here? He'll be as dumb as an oyster about it. Here's the truth of the matter, friends. There isn't but one family involved here. It so happens that there's an old brother down at Stephenville, Texas that gave them a farm that was worth $150,000 or more, and they use the facilities down there to provide for some of the children down there, but there isn't but one organization, and that's all operated like these twelve cottages are here. The only difference is that these cottages are farther away from the office than the others are. That's the only difference. When a fellow has to come up with that as opposition, he's getting on mighty weak ground.

"Oh," he said, "brother Woods came over here and asked him a question and demanded an answer, and he already had the answers written out." Well, I knew that, and I'd read them. I knew that he hadn't answered the question. Sutton, can the church operate a kitchen in the basement of this building? Now, friends, do you know why he won't answer that? That's not a hard question, is it? Now, do you think Sutton doesn't know the answer? It isn't that he doesn't know the answer. It isn't that he hasn't any convictions on it. It isn't that he hasn't been preaching on it around. It's just that I've got him backed up in a corner over there, and he can't answer either way without cutting his theological throat. That's the reason he doesn't answer. Now, I wouldn't answer myself if I was in the shape he's in. I couldn't and stay in the debate. Now, Sutton, why don't you answer that question? I'd answer it. If my tongue had to cleave to the roof of my mouth, I'd answer it. I wouldn't let somebody come over me and demand that I do something I couldn't do. I wouldn't do it. Sutton, up here's a little line I'm going to put out here. That's to remind you of the fact that I'm asking you the question, brother Sutton. You're going to have to answer it, and you will before this debate's over. I don't want to prolong the misery for you. Why don't you go ahead and answer it? You're going to have to. You can't stay in the debate. If you do or you don't, you're going to have to answer my question. I'll give up half a minute of my time right now, to get up and answer it. Friends, that's the shape you get in when you defend an unscriptural position, and one of the tragedies of the era is that good men, men of ability, like a lot of these fellows are have destroyed their usefulness and are, as many as they can, destroying the work of the church by following these positions. It's a sad situation, I tell you it is.

Now, again, here's another argument I want to make. I've got how much time? [TOTTY: Four minutes.]

Alright, yes. Now, get this, friends. This is an argument that I want you to get now. I have shown you that there are church duties and family duties. Now, get this. For every legitimate function of the church there is a specified functionary and his qualifications are given in the Bible. I want brother Sutton to notice this and, if he won't, why won't you notice it? There must be oversight of the church; hence, the elders. There are functions for the church to perform that must be performed by the deacons. There must be evangelists to preach the

84

word. Elders, deacons, evangelists are mentioned, designated. Their qualifications are given. There must be personal workers. They are mentioned. Their qualifications are given in 2 Timothy 2:2 and so on. For every legitimate function of the church there must be a functionary, and he must be specifically mentioned in the Bible and his qualifications given. Now, then, let's have the chart over here right quick. Now, then, if it's the function of the church not only to supply the means but also to actually envision this, then there would have to be nurses, doctors, hospitals. Now, I might ask you: Can the church operate a hospital? Well, you could say it could buy the services of one. That's using another organization. If the church is all-sufficient, why would it have to buy it? If it can, if it can legitimately do it, it wouldn't have to buy it. If it has to buy it because it can't do it, then it's not a work for which it was cut out to do. What about supervision, discipline, recreation, and so on? I was debating a fellow down in Florida a while back on this who was taking the same position that Sutton does that the church can perform every family need of a child, and I forced him, he had more courage and conviction than Sutton, I forced him to admit that it would be a part of the work of the local congregation to have a baseball field out here on the church grounds and for the elders to appoint a man to umpire a baseball game and that the umpire would be performing a part of the work of the church umpiring a ballgame. You know why he took that position? In his effort to be consistent. In an effort to show that the church can perform every function. Now, Sutton, can a church provide an umpire for a baseball game for a bunch of boys? It isn't funny. It's not funny at all to me. It's serious. I wish you'd answer that. Why don't you leave him alone, Holt? He's in enough misery as he is.

Now, friends, do you think that he's going to answer this? Of course, he isn't. I derive no pleasure in embarrassing brother Sutton. I don't want to do that. I would be glad if he stood by my side and helped me to fight the battles for truth, but just as long as there are men like him going about all over the country preaching these doctrines that divide, we're going to oppose him, and you're going to see the state they get in.

TOTTY: We will now, have about five minute's intermission before the next speech. [BREAK]

TOTTY: Concerning the new material brother Sutton is threatening to use in the last speech, the rule is generally, as brother Woods said, we've always, most of us, agreed to be governed by Hedges Rules of Logic, and even though they are not signed, his—the ones who are with him—have asked in different debates, such as Curtis Porter and fellows like that, that we use those rules. Those rules are that the opponent must weigh his opponent's arguments with fairness and candor, and that there cannot be any new material introduced in the last negative speech. Now, if brother Sutton persists in that, we are going to answer it, and you can just get ready for that, because we expect to be treated fair, and we are expected to treat him fair. He did sign a proposition that we would act and conduct ourselves as Christian gentlemen, and that means to be fair. Do unto others as you would have them do unto you. Now, brother Sutton may start his next speech.

HOLT: The audience can judge as to how fair brother Sutton and those here have tried to be, and also brother Sutton was under the understanding that in the last night on the proposition—each proposition—there would be no new material brought in by the person in the negative.

Brother Sutton has no intention of bringing in any new material. He never did have any intention of bring in any new material in the last speech in the negative, and he had no intention of taking advantage last evening. So, these people can just rest assured there will be no material, new material, brought in in the last speech tonight.

TOTTY: Thank you, brother Holt. That settles it. If brother Sutton had said that in the beginning it'd been alright. But I wonder how brother Holt knows what brother Sutton has always had in his mind. That's a thing we'd like to understand, all right.

HOLT: When brother Sutton has told me things, I've always found them to be true. I don't know what's always in his mind or other people's mind, but I do know that's the reason I said what I did.

TOTTY: Thank you, brother Holt.

Carrol R. Sutton's Fifth Negative Speech

Gentlemen moderators, brother Woods, ladies and gentlemen:

I'm glad to appear before you for the next twenty minutes in defense of the truth as revealed in the Bible. After all, we're here discussing, at least we're supposed to be discussing, as to what is scriptural. Brother Woods signed to affirm this proposition: "It is in harmony with the scriptures for churches of Christ to build and maintain benevolent organizations such as the Tennessee Orphan Home, Boles Home, Home for the Aged, and other such organizations for the care of the needy."

Brother Woods has one more speech tonight to produce that scripture. He hasn't done so yet, and every person in this audience knows that to be so. I'm not saying brother Woods hasn't referred to some scriptures, but not one of the scriptures that he referred to even refers in the remotest sense to a benevolent organization such as those mentioned in the proposition. Brother Woods can follow any course he sees fit to follow, but I intend to hold him to the proposition that he signed. Keep this in mind, brethren.

Tomorrow evening beginning, the Lord willing, I'll be affirming that it is not in harmony with the Scriptures for churches to build and maintain these organizations. I'll take up scriptural arguments, you can rest assured of that. We'll not deal in a lot of matters like he's brought up tonight and last evening. We'll deal with issues. Now, I've been following him last evening and this evening but tomorrow evening I will be in the affirmative. I've been simply showing, last evening and this evening, that he hasn't produced the authority from the scriptures. That's all I'm obligated to show, but I'll go further tomorrow evening and the next evening and show what the scriptures teach relative to these issues. Further, I'll be in an affirmative position tomorrow evening, and I'll introduce arguments based on scriptural principles.

I'm still asking you, brother Woods, to produce the passage of scripture—not that justifies the church, not that justifies the family, but the one that justifies your benevolent organizations such as Tennessee Orphan Home. Now, brother Woods has put on the board here Matthew 16:18 that mentions the church. I knew that, brother Woods. Jesus says, "Upon this rock I will build my church." Now, what does that have to do with churches building and maintaining benevolent organizations? We notice also that he mentions the scripture over here that mentions that the church is to relieve. That's what I've been advocating all the time. That is the organization that God specified. But where is his benevolent organization? Then he mentioned James 1:27 shows an obligation. I agree with that, but where is his benevolent organization such as Boles Home, Tennessee Orphan Home, etc.? Then he also mentioned the family. Brother Woods, I'm not asking for the passage of scripture that justifies the family. I'm asking for the scripture that justifies benevolent organizations, such as families. No, sir. Such as the Tennessee Orphan Home, Boles Home, and etc. I'm still asking for the passage of scripture, brother Woods, and I'd appreciate it if you'd give it to me when you come before this audience, if you have it. If you don't have it, be man enough to say, "Well, brother Sutton, I can't get it." Don't do like some people do, offer passages of scripture that deal with other matters and say, "Here it is!" Either produce the scripture that deals with what the proposition says or simply admit defeat, we'll close, and go home. Isn't that fair enough?

I'd like to mention a thing or two about the questions that I asked brother Woods last evening and this evening: Question 1 is, "Is the church a benevolent society?" Brother Woods say, "No, not in the sense in which you use the phrase." It just happens that my adversary has printed a book. This is the ***Woods-Porter Debate*** conducted in Indianapolis in 1956. On page 255 brother Woods said, quote, "I said that the church is not an orphan home. It is a benevolent society." (end of quote). But brother Woods said, in the question that he's written the answer out to, that the church is not a benevolent society. Now, which time did he tell the truth about it? In one situation he says it is a benevolent society, in the next situation he says it's not.

WOODS: You're not answering, not reading, all the answer.

SUTTON: And so, neighbors and friends, you can see...

WOODS: I insist you read all the answer. I explained what I wrote in your answer.

SUTTON: Let me make a point of clarification.

HOLT: Just a minute. It's left up to brother Woods to show he's not reading it all.

WOODS: Let me have the answer, and I'll read it. He's suppressing part of my answer there.

SUTTON: Hold my time.

HOLT: Brother Woods has his time. He's doing on his time.

TOTTY: Brother Holt, you mean to be that unfair; that you'd hold back part of that answer? Is that your way of debating? I demand that he read all that answer. Go ahead and read it.

SUTTON: Start my time. Neighbors and friends, we have tape recorders going here. These tape recorders will show that I either read all of the answer or I didn't. I maintain that I did read all of the answer brother Woods wrote to question number 1 and, if that isn't the case, tomorrow evening let him play the tape and prove that it's not so.

WOODS: In the first place, there won't be people here tomorrow night that are here tonight.

SUTTON: Hold my time.

WOODS: When he read the thing over at first, he read the words I said, but when he made the application he left off the qualification, and I insist that that's a misrepresentation. I said, "No, not in the sense in which you're using it," and that's right.

SUTTON: Start my time. Anyone who cares to see the answer that he gave and listen to the tape after service, you can know that I read exactly what he said. Now, I can't help it if he said it. You want to take it back? If you want to take it back and apologize for it, I'll let you do that brother Woods.

WOODS: No.

SUTTON: Hold my time.

WOODS: That's exactly what I mean. Exactly what I said there. Not in the sense in which he's using it.

SUTTON: Alright, start my time.

TOTTY: May I just clear up, a minute...

SUTTON: Hold it.

TOTTY: When he comes over to ask brother Woods a question, brother Woods answered it. If they hold that time, we'll give brother Woods that much time, too. Now, if brother Woods says something when he doesn't ask him a direct question, they may take time. He asked a direct question. Brother Woods stepped up to answer him. Then we give brother Woods just as much time as they hold out.

HOLT: The whole situation started when brother Sutton first was asking questions. Brother Woods didn't like that. Then this came up when he wasn't asking questions. So far as we're concerned, he can go ahead.

WOODS: Just so he doesn't continue to misrepresent.

SUTTON: Start my time. I appeal to the honesty and sincerity and integrity of each one of you in the audience to consider for yourself as to the fairness involved in the interruption of these various speeches. Now, my sense of fairness is that when he's on the floor having his speech, he can say what he pleases. Now, I don't interrupt him during his speech. Now, if he wants to interrupt me during mine, if he considers that conducting himself as a Christian, like he wrote the rule and I agreed to it, then he's got it. He can follow it. That's not my way of doing things.

We notice the question still reads just like it did. I asked him, "Is the church a benevolent society?" He said, "No, not in the sense in which you use the phrase." Well, I was just asking him if it was. I wasn't even using it in this question here, I just asked him simply. He said, "No, not in the sense you use it." Well, I simply asked him if it was, and we read on page 255 of the **Porter-Woods Debate** where that he said the church is a benevolent society. Now, which time did he tell the truth, brethren? Now, that's him for that. I can't help it if he got in that condition. That's what false doctrine does for a man. It's not my fault, brother Woods.

Then further I asked him, "Are benevolent organizations such as Boles Orphan Home, Tennessee Orphan Home, Cherokee Home for Children, Sierra Children's Home, and Florida Christian Estates divine institutions?" He said, "I never heard of Florida Christians Estates before. The legal families which constitute Boles, Tennessee Orphan Home, etc. are divine institutions." I thought he believed in giving

90

direct answers. You know he's been chiding me because I answered and explained my answers. That's real direct, isn't it? That's really a direct answer, but it just so happens that brother Woods is contending for benevolent organizations that he says are divine institutions. Every person in this audience has heard him say that but the Superintendent of Tennessee Orphan Home says that Tennessee Orphan Home is a human institution, brother Woods. Brother Richter, who's the Superintendent of Tennessee Orphan Home, says it's a human institution, but brother Woods says it's a divine institution. There's the Superintendent, who has been a Superintendent for a number of years. Here's brother Woods who never has been. Brother Woods says it's divine; brother Richter says it's human. I wonder which one of them is telling the truth about it. What about that, brother Woods? Is he defending human organizations? Brother Richter says he is. I say he is. Are they human or divine, friends? Not only that, but it just so happens that brother Cannon, Superintendent of the Sierra Children's Home of California, says the same thing about that one, brother Woods. You say it's divine; Superintendent says that isn't so. It's human. It just so happens brother Alexander, who's the Superintendent of the Cherokee Home for Children, says that it's a human institution. Brother Woods says it's divine. Those men are in position … they operate these things. They ought to know, oughtn't they, brother Woods? Brother Woods says they're divine institutions. These men say they're human, yet he gets on to me because I call them human. I call them what the Superintendent said about Boles Home, brother Woods. In case he wants the proof of it, I've got it right here in the folder, every one of them that I've mentioned. Are they human or divine, friends? I maintain they are human organizations. That's what brother Woods is defending.

Another question I asked brother Woods was, "Were the seven men who were selected to dispense food in Acts 6 set over the work of the church or the work of the home?" He said, "In receiving the funds, they performed the work of the church. When the money was turned over to needy families, it became the work of the family to spend it. Church work is not family work. Church work is not state work." Well, that's very enlightening, isn't it? That's real direct. He believes in answering questions direct, doesn't he? That's very enlightening, brother Woods, and in view of the fact that you've chided me because I answered and explained my answers, that's very enlightening. But notice what he says here. He's saying now, that in receiving the funds the Seven performed the work of the church. I didn't ask anything about any receiving the funds. I said, "in dispensing food," brother Woods. He evaded it. He didn't answer it. I asked him about when they dispensed the food, like he said last evening that they did dispense food. See, he didn't answer the question yet. He said something about my not answering questions.

I asked him also, "If the benevolent organization, known as St. Louis Children's Home and School, were to build and maintain fifty orphan homes in the state of Indiana, could churches still scripturally make contributions to it?" Here's his answer, very direct. Quote: "If the legal parents of St. Louis Children's Home should build fifty places to take care of children, I would rejoice and support the effort. I would urge congregations to support such." (end of quote). Isn't that direct? Isn't that answering that just forthright? He just steps right up to the question, no doubt about it, and then he kind of drops off. You be the judge. But that's alright; he has the right to answer like that if he wants to. We agreed to answer questions; not like each other wanted us to. So, I'm not complaining about it. I'm just showing how that he's guilty of the very same thing that he accuses me of.

We notice a chart here on "Consider the Word 'Visit'" in James 1:27. Does it authorize churches to build and support or build and maintain benevolent societies such as Childhaven, Tennessee Orphan Home, and so forth? Does that word "visit" do that in James 1:27? It's not discussing church work at all. Now, if so, the word "visited" in Matthew 25:36 and 43 authorizes churches to build and support sick and prison visiting societies such as hospitals, etc. If not, why not? There's the same word in both passages. How can we reject one and accept the other? When the Bible says, "visit those in prison," does that mean the church can build and maintain prisons or to build and maintain organizations which in turn will visit those in prison? It says "visit." He says the word "visit" in James 1:27 brings in churches building and maintaining these benevolent organizations. If one, why

92

not the other?

Then we notice brother Woods had quite a bit to say about the preacher's home and the church building. In fact, we might notice his chart along that line. I believe brother Woods has it right here. He says, "Here's the church and the Board of Directors and the Orphan Home and then here's the church, Board of Directors, and the preacher's home. So then," he says, "now, if we can have this Board of Directors in the case of the preacher's home, then why can't we have it in the case of the Orphan Home?" It just so happens that brother Woods has shifted gears on us on the use of the word "home." He told me that every time he used the word "home" up here that he's talking about a family. You heard him say it. He says, "Now, I want brother Sutton to realize I'm talking about the family." Notice this. He says here's the church, the Board that provides the orphan's "family" based on his definition of the word "home." But notice now, here's the church, the Board of Directors that provides the preacher's "family," brother Woods. You see? I don't know of any church that provides the preacher's family, do you? Do you, friends? The church here doesn't provide my family. I don't know about his, it doesn't mine. Not only that, brother Woods, there's not a Board of Directors between the church building and the preacher's home here. No, sir. That's a false accusation when he leaves that impression. That isn't so. It ain't right (with a capital A). It ain't so, brother Woods!

Then he talked a lot about this incorporation. He said the church here one time—he said had been, then he said it may be still. Then he said it is. Well, that isn't so either, brother Woods. It just so happens that those who incorporated it, brother Woods, in the main when they did, agreed with you, and then we straightened it out later. That isn't so. That's a false accusation, brother Woods. He doesn't know what he's talking about, friends. See, he doesn't know any more about these matters than he does about what the Bible says. Now, I wish I didn't have to mention those things, but he's leading, and I ought to follow, I guess. I guess I ought to. I don't like to, but I guess I ought to. I won't tomorrow night and the next night, though. He will have to follow or go by himself one. I don't intend to follow him tomorrow night. No, not in the least.

Let's notice something about the preacher's home. Now, brother Woods said in the **Porter-Woods Debate**, page 215, "The same argument that justifies the preacher's home justifies the home for the aged. The same argument that justifies the church building justifies an orphan home." Now, notice what he has. We notice in this case, here's the church that provides a preacher's home. 1 Corinthians 9 shows that the church ought to support the preacher. In Hebrews 10:25 he showed the church ought to assemble. Therefore, then, that justifies the church providing a church building. He says, "Therefore, then, that justifies the church providing a building for orphans or a home for those who are needy." We agree with that, brother Woods. Why sure, that's what I'm contending for. That's my argument, not his. But let me show you what he's contending for. Now, he's contending that the church can build and maintain benevolent organizations between the church and the home that's provided for the orphans. Here's that benevolent organization that's between that. That's what I'm against. We notice how that if that's so, then in case of the church putting up a church building, it could send funds to a church building society and let it put up church buildings. Now, that's his parallel. He doesn't want it, but he'll have to take it anyway, won't he? Then on the same basis, the church could send funds to a preacher supporting corporation and let that thing provide the preacher's home. Yes, brother Woods, I agree with that argument, but not your application of it. Yet, he said, "Brother Sutton won't say anything about this, will he, this preacher's home business." I guess he wishes I didn't. I wouldn't be surprised, but I'll let you be the judge.

I'd like to have chart number 23 on this side over here please, sir. How much time? Alright. Brother Woods said, "Brother Sutton, is your family a benevolent organization?" You know, it just so happens, that my home is not a benevolent organization such as the TENNESSEE ORPHAN HOME, and that's what his proposition says. My home, brother Woods, or my family, brother Woods, does not have a Board of Directors with a president, vice-president, secretary, and treasurer. Does your home have, or your family have, or do you have a family? I don't know, I'm just asking. I mean, I don't mean to be prying. It doesn't really matter, but the point is that certainly my home is not a benevolent organization in the sense of the TENNESSEE ORPHAN HOME like this proposition says, and he won't say that his family is either. So, they're not parallel.

We might notice this also: some differences in these benevolent organizations and the private family. Children are born into the private family, but they're not born into these benevolent organizations such as Tennessee Orphan Home. The parents in the private family feel obligated to expend their own resources in caring for their children; not so in the case of these benevolent organizations. The parents in the private family lives with their children; not so in the case of these benevolent organizations. The parents in the private family usually will what they have to their children, but not so in the case of these benevolent organizations. So, there's a vast difference between private families and benevolent organizations like he's contending for. No, my family is not like these benevolent organizations, brother Woods. Not in the least.

Then brother Woods had something to say about this little square in the kitchen. What does that prove about benevolent organizations? What on earth, friends, does that have to do with a man showing that it is scriptural for churches of Christ to build and maintain benevolent organizations such as Tennessee Orphan Home? That's really scripture for it, isn't it? I'll tell you what, if brother Woods wants to prove his proposition, let him put the scripture here that justifies his benevolent organizations. I've already answered his questions with respect to the kitchen the very first night, and I asked him that if he wants the answer given again to read what I answered, what I wrote down, on the question the first night he asked me.

Guy N. Woods' Sixth Affirmative Speech

Gentlemen moderators, brother Sutton, ladies and gentlemen:
I still want to know if it would be scriptural for this congregation to have a kitchen in the basement? I haven't got the

information on that, Sutton. You said you told us last night. Is there anybody here in this audience that will volunteer the information whether he said if you could or couldn't? Now, I thought I was here last night. I have a vague recollection of being here last night, but I don't have any recollection of the answer to that question. He said he answered it last night. Now, Sutton, you're just dodging more and more and more on it. He said, "What is that to do with the issue?" It has everything to do with it. Here's the reason, friends, that I inserted this. It is Sutton's contention that the orphan home is useless, that the church can take over every operation of the home and operate as a part of the church organization. That's his contention. Now, these brethren believe that it's right to have a storeroom in the basement. I take it that he'd have no objection to having some can goods down there to administer. I just want to know if you could heat the food that you got down here in your storeroom? Could you have a stove down there and heat it or do you have to feed it to them cold? Now, I don't see why he didn't answer that.

Here, friends, is the thing about it that's vital to this question, because he knows that he won't answer it. He's preached all over this country that it's sinful to have a kitchen in the basement. His argument would necessitate that, and he, therefore, doesn't have the courage of his conviction. He said that I took the position, in the Porter Debate, that the church is a benevolent society. If you let me define the terms of the proposition, as I did here, I would accept that. It's strange that he didn't read the statement. He took one little statement out of the context. Here's what I said: "Brother Porter puts some words into my mouth,"—they have a way of doing that I might intersperse here— "Brother Porter put some words into my mouth, and I want to correct him on that." He did that two or three times. He said that I said the church was God's missionary society, but the church wasn't God's benevolent society. I did not say that. That's putting an interpretation on what I said. I said that the church is not an orphan home. It is a benevolent society. It is also a missionary society. Now, why didn't he read that? "It is also a missionary society, but it's not a gospel meeting, so it arranges a gospel meeting. The church is not an orphan home, so it arranges an orphan home." Now, why didn't he go ahead and explain the context. I showed that I was using it in a sense other than that of a missionary society idea. Well, you'll decide that.

Now, he said next that I answered the question "no." It's very true that I did, but I went on to say, "Not in the sense in which you use it or in the sense in which you use the phrase." That's what I said about it, and it would have been fair for him to say it.

Now, he said that the superintendent of these homes, some of them, say they're human institutions. Well, I say they're human institutions in the same sense that I say the church is a human institution: made up of human beings. But I happen to know that some of these brethren, at least that he's representing, I can't speak for all of them because I can't do like Holt. I can't sit beside a man and tell you everything he thinks and knows. But I do know this, that these brethren believe exactly what I do with reference to the right of these homes to exist. This man thinks he can do a better job of debating with these superintendents than he can with me. Wait until you get into a debate with them, Sutton, and then deal with the matter.

Now, he says, "You say that they can dispense food. Over whose work were those men exercising control?" Why, just the same as it would be in the matter of money. I answered that awhile ago. These seven men had supervision of the means that was placed at their disposal. That wouldn't make any difference whether that was money or whether that was food. They took that and turned it over to these needy families. But these needy families took that money or food, whichever it was, ate the food and spent the money. And it was the duty of the family to spend the money; it was the duty of these men to supply it. That's exactly what Paul teaches in 1 Timothy 5:16, and that's exactly what we have here on our chart. If this home falls into need, the church comes to its aid. If the home is broken and it's reestablished, in the sense of a family relationship, the church comes to its aid. The church provides the money. It relieves, but it's the home that does the actual work.

Let me tell you this, ladies and gentlemen. If there were to be a group of babies abandoned here on the steps of this building, and you moved them into the basement of this building and moved in a bunch of beds and stoves and cooking utensils and started taking care of them down there, that wouldn't be a church operating in the basement. That'd be a home being conducted in the basement of a church building, because it's not a function of the church to serve as a home. That's what we're saying, and that's what we've said all along, and this man hasn't touched top, side, edge, or bottom of it.

He said, "Why Woods takes the position that if St. Louis should establish 50 places that the church could come to the aid of each of them." Why, I think so. The implication of his objection is that the church couldn't help but one group at one time according to that. According to Sutton, if the church is helping one group, then it's got to help that group exclusively, and it couldn't help any other. I think the church could help 50 families if it had the money to. Just like I think that the church could contribute to 50 places. That's a silly and ridiculous argument.

Now, let's have his chart on "Visit" over here that he had. He made no argument on it, but I want to deal with it. You know a fellow that has to have as many charts as he has to prove this thing, he couldn't prove it anyway. Alright, now, consider the word "visit" in James 1:27. Does it authorize churches to build and support benevolent societies as Childhaven? If so, the word "visited" in Matthew 25:43 and 36 would authorize churches to build and support sick and prison visiting societies such as hospitals. If not, why not? Same word in both passages. How could we reject the one and accept other? Now, in so far as the matter of providing prison societies, it's not a part of the work of the church to provide prison societies or to even provide the money with which to provide such. It so happens that there's a difference between providing societies for prisons and providing homes for needy children. But let me take the part that does apply here. The visiting there, of course, means to call upon them and render them aid and one could do that even in prison. The word "visit" is a generic term. It doesn't mean just to provide a home or the means of a home. It means to do them good. But one of the ways of doing good is to provide a home for the homeless. But now, look here. What about the sick? Suppose you got one sick person in the congregation and this person is indigent and in need. Could the church supply a nurse and doctor and medicine to take care of that person? Could you provide a

98

room for them? Suppose that instead of having 250 members you had 25,000 members. The church in Jerusalem had at least 40,000 or more. Suppose you had 60 of these people. Could you have 60 rooms and 60 nurses at the same time taking care of them? I say you could. That is, I say you could support the work out of the church treasury. Now, get up here and say, "Well, Woods thinks that the church can operate a hospital like the Methodist Hospital." I never said anything of the kind. Those organizations are operated for profit. I'm talking about sick and indigent people. Let him answer the questions. I don't think he will.

He said, "Oh, we straightened out matters here." He said, "People that agreed with me arranged the thing." Well, I happen to know that these brethren believe that it's right to have an incorporation by which to operate a church building and a preacher's residence. I know that they believe in that. Some of them do. Are you taking the position, Sutton, that that's wrong? You said they straightened it out, therefore, you don't believe that the church can have an incorporation, and this incorporation can own a preacher's residence. You said they straightened it out. Now, if they straightened it out, they fixed it otherwise than that, and he's taking the position that those places that have such are wrong. You fellows remember that when you write this up, will you? Please remember that now.

But now, another thing about that. They straightened it out. Did you straighten it out by paying the money back to the people that paid for the building? How far did you go in straightening the thing out? You said that they're gone, but did you pay them back for what they put into it? I'm interested in the answer to that question.

Let's see this chart here. Is that the one you had up when I got up here? When you got up here awhile ago or did you change it? Oh! While this is up, let's just deal with this and then we'll get to the other one here. What about a preacher's home in a church building? He said, "Now, Woods has changed the use of the word home." No, this is the argument you made. I was using it in the sense in which you do and told you that this is the representation that you have right here. Why I don't think that a home is a house in the sense in which you use it. I use the word "home" synonymously with family, but Sutton says that the word "home" just means the house. That's his position. He said it in the Blazer debate, and if he questions it, we'll produce it. So, all of this then has nothing to do with that. The same argument that justifies the preacher's home justifies the home for the aged. The same argument that justifies the church building justifies an orphan home. "Well," he says, "yes, these justify this. The church provides a preacher's home, provides a church building, provides an orphan home, but these are not justified. The church provides funds to give to benevolent societies which provides the home." Well, nobody claims that it does. That's not what I'm defending. I told you that the organization is itself the home. This is his argument, not mine. "Well," he says, "the church provides funds for a church building society which provides the church building." Alright, are all of these places where they've got trustees sinful? Now, I want to know, Sutton, the passage of scripture that justifies the trustees. According to him, whenever you have the church giving money to an organization which provides a building, you've got an in between affair. Alright now, I know you got trustees here. I know you didn't straighten that out. No, you didn't straighten that out because you can't own property. A church can't. You got to deed it to trustees. I know you got the trustees. You can't come up here with anything on that that's been straightened out. Alright now, where are these trustees? Are they between the church and the congregation? Where are the trustees in this deal? When we have that answer, which we will never get, then we'll know more about it.

He says his home is not a benevolent organization. Now, suppose I'd stop right here. I'd be doing him like he tried to do me. I said, "Brother Sutton, is your home a benevolent organization?" He said, "No." But he went on and said some more. Suppose I just stop here and say, "Well, the word 'benevolence' means doing good and 'organization' is a systematized method of procedure. Therefore, his home, his family, doesn't do anything good." I'd be doing exactly what he did. I'd be misrepresenting him in a ridiculous fashion. I just don't do that. He knows that his home is a benevolent organization. I know it is, but he thinks that I'm using it in a peculiar sense. Well, I give him credit for qualifying his answer, but he didn't deal that fairly with me, did he? There are a lot of people around here that are going to remember these things, Sutton, from now on. They're going to

100

remember these.

He was going to prove to me why the orphan home differs from his home. He said that the children are born into a natural home but they're not born into one of these orphan homes. That's his argument against the orphan home. Listen friends, it happens that I'm staying with a wonderful family here in this debate, the Keplingers. They have a very fine little adopted boy. They're practicing benevolence, both collectively and individually. That little boy wasn't born into their family. I wonder if he thinks that little fellow has a family. Sutton, what do you say about it? What do you say? How many children, how many adoptive children, are born into this family? Do you have to be born into a family to be a part of it? That was your implication. That was the effort you intended to leave with this congregation here tonight. What about it? Now, friends, that covers his speech, except that in his desperation to avoid this over here, he comes up here and says, "But in this square, now, the passages of scripture that justify benevolent organizations such as Tennessee Orphan Home and Boles Home and so on." Well, I put it all over the board nearly every time I got up here. But I'm just glad to satisfy him. Incidentally, there's a passage right close to it. If he'd just extend the square on over here, like that, he would of had it. He didn't see that. Made no mention of it. Made no reference to it whatever. Now, you get up here when I have no chance to reply, quibble around about that because what does that say? That says that God puts the solitary in families, hence the family is a divine institution. But you can't have a family of seven children or more, who are not related to you, without having a license from the State. Incidentally, I referred to the Keplinger family; they have a license from the State in order to operate. It is a private family, but it is operating as a State foster home, licensed by the State to that end. Alright, that's not wrong. That's what the orphan homes do. You have to meet certain specifications regarding the size of the property to maintain a home of seven or more children. You have to conform to the law of the land. You have to have a board of at least seven directors in the State of Kentucky. I read that last night. He made no mention of that whatever. I've shown you, step by step, that these items are scriptural. Now, then, if each item of a given series is a scriptural item, when you put them all together they're still all scriptural, aren't they? I have proved every item essential to my proposition to be scriptural. I have shown the right of the family to exist. I have shown the right of the church to support that family. I have shown that when you get seven children in that family, you fall under State laws. I have shown that the State law, at least in some States, require a board. I have shown that it is right in connection of the church building and practiced by him to use trustees. I showed that we proved the items of worship and the plan of salvation in the same way that a series of scriptural items is itself a scriptural series. Since I have proved each one of these items to be scriptural and since, when you put them all together, you have a total situation which is scriptural, I have proved by argument to be scriptural.

Now, there it is, Sutton. Just include this as well as all these others here: James 1:27; 1 Timothy 5:16; Mark 14:6; Acts 20:35 and the many other passages that I have given. [TOTTY: Three minutes.]

Thank you. I include all of these in that.

Now, Sutton, look up here just a minute. This is my last chance tonight, in the affirmative, to know whether or not you are really sincere in your position regarding the church's performing the function of the family. I want to know, Sutton, look up here just a minute, sir. Right up here. You see this square right over here? Just write into that some sort of an answer with a reference to whether or not a church can operate a kitchen in the basement. These people are going to think you've waited a mighty long time when you answer it after I've had no chance to reply. It will be too late next week when I'm gone. Oh, he'll tell you a lot about it then. You wait and see. These fellows usually conduct them a meeting right after one of these debates to patch up all the difficulties they get into in a debate. I haven't heard them announce anything like that here, but I'll be surprised if they don't. But at any rate, whether they do or not, he'll try to patch it up. Right now, would be a good time to tell us. I'd like to know, Sutton, what your position is. These people are going to wonder, and they're going to leave here tonight wondering, why is it you're so bold when you're on the radio by yourself or when you're preaching out over this country, but when you face Woods or somebody else, then you get as dumb as an oyster

102

about it. You haven't answered that question. This audience knows you haven't. You don't intend to. You can't, and I'd be ashamed of myself to get in a position with a doctrine where I had to brow beat like you're suffering here tonight. I feel sorry for you.

Alright, it's a shame for a man who claims to be a gospel preacher to have so little courage that he won't come up and say— Why, I'd say it if my right arm wasn't—I would. Sutton, can you put a kitchen in the basement? Well, if you know the answer, you tell it. It doesn't make any difference with me which one of you tell me. Holt, do you know? Just any of you. Be glad to have the answer. These people around here are going to wonder why it is that Sutton is so bold when there's nobody around to call his hand, but when the time comes that he has to walk up to the lick log and face it, you see what he gets into. The reason is that he's got a false position, and I urge you people, who have any regard for the truth whatsoever, to repudiate him and it and stand for the truth like most of the brethren are over the country.

We're not contending for human organizations to do the work of the church. We're not contending that the church is insufficient in its field. We're contending that the church ought to be the church and the home, or the family, the family. That God gave duties to each. That one can't usurp the functions of the other. That we mustn't try.

I charged Catholicism on him in the first night. He's made no read effort to deny it because he can't. Remember, that, if you can turn a home into a church, you ought not to stumble at the idea of turning a State into a church. Sutton's position is right if the church can take over the family and operate it as a part of the church. Then he ought not object to the idea of the State doing the same—or the church doing the same.

Carrol R. Sutton's Sixth Negative Speech

Gentlemen moderators, brother Woods, ladies and gentlemen:
I'm glad to come before you in the last speech of the evening in

defense of the truth.

I'd like to read, first of all, the proposition that brother Woods is supposed to be affirming for fear that some of you may think that I'm supposed to be affirming that it's scriptural for churches of Christ to build and maintain and operate kitchens in church building basements. I'd like to read the proposition for you again. "It is in harmony with the Scriptures for churches of Christ to build and maintain benevolent organizations such as the Tennessee Orphan Home, Boles Home, Home for the Aged, and other such organizations for the care of the needy." Now, that's what brother Woods signed to affirm, yet he talks about brother Sutton and the kitchen and this thing and that thing. Well, if I didn't have any scriptures for benevolent organizations, brother Woods, I'd talk about the kitchen, too. You wait till tomorrow evening and see if I start talking about a lot of other matters other than those things that pertain to the proposition that I'll be affirming.

Alright, let's read the proposition again. The proposition says: "It is in harmony with the Scriptures for churches of Christ to build and maintain." That means to establish and support. What does it do? It builds, it establishes, and it maintains. It supports. Brother Woods still says he believes that, but at the same time he says that the church can only send money. Well, that doesn't build it and maintain it both, just to send money. Incidentally, brother Woods, I just wonder if...

TOTTY: Point of order. Just a minute.

HOLT: Hold his time.

TOTTY: Brother Woods didn't say any such thing. He didn't have the word "only" in it. Brother Woods said you could send either money or food, and he said that brother Woods said you could send only money. That isn't so.

SUTTON: Just hold my time, brother Holt. It just so happens, I have a little book here by brother Guy N. Woods. It's entitled *A Defense of Orphan Homes*. On page 14, here's what he had to say: "The church is not an orphan home or home of any kind. It is a divine missionary society. When the human society does its work, nothing remains for the church but when the church, in its organized capacity, does all it is authorized to do, that is, supply the money for the needy, the work of actual care must yet be done." There it is. There's proof of it.

TOTTY: Just a point of order. That isn't proof of it. Brother Woods said in his other speech it could send either money or food. He didn't use the word "all" there in the sense of only money, did you, brother Woods? No. You're just quibbling. Just hold it a minute. We'll settle that thing right here.

MAN FROM AUDIENCE: Brother Sutton, are you supposed to be debating one guy or two guys?

WOODS: We might ask brother Holt that. Yeah, I would suggest you ask him that.

MAN FROM AUDIENCE: I'd like to ask if he has to debate two guys? It's a little unfair.

TOTTY: That's alright. I'm a moderator. If you know what one is, you'll keep your mouth shut.

There's brother Woods' speech, everybody look at it. That looks like "only"? Look over there. A place, food, clothing, education, superintendent, and medical care. Now, go ahead with your speech and answer that.

SUTTON: Start my time, brother Holt. I've already suggested that brother Woods admitted last evening that the church could send money and also dispense food. I suggested that. I knew that he said that last evening, but I knew, also, that he had already said, right here, that when the church does all that it's authorized to do, that is, supply the money for the needy. I can't help it if he contradicted himself. That's exactly what he did.

TOTTY: Just a point of order again. That isn't a contradiction. Brother Woods said when it furnished the money that is to buy the food, and he explained that tonight that it can be either food or money. He didn't say "only" in that now, brother. You said he said "only." Now, he didn't have that in there. Now, go ahead.

SUTTON: Let me read it again. "But when the church in its organized capacity does all that it is authorized to do." It does "all" that it's authorized to do. That is, supply the money for the needy. The work of actual care must yet be done. We'll let it stand with you. You can read it for yourself.

TOTTY: No, we won't. You read the work "only" in there.

You said he said "only." You put that in there. Now, here's what he said right here. Now, read the word "only" and then go ahead or take it back, either one you want to do. You said that he said that you only furnish money. He didn't say any such thing. There it is. Now, if you want to make a speech, make it fair and go ahead and tell what he did say.

SUTTON: Start my time again, brother Holt. Let me read it again. Quote: "But when the church in its organized capacity does **all** that it is authorized to do; that is, supply the money for the needy, the work of actual care must yet be done." End of quote. I'll leave it with you.

We might mention also a thing or two that brother Woods had to say about his "Component Parts" argument and his "Total Situation." You know sometimes these total situations get a man into a bad situation and, of course, it's not my fault that it does. I want us to notice, for example, brother Woods said that with respect to the plan of worship. That the various items of worship constitute then a total situation that is scriptural. I agree with that because there are scriptures authorizing each one of those component parts.

The same thing is so with respect to the plan of salvation. When you have each one of the parts—faith, repentance, confession, and baptism—you have a total situation that is scriptural because each one of these are authorized by the Scriptures.

In his total situation, he hasn't produced a scripture for his benevolent organization. That's the very thing that he signed to affirm that he hasn't shown the scripture for. So, his total situation is not a scriptural situation. And let me show you something else. He says, in the case of worship, that this constitutes a total situation that we're to follow. There is a pattern involved. He says the same thing about the plan of salvation. There's a pattern to follow. I wonder if brother Woods thinks that these benevolent organizations constitute a pattern in benevolence? You know, he said you couldn't do it the wrong way in substance awhile ago. Is that a pattern you must follow? You know, some of these preachers say there is no pattern in benevolence, but brother Woods' logic leads him to the conclusion that what he's contending for is a pattern because he's paralleled it to the plan of salvation and the plan of worship. Brother Woods, you've got a pattern, haven't you? What about that, friends? Yet, he says there is no pattern in benevolence. He gets on to me because I say that when the Bible says the church is to relieve, that the church ought to relieve and not some other organization doing the work of the church. Thank you, brother Woods. You know, those total situations do get a man into a bad situation sometime, don't they?

WOODS: You're a good demonstration of it.

SUTTON: You and the audience can be the judge. At least, my seat hasn't gotten hot enough that I've been popping up, has it? You know, over at Newborn brother Woods said that when a man popped up from his seat, it was getting hot. Well, I'm just accepting what he said now. I haven't been popping up, so I don't know whether a man's seat gets hot or not when he pops up, but he's in position to know. I don't know.

Then, of course, brother Woods has mentioned the case of this home restored. The home is broken, or the family, he says. After the original family is broken, then there's the family restored, and he says the church moves on parallel lines with it. He still doesn't have his benevolent organization. That's what his proposition says, but let's think about this, friends. Let's say then since he says there are three divine institutions—the church, the family, and the State, here's the State moving on parallel lines. Suppose the State breaks down. Can the church restore the State? "Divine institutions," he says. Upon the same basis that the church can restore this family that he's talking about, why can't it restore the State? Yet, he talks about the Catholics binding church and State. I don't think I'd oppose it if I had his position. Thank you again, brother Woods.

Then he talks about the fact that we must conform to the state law. Brother Woods, I just wonder? If the state law were to require the setting up of a missionary society for the church to perform its missionary work, would you conform to it? I just wonder about that. He talks a lot about the state law, but I'd like him to produce the law that requires churches to build these benevolent organizations before the churches can do their works of benevolence. I challenge him for the law. He hasn't shown the law. He's talked about in the state of

Kentucky that there must be a license required and this thing and that thing required. He hasn't shown where that the church, to do its benevolent work, must form an organization out here apart from the church through which to do the work. I challenge him for the proof of it. Wait and see if it's forthcoming.

Then, of course, he said something about Boles Home and he said, "According to brother Sutton, just because you've got Boles Home Corporation here and then you've got over here cottages and down here one, he thinks you've got two homes." Well, it just happens, brother Woods, that brother Oler, who is superintendent of that thing, thinks he's got two down there, too. You know, that's kind of amusing, isn't it, that brother Oler superintends Boles Home and he thinks they've got two down there? Here's **Boles Home News**, Volume 17, Number 13, and it mentions the Sherwood-Myrtle Foster Home, and it says the new home was dedicated to the cause of Christ by brother and sister H. S. Foster of Stephenville. It goes on to mention the fact that they arranged for the Home to be under the supervision of the directors of Boles Home. Then it talks about the manager of the Home. That's the one down at Stephenville, Texas, 150 miles away from the Boles Home that's in Quinlan, Texas.

You know, last night he gave an illustration about the fact that down in Tennessee a few years ago, out in the rural area where he was born, that they had a little breezeway between one side of the house and then the other side of it. You know that 150 miles between Boles Home and Sherwood and Myrtle Foster Home is a mighty wide breezeway, isn't it? That's a mighty wide breezeway, brother Woods.

WOODS; They've got automobiles now. And, besides that, that was in Texas.

SUTTON: Well, anyway, brother Oler says there's a Home here and that's what I said, so he agrees with me on that.

It just so happens, I also have **The Potter Messenger**, and the superintendent of the Potter Orphan Home, another one that brother Woods defends, he thinks that there's a separate Home there, too. Notice for example here, November 1961, on the back of it says, "Twenty-eight homes are now, supported by churches of Christ." The first one listed is Boles Home in Quinlan, Texas. The last one listed is

Foster Home in Stephenville, Texas. Separately listed! If they're one and the same thing, you didn't have but 27, brother Woods. The superintendent of Potter Orphan Home thought they had 28. Not only that, the author of **The Christian Chronicle** thought the same thing because he said they had 28, and he listed these as two separate Homes in Texas. Then he asked for proof. Brother Woods, you ought to learn that I don't say things I can't prove. If you haven't, you will.

Then we notice also that he talked about Boles Home, and he said down here it's Sherwood and Myrtle Foster Home. Brother Foster and gave them a $150,000 farm. Well, that sounds like a destitute saint, doesn't it? There's Boles Orphan Home that in 1955 had about 2,000 acres of land. It had $706,000 worth of fixed assets and then, here a little bit later, we have somebody giving a $150,000 farm to them, and yet they're destitute saints. They're begging to provide for their children. 1 Timothy 5:8 says, "If any man provide not for his own, he has denied the faith and is worse than an infidel."

WOODS: I say that's new material. I have no chance to reply. He's misrepresenting these things, friends.

SUTTON: Hold my time.

WOODS: He's introduced this in the last speech when I have no chance to reply. They got about 300 children down there. They don't get a dime out of that $150,000 property except from the proceeds of the farm. You can't turn dirt into food and eat it. You may think that orphan children can survive on a diet of dirt, but I don't agree.

SUTTON: Start my time. I'd like to mention this. Last evening I mentioned the fact that it had 2000 acres of land and about $706,000 worth of fixed assets, so it is not new material. Brother Woods introduced the $150,000 farm that was given, so that's not new material. So, I deny the allegation and charge the alligator … that he's charged me falsely. You be the judge in it.

WOODS: I didn't say they had 2000 acres. I don't know how many acres they got, and I really don't have any idea. I really didn't say anything of the kind.

SUTTON: The tape will show that I didn't accuse him of saying that. I accused him of saying that there was $150,000 farm given to them. That's all I accused him of. Brother Woods ought to apologize for that.

TOTTY: You just said that a few minutes ago when he said they had 2000 acres. It hasn't been five minutes since you said it. Now, turn around and say he didn't.

SUTTON: I believe the tape will show exactly what I said.

TOTTY: It will show you said 2000 acres, too.

SUTTON: It will show that I said they had about 2000 acres and I said they had about $706,000 worth of fixed assets and I...

TOTTY: Point of order.

SUTTON: And I said that brother Woods said that there was a $150,000 farm given to them.

TOTTY: Point of order. You said brother Woods said it. Play back the tape. I challenge you to play the tape back.

SUTTON: Stop the time. Back the tape up. Everybody keep real quiet so you can listen, and if I did say that brother Woods said that they had 2000 acres of land, I'll apologize for it. If I didn't do it, I'll expect them to apologize for accusing me of it. Well, somebody can apologize then and if it's me, I will.

[Listening to tape.]

SUTTON: Stop the tape there and let's put it on this machine so it will play louder. Everybody just be real quiet, please. Set it up over here and back up and give you this context, and we'll see what was said.

[Listening to tape.]

WOODS: The context in which that was said led us to believe that you were charging in connection with the $150,000 farm the 2000. So far as I'm concerned, I don't know how many acres they got now or then, and I didn't say that. And the context in which you made the statement led us to believe that you said it. If you wish to make clear the statement that you're not charging on me the statement ...

SUTTON: Brethren, I said that if I ...

WOODS: Just a minute.

SUTTON: Just hold it until we get it settled. Brethren, I said that if I had accused brother Woods of saying that they had 2000 acres of land and $706,000 worth of assets in 1955, I would apologize for it.

110

You heard the tape. Therefore, I don't owe anybody an apology, but brother Woods and brother Totty owes me an apology for falsely accusing me.

WOODS: Now, may I say this. I have no desire to falsely accuse brother Sutton or anybody else, and I honestly thought that in the context in which he made the statement, he was charging it on me. He made the two statements together. He says that I said they had $150,000 farm, and I thought that, in connection with that, he meant that I also made the other statement. Now, I honestly understood that. He says he didn't. The tape shows he didn't. Brother Sutton, I'm sorry I said it.

SUTTON: Thank you, brother Woods. We're making a lot of progress.

WOODS: I hope so. I want you to tell me if you can have a kitchen in the basement.

TOTTY: Brother Sutton, I also apologize for saying that.

SUTTON: Thank you, brother Totty.

TOTTY: I think you ought to prove that they have 2000 acres of land.

SUTTON: Hold my time. It just so happens I have here a letter that's dated March 24, 1956, a photocopy of the letter that brother Gayle Oler wrote to brother W.W. Otey. It's on Boles Home stationery. Here's the letter in its completeness: "Dear brother Otey: In reply to your letter requesting information, let me say that Boles Home has some 230 children, approximately 2000 acres of land, and total fixed assets of $706,713.83 as of July 1, 1955. Faithfully and fraternally, Gayle Oler."

The only thing is that they had $713.83 more than I said. I gave round numbers and there's nearly another $1000 more than I'd mentioned. So, there's the proof of it. If you doubt it, you can look at it and then give it back to me. Alright. I still suggest to you that I don't say things I can't prove. And I do appreciate very much though the willingness of these men to apologize for these matters that they find out they're wrong in. If they'll continue to do so as the debate progresses, I believe that by the end of Friday evening that we'll be together on these issues. If they're willing to accept whatever the Bible says, and not try to defend these human institutions, I believe that we'll be together before the debate's over.

Then, of course, brother Woods had something to say … in fact, he did say something about the kitchen, didn't he? The best I remember he said something about it either last evening or this evening one. It just so happens that last evening I said, "Awhile ago last evening, I answered it on the written questions." I want to read his question and read my answer. That ought to settle it. He makes like I haven't answered it, and he keeps saying, "Why don't you answer it?" Brother Woods, if you can't understand it when it's written out in front of you and you've read it, you wouldn't if I told you, I don't believe. Here's what the question was: "May the church, in its organized capacity, operate a kitchen and provide meals for needy saints from money out of its treasury?" Answer: If by 'operate a kitchen and provide meals for needy saints' you mean provide the necessary facilities and dispense food to hungry saints for whom the church is responsible, yes."

WOODS: Can they do that in the basement? That's what I asked you.

SUTTON: "However, the church would not become a kitchen any more than it becomes a meeting house when it provides a meeting house." That's what he didn't read last evening when he read my answer.

WOODS: Brother Sutton, can they do that in the basement? That's what I'm asking. I wasn't asking if they can operate something. Can they do it in the basement of the church building?

SUTTON: Did you read the answers to the questions I gave you tonight—or you gave me tonight? The questions you gave me when I gave you the answers back, did you read the answers? Did you understand the answers?

WOODS: Tell the audience.

SUTTON: Did you understand the answers? He knows exactly what I said about that, too. If he doesn't understand by tomorrow night or the next night, I'll get up and read it off, too.

Then, of course, he made mention of the fact that in the ***Porter-Woods Debate*** on page 255. He said in the context that he said that the church is a benevolent society, that the church is a missionary society, that the church arranges an orphan home, and it arranges a gospel meeting. Now, brother Woods, that's exactly what I know you said, and that's what I accused you of saying. I accused him of saying that the church is a benevolent society. In fact, he thinks it's a benevolent society and even can arrange an orphan home that does more than provide money. That does the arranging of it, isn't it? He said this like it can arrange a gospel meeting. Well, it provides money for gospel meetings and the oversight, too. The same thing would be so then, according to what he said in the ***Porter-Woods Debate***, about his orphan home. That gives up his contention then that the church cannot engage in this work of relief or benevolence as far as getting out the work is concerned. Thank you, brother Woods.

Then he said that, "Brother Sutton should debate the superintendents because he said they said they were human institutions," and said, "I say they're divine, so he ought to debate with them." Well, no, brother Woods. They agree with me on it. You ought to debate with them. Brother Woods says they're divine institutions and the superintendents say they're human. He says, "I should debate with the superintendents." No, they agreed with me, brother Woods. You ought to debate with them. How confused can a man get? I don't know any use of us debating because we agree on that matter. It's you and them that ought to do the debating, brother Woods.

Then, of course, he had something to say about the fact that the church cannot serve as a home. Well, I agree, brother Woods, that the church doesn't serve as a home. You know the church isn't a home, just like the church is not a gospel meeting, but it arranges one, doesn't it? The church is not a meeting house, but it arranges a meeting house. Now, the church doesn't serve as or function as a meeting house just because it provides a meeting house, does it? The church is not a preacher's house, yet it may provide a home for the preacher. And so, the church may provide a place, necessaries, and personnel, and evangelism, but it's still the church. Upon the same basis the church may provide a place, necessaries, and personnel for relieving the needy and still be the church. That exactly what I'm contending for. No, it doesn't cease being the church and become a home any more than it becomes a meeting house when it arranges a meeting house. That's my argument, brother Woods.

Now, brother Woods is the one that must believe that the church is a home because a benevolent society is a home because it provides a home. Then, according to brother Woods, the church is a home because it provides a home. So, his logic would lead him to believe that thing if he took it to his logical deductions. He's the guilty party.

Then, of course, he had quite a bit to say concerning the trustees. He said you can't have a church building without trustees. Now, brother Woods, I demand the proof of that. I demand that brother Woods produce the law that requires churches to have trustees before they can have church buildings. I deny the charge, brother Woods. Now, brethren, I said that I didn't make statements I couldn't prove. Brother Woods says, "I know you can't have a church building without there being trustees."

WOODS: Brother Sutton, the proof is this: Under the common law of this country and all of 48 states, a church cannot receive property, cannot make a deed to a church building. I have admission of the law from Texas and Tennessee. I can practice up to the Supreme Court. I know it to be the law of the land. Any lawyer in the country would tell you that. Anybody that's had any dealings at all with church property knows that you have to make the property to trustees to hold in trust for the church group. I'm surprised that you would exhibit your ignorance in that area.

SUTTON: Hold my time just a minute, brother Holt. I'm asking brother Woods to cite me the law that requires ...

WOODS: I don't have the statutes of the state of Illinois here on this table tonight. I can't read from the law, but anybody that's had any dealings in that field at all knows that I'm telling the truth. Maybe you're appealing to the ignorant.

SUTTON: I may be, brother Woods, in your estimation, but it just so happens I don't make statements I can't prove, brother Woods.

WOODS: Prove it, brother...

SUTTON: Hold my time, brother Holt.

WOODS: No. Don't hold his time.

TOTTY: Just a point of order. You're proving that; your time goes on, brother, and if you don't, we'll take the same amount he holds back on you.

SUTTON: I'm not speaking for it.

TOTTY: Well, you're proving it though, and you're trying to look up your proof.

SUTTON: Well, that's not proving it.

TOTTY: Well, it's trying to prove it. Well, you better let his time go. If you don't want us to use it.

WOODS: And besides, that's new evidence. I don't know what you fellows are trying to do here tonight unless you hold all this out to the last speech. I'd suggest, brother Holt, that you rule on the questions whether this is new evidence.

SUTTON: They asked for it.

HOLT: Did you ask?

WOODS: Only after he said that this was ignorant. Okay, let's have it. Alright, let's have it.

HOLT: Just a minute, brother Woods. The audience has been wonderful, and I know tonight has been tiresome and insensitive because we've been interrupted so much. We appreciate your patience, and I do ask that order continue, and I believe that you will cooperate. Do you want to prove it?

WOODS: Let the audience have it. I say that there isn't any such proof existing. I say that anytime a church owns church property it has to be held in trust by trustees. Now, if he has any proof laying around, let him prove it.

SUTTON: Now, I'm in a dilemma. I don't know whether to produce what I've got or save it to tomorrow night. If I knew all you would come back tomorrow night, I'd just wait and show it tomorrow night. That way, he couldn't accuse me of bringing in new material tonight. Yet he asked me to do it tonight, and yet he says it's new material. So, I don't know what to do.

WOODS: Go ahead and present it.

TOTTY: Go ahead and read it.

WOODS: Now, remember, this is the law of the land.

SUTTON: It just so happens, brethren and neighbors and

friends, that I have here in my hands a photocopy of a warranty deed for a church building of the church of Christ at Vinemont, Alabama. Now, here's how the deed reads. It says, "Have this day bargained, sold, and conveyed and do by these present to the said church of Christ at Vinemont, Alabama." It doesn't have a name of a trustee on it. Just hold the time.

WOODS: Go ahead.

SUTTON: I want to see if he accepts the proof.

TOTTY: Go ahead then.

SUTTON: Now, let's just hold the time.

HOLT: I believe I'd go ahead, brother Sutton.

WOODS: Now, right here, friends, is evidence of the fact that this fellow is not interested in the truth. Listen here on the top of this which he neglected to read. This is a correction deed of one given to L. P. Whaley, G. G. Thompson, and F. M. Ingram and recorded in vol. 79, p. 193. It was made to trustees, and then in order for some reason or another, in harmony for their law down there, they issued this correction and filed it with it. But it's based upon the real deed, and this is merely a warranty deed anyway. So, he has misrepresented the matter again.

SUTTON: Read the trustees on there again, brother Woods.

WOODS: Why, here they are: L. P. Whaley, G. G. Thompson, and F. M. Ingram. Were they the church at Vinemont?

SUTTON: Brethren, that isn't so. It was taken away from those trustees and deeded to the church by virtue of the fact that it is a corrected deed. He knows so, and you can read it after the service if you want to. It just so happens that I have another one here of the Washington church of Christ, and you find in it where there's a correction deed involved here, brother Woods.

WOODS: Is that in Russellville, Alabama?

SUTTON: No, sir. It's in Washington, Illinois. Just hold the time. Now, let's get it straight while we're at it. It doesn't have the name of any trustee on it to whom the property is deeded.

WOODS: In that case, it's to a corporation.

SUTTON: No, it isn't.

WOODS: "The matter raised by the church, a religious

116

corporation of the city of Washington, in the county of Woodford, state of Illinois for and in consideration of $4,710 and hand paid and conveyed the Washington church of Christ of the city of Washington the following real estate." Then it goes on to describe the bounds of it "situated in the state of Illinois hereby released by waiving all rights under by virtue of homestead exemption of the laws of this state." I don't have time to read all of it, but I call your attention to the fact that, in this instance, the grantor was a religious corporation by the grace by the church.

SUTTON: But the one that received the property is the Washington church of Christ, and it is not incorporated, and I challenge him to produce proof of it. That being so because there are brethren from Washington here tonight who know that the church of Christ is not incorporated. Brother Woods knows it's not on here. Thank you very much, ladies and gentlemen.

Third Session

May 31, 1962
7:30 p.m.

Carrol R. Sutton's First Affirmative Speech

Gentlemen moderators, brother Woods, ladies and gentlemen:

I'm glad again to appear before this audience for the purpose of discussing that proposition that's been read in your hearing. I'd like to express my appreciation to each of you for coming tonight for this study. I trust and pray that all of us will realize that truth is important, and we'll be desirous of ascertaining what truth is.

Our Lord, in one occasion as in John 8:32, said, "And you shall know the truth and the truth shall make you free." In John 18:38 Pilate asked Jesus saying, "What is truth?" On another occasion, as we find in John 17:17, Jesus said, "Sanctify them through Thy truth: Thy word is truth." Now, that's what we're concerned about this evening: What is truth as contained in God's Word?

We notice in 2 Peter 1:3 the apostle Peter says, "According as his divine power hath given unto us all things that pertain unto life and godliness...." Now, anything that pertains to life and godliness we can find ourselves furnished unto by the Scriptures. We notice in 2 Timothy 3:16-17 the apostle Paul says, "All scripture is given by inspiration of God, and is profitable for doctrine, for reproof, for correction, for instruction in righteousness: That the man of God may be perfect, thoroughly" (or throughly) "furnished unto all good works." So, if a thing is a "good work," we can find it in the Scriptures. We can find the authority for such in the Word of God. Hence, in 1 Peter 4:11, the apostle Peter says, "If any man speak, let him speak as the oracles of God." We have that responsibility tonight, as on all other occasions, to speak as God's oracles.

118

We notice in 2 John 9 that John says, "Whosoever transgresseth, and abideth not in the doctrine of Christ, hath not God. He that abideth in the doctrine of Christ, he hath both the Father and the Son." We can see then the need of abiding in the doctrine of Jesus Christ, because if we go outside of the doctrine of Christ, go beyond, then we do not have God the Father nor Jesus Christ the Son.

We notice also that in Ephesians 5:10 the apostle Paul says, "Proving what is acceptable unto the Lord." For three nights or rather for two nights prior to this, we've been discussing what the word of God teaches. We need to prove by the scriptures what the Word of God shows. We need to show by the scriptures whether a thing is authorized or not. I'm here tonight in the interest of truth only. I'm not here to please men but God, Galatians 1:10. I'm not here to win a personal victory but a victory for truth. I'm not here to defend human institutions, but I'm here to oppose human organizations, such as Tennessee Orphan Home, Boles Home, etc., being set up to do the work of the church. I'm here to defend a divine organization, the church of the living God, and it being sufficient as God planned it by God's divine wisdom as Ephesians 3:10 shows. This has been an all-sufficient organization to do all that God requires of His people in organized capacity. I am thus here to defend and "contend for the faith which was once delivered unto the saints," as we find in Jude 3.

Now, let's read the proposition again and define the terms thereof. "It is not in harmony with the scriptures for churches of Christ to build and maintain benevolent organizations such as the Tennessee Orphan Home, Boles Home, Home for the Aged, and other such organizations for the care of the needy." I am affirming that proposition. I believe that with all my heart, and anything that we could find in the Scriptures that would be contrary to this proposition, if such were to be so, I'd be glad to accept that and thus lay aside my views right now. If brother Woods can produce the passages of scripture that would authorize these things, I'd simply quit contending that these things are wrong. But they are not authorized by the word of God.

Now, by the expression "it is not in harmony with the scriptures," I mean that it is not sanctioned nor authorized in the Word of God as contained in the 66 books of the Bible. I mean, there is no authority for such; there is no precept, no divine example, no necessary implication in the scriptures. It was without divine authority; therefore, lawlessness in the sight of God Almighty.

Now, by the expression "churches of Christ," I mean local congregations composed of Christians.

By "to build and maintain," I mean to establish and support. Not only to send contributions to, but to establish and then to maintain or send contributions to or support in some way.

By the expression "benevolent organizations such as Tennessee Orphan Home, Boles Home, Home for the Aged, and other such organizations," I mean human benevolent or charitable organizations or societies or associations as those mentioned in the proposition. These organizations or societies or associations are not families, they're not homes, but they in turn provide homes for the needy.

Now, by the expression "for the care of the needy," I mean in order for the destitute to have their needs relieved.

Now, before considering some scriptural arguments in proof of the proposition, let's consider a few things that I believe will help to clarify the issue that we're discussing. Back in the 1800's, when the question and problem of the missionary societies arose among the people of God and divided churches and alienated brethren, there were many brethren who failed to understand the truth because they did not know what the issue or question of difference really was. Now, the issue of difference back then was not: Should the gospel be preached? It was not: Was the church obligated to preach the gospel? It was not: Could a place be maintained in which the gospel might be preached? It was not a matter of systematic arrangement. It was not a question or matter of how with respect to means, modes, or methods. The issue back then was: Is it Scriptural for churches of Christ to build and maintain missionary societies for the purpose of preaching the gospel?

Now, the issue tonight is not: Should the needy be cared for? I believe they ought to be cared for. It is not: Is the church obligated to care for some needy? I believe that it is. It is not: Can a home be provided for the needy? I believe that a home may thus be provided. It is not systematic arrangement. It is not a matter or question of how with respect to means, modes, or methods. But the issue is this: Is it scriptural for churches of Christ to build and maintain benevolent organizations such as those mentioned in the proposition; benevolent associations, benevolent societies, through which the church might perform works of benevolence.

I believe all of us can see tonight that it's a question of authority. Are these things authorized in the scriptures? It is a matter of what does the word of God say. Do these things constitute good works? If so, the word of God would furnish us unto them. Do they pertain unto life and godliness? If so, they're thus revealed in the scriptures, and so then, we can see the need of appealing to the word of God that we might thus see scriptural principles applied to these particular questions that we're concerned about tonight.

Now, chart number 1 is entitled "COMMANDS: GENERIC OR SPECIFIC?" We have in one column "COMMANDS," another "GENERIC TERMS," and another "SPECIFIC TERMS." As in the case of the command in Genesis 6:14, Noah was to build an ark. God did not give a generic term "wood," but God specified a particular kind of wood. God said, "gopher" and, hence, that ruled out other kinds of wood. We notice in 2 Kings 5 that God's prophet told Naaman, "go wash in Jordan seven times." He did not give a generic term "water," but he specified a particular body of water. He said in "Jordan"; therefore, other bodies of water were eliminated. We notice also in Leviticus 14:12-13 that God gave a command to offer. God did not simply say, "offer an animal," but God specified a "lamb" and, hence, that ruled out other kinds of animals. The lamb was what God specified. We notice in the case of John the ninth chapter that Jesus said to the blind man to "go wash in the pool of Siloam." Had Jesus Christ simply gave the term "water," it would not have mattered what body of water he washed in, but Jesus Christ did not do that. He specified a particular body of water. Jesus Christ said, "in the pool of Siloam." That ruled out other bodies of water.

Now, we're going to apply these very principles here to the issues that we're discussing tonight. We notice in the case of evangelism, or preaching the gospel, that Ephesians 3:10 shows that the church makes known God's manifold wisdom. We notice that in 1 Thessalonians 1:8 that Paul says, "For from you sounded out the word of the Lord not only in Macedonia and Achaia, but also in every place your faith to God-ward is spread abroad; so that we need not to speak anything." Hence, here's a congregation sounding out the Word of the Lord. God did not simply give a generic term "organizations," but God specified the church and, of course, the organization of the church is the local congregation. So then, God specified the local congregation, the church, that is the organization that is to do that particular work. That rules out other organizations. We note that is doing the work of the church.

We notice also in the case of edification that Ephesians 4 shows that the church edifies itself in love. Had God simply said to the apostle Paul "organizations are to edify the church," it would not have made a difference which ones, but God gave a specific term, church. Therefore, that rules out other organizations.

We notice in the case of relieving, and this brings us to the very heart of the issue that we're discussing tonight, in 1 Timothy 5:16 the apostle Paul says, "If any man or woman that believeth have widows, let them relieve them, and let not the church be charged; that it"—it what? The church—"That it may relieve them that are widows indeed." We have in Acts the sixth chapter an example of the church performing works of benevolence, as we've noticed in times past. There were seven men chosen by the church from among that local congregation that they might thus have the oversight to be set over the business of serving tables in the daily ministration. They thus dispensed food as some have suggested. So, we notice here God did not give a generic term "organizations," but God specified the church, the local congregation. Therefore, that rules out benevolent societies such as those mentioned in the proposition. Now, keep this in mind, brethren, that we're discussing the work of the church. We're not discussing the work of a private family. We're discussing the work of the church. So, God specified the church as the organization to do that. Therefore, when God specifies, others are eliminated.

We notice now, chart number 2 that's entitled: "AIDS AND ADDITIONS." We have in one column "COMMANDS," another "AIDS," and another "ADDITIONS." We notice, for example, the command in Matthew 28:19 was "Go teach all nations, baptizing them..." So, the command to baptize.

We notice Romans 6:4 shows how that baptism is a "burial," and so then the command is to baptize or to bury. Now, in carrying out the command to baptize, there may be such things that would AID such as a baptistery, or heating the water in the baptistery, or clothes provided, etc. But suppose somebody were to say, "Well, sprinkling is baptism", so we can baptize by sprinkling. You and I would recognize that as an addition to what God said because God said to "bury" in baptism, and sprinkling would be another kind of action. Hence, an addition to the word of God.

We notice in the case of 1 Corinthians 11:23-29 the apostle Paul shows that we're to eat bread with respect to the Lord's supper. Now, in eating bread, with respect to the Lord's supper, there are things that might aid us. There may be those who are serving the congregation or serving in that capacity of passing the bread around. There may be plates or things of that nature. Those things would be aids in doing what God said do. They would not be additions. But suppose somebody were to add beef on the Lord's table. That would be an addition to the word of God, because there's another kind of food involved. God said what to do, but here is another kind of food involved.

We notice in the case of Ephesians 5:19 where it says, "Singing and making melody in your hearts to the Lord." Colossians 3:16 also says to "sing with grace in your hearts to the Lord." So, there is the command to sing. In our singing we may use such things as the song books, the pitch pipe, or the lights in the building that will aid us in doing what God said do. But suppose somebody were to use mechanical instrumental music. There is another kind of music involved. God specified singing and, hence, that eliminates playing.

We notice also, in the case of the work of the church, in Ephesians 3:10 and in 1 Thessalonians 1:8 that the church is to evangelize or make known the gospel of Jesus Christ. It's to preach the Word of God. Now, in preaching the word of God, the church may use such things as literature or the radio or classes or the pulpit that it might aid in carrying out the command to preach. But suppose somebody would add a missionary society. That would not aid the church but be an addition to it because another kind of organization is involved. God specified the church which is a divine organization, but there is a missionary society which is a human organization. So then, that is ruled out as an addition to the word of God.

We notice in the case of the church edifying in Ephesians 4 that the place or facilities or teachers, etc. would fall in the category of aids. But suppose somebody were to organize a Sunday school society. I'm not talking about Bible classes, but I mean an organized Sunday school such as sectarians operate with their president, vice-president, etc. Now, that thing would not aid the church in edifying but be an addition to the word of God, because it's another kind of organization; a human in contrast with the divine, the church.

We notice now, in the case of relieving the destitute that we've read in 1 Timothy 5:16 the obligation upon the church to do it. We showed Acts 6:1-6 where the church did that. In Acts 2:44-45 the Bible shows the church engaged in relief work. Now, engaging in the relief work, as aids, the church might provide a building or facilities and personnel. Whatever might be required in carrying out this command to relieve those who are destitute. But suppose somebody comes along and adds a benevolent society. That could not fall in the category of aids because here is another kind of organization involved. It is a human organization, and God specified a divine organization, the church. Hence, we can see then the difference in aids and additions.

We notice now, chart number 3 that says, "IS THE TENNESSEE ORPHAN HOME A BENEVOLENT SOCIETY?"

We've shown this chart before. We have here churches sending to a body politic and corporate. A human corporation afforded the records which in turn provides a home, necessaries, and personnel for orphans at Spring Hill, Tennessee. The charter of incorporation shows how that it is a body politic and corporate by the name and style of "The Tennessee Orphan Home." So, it also says the corporation may establish branches in any county in the state. So, this one corporation operates, at the present time, a home and necessaries and personnel in Spring Hill, Tennessee, but it could do the same thing for orphans at Memphis, Tennessee. It could do the same thing for orphans in each of the other 93 counties in the state. So, here is one organization that could provide 95 homes for orphans if they wanted to and could beg enough money from the churches to so supply the needs. So, here is a thing that is not a home. Here is a thing that is not a family. Here is a thing that is not a church. I maintain it is an addition to the Word of God because it does not and cannot fall in the category of aids. When God specified the church, a divine institution, that rules out this human organization thus known as a Tennessee Orphan Home. Now, if that's not a benevolent society, friends, suppose we've got this thing set up identically down here, but instead of doing benevolent work this thing engages in missionary work or evangelism. Would that be a missionary society? If not, why not?

We notice also now, a chart that's entitled: "IS BOLES ORPHAN HOME A BENEVOLENT SOCIETY?"

We have, as we showed last evening, churches sending funds to a human corporation that's known as Boles Orphan Home. Here is a Board of Directors who supervises a place, facilities, necessaries, and personnel at Quinlan, Texas for the needy. Now, this here consists of several cottages and all of these cottages combined over here at Quinlan, Texas are known as Boles Home. Then 150 miles away, brethren, there is another place, facilities, necessaries, and personnel which also consists of a number of cottages and it's referred to as Sherwood-Myrtle Foster Home. It's operated by the same Board of Directors but 150 miles apart. We showed last evening from a *Potter Messenger* that they have listed the Boles Orphan Home as one orphanage. They have also listed the Sherwood and Myrtle Foster Home as a different orphanage, but there is two of them under the same board, this human organization. That's what I'm opposing tonight. That's the thing that we can't find authority for. That's the thing that's an addition to the Word of God. We've shown how that God specified the church. That rules out this human organization. It's not a family, brethren. It's not a family in form nor in origin nor in function. It's simply not a family at all. Yet, here is a human organization, an association, that exists by human authority alone and is engaging in providing the Boles Orphan Home or supervising it and also the Sherwood-Myrtle Foster Home 150 miles away. I ask, is it a benevolent society? If not, what is it? It is not the church. It's not a home. Somebody said, "Well, you call it a home." That's the name of the corporation. You can form a corporation and call it a church if you want to, but that doesn't necessarily mean it was a church. Thank you.

Guy N. Woods' First Negative Speech

Brethren moderators, brother Sutton, ladies and gentlemen:

I should like to say that it's a genuine pleasure to me to be before you tonight. I am enjoying especially my visit to this lovely city of Peoria. I'm happy to be associated with so many fine people and to speak to you from night to night in this discussion.

Now, in order to facilitate the matters of handling these charts because I shall take them up one by one, I shall go in reverse order here so that we may turn them back as they were after I have noticed briefly some of the preliminary remarks of brother Sutton.

He started out by calling attention to the importance of the truth: John 8:32; 18:38; and 17:17, part of which has no bearing whatsoever regarding the issue involved. We believe that we must go by the truth, and so we do not question that. We're agreed that the Scriptures supplies in all matters that pertain to life and godliness, and that it's all inspiring and that we must speak as the oracles of God and that we cannot go beyond or transgress the law of God and that we must prove that which is good and acceptable. All of this we accept without hesitation, and so that was just so much time that he might have spent in dealing with passages that have to do with the question of benevolence. That's the subject under consideration here tonight.

May I point out to you now, that we answered this last evening, and we submitted to him some difficulties regarding his position on it which he did not notice. We pointed out to him, first of all, that in so far as Boles Home is concerned, there is but one legal family and, if his argument possesses merit, that he ought to say there are 13 homes because there are approximately 12 cottages and then there is one cottage that is farther removed than the others. There is but one organization there, but if he chooses to call each of these separate cottages a different home, I'd like for him to wrestle with this.

He pointed out to us that in Acts 6 that seven men were selected in order to administer funds for the needy in Jerusalem. Does he mean to imply that there was but one home involved in that administration? So far as we know there were a hundred. At least, we are proper in drawing the deduction that there were many such homes involved. His argument, if it has any merit at all, is that a legal family can operate but one home at a time. I asked him last night, what about a man who sends his son and daughter off to college? Is he operating two families? What did he say about it? He said not anything at all and, of course, he won't.

Let's have the next chart now: chart number 3. In this instance we've also answered this each night thus far. We pointed out to you that his argument here is a figment of the imagination. Now, he maintains that there is a corporation between the church and the work that's being done. Then we insisted that the corporation itself is a part of the organization itself. But now, get his argument, and brethren use your heads a little. Don't allow him to mislead you on a matter so obvious. Now, look. "This is wrong," he says, and it proves that this is separate from this because this provides this. Because this is provided by that, that can't be any part of this. Now, look. According to that argument, a man provides for his family but that which does the providing is no part of that which is provided for. Therefore, the man who makes the living is no part of his family. If not, why not? I say that needs an answer. If his argument has any merit at all it is that because the corporation provides the necessities that it's not part of that which is provided. Of course, he's wrong about it as he is on everything else that's peculiar to his position. Now, we insist that that must be answered. Will you say something about it? Just say something about it when you get back up here, Sutton.

Chart number 2. Now, you'll note here that he has the long

column here under "AIDS" and under "ADDITIONS." The implication being that an 'aid' is permissible but an 'addition' is wrong. Why I think that's right. I think the principle of that is correct, but let me call your attention to this fact: We do not maintain that the orphan home is either an 'aid' or an 'addition' to the church. It's neither and 'aid' nor an 'addition.' It's a separate organization, a separate institution. Now, once again get it, ladies and gentlemen. God designates what organization is to perform the actual work. Psalms 68:5-6. "God setteth the solitary in families...." That tells us that the family is the organization that is to engage in actual child care but observe this please. It is the obligation of the church to assist the needy: James 1:27; Galatians 6:10; Acts 20:35; Mark 14:6 and so on. We've presented it repeatedly. Now, what is it? There is an obligation of the church. There is an obligation of the family. We have seen that it is the family work to provide the actual care. It's church work to supply the means. You have the organization, the church. You have the organization, the family. Neither usurps the function of the other. But this family must comply with state laws. It must be licensed. It must, in order to follow good business practice, be incorporated. Now, when that's done it's nothing but following legal procedure. Sutton implies that that's one of the things that makes it wrong. He is telling you that it's wrong to do right and he's encouraging you to believe that you should violate the law of the land in taking care of orphans because he's telling you that when we comply with the law and have a Board of Directors and the organization licensed, that such is wrong. Now, get this. Sutton is not about to start an orphan home, but if he were to and he practiced what he preaches, he'd get put in jail. Now, I won't have much trouble proving that. That's exactly right. In the first place, he's not about to do it and I want to show you the insincerity and the hypocrisy that's involved in these charts.

You would get the impression that Sutton believes that it's right for the church to help orphans. You'd get that impression, wouldn't you? That's what he is opposing. He's opposing another organization doing it, but that the way to do it is for the church to do it. Now, ladies and gentlemen, he doesn't believe a word of that.

128

Not one word of that does he believe when he puts that on the chart here and tries to make you believe that he thinks that it is the church that ought to relieve the orphans. He doesn't believe one word of that. He doesn't believe that it is right to take one single dime out of the church treasury in order to feed a starving orphan. Not a dime. He thinks it's all right to buy fertilizer to feed the grass on the preacher's yard, but it's sinful to buy a bottle of milk to feed a starving orphan out of the church treasury. Now, ladies and gentlemen, that's right or it's wrong. It's either right or it's wrong. If I am wrong about that, you get up here and tell us, Sutton.

I want to tell you friends, thank you, some of the things that he believes about. He thinks that if there should be an automobile accident out here in the street, that if it involved members of the church, you could bring them into the building and minister to their needs. But if there were babies, not old enough to be Christians and whose parents were not members of the church, you couldn't scripturally wet a rag at that drinking fountain down there in the basement and wipe the blood from their faces. He doesn't believe that would be scriptural in principle. He doesn't believe that it's right to let a baby, that's not a Christian, sleep in a crib back there, if he is consistent in his position. Now, again I say I'm either telling the truth or I'm not. He knows that I'll produce a tape recording that states exactly in principle what I'm saying here tonight if he denies it. Now, that's what you fellows have accepted when you follow Sutton or else you are supporting and defending a fellow who teaches a doctrine that is so repulsive that I don't see how you can stomach it. I don't! No, friends, he doesn't think that the church can help orphans. Not one dime, does he think, can be spent in that venture.

Now, let's have his next chart: chart number 1. Here is the same situation. You'd get the idea from this, and I told you the other night that there is no issue with reference to this, although if he'd been back there in Noah's day he probably would have said, "Well, now, I'm going to tell you what kind of wrench you can use or what kind you can't use or what kind of hammer you can't use." I think he would have told him what kind of tools to use, but at any rate, you'd get the idea that he thinks that the church can relieve orphans because that's what we're debating tonight, about how to take care of orphans. You'd think that he believes the church can do it. He doesn't believe one word of that, ladies and gentlemen. That is hypocrisy pure and simple to put that on there because he doesn't think the church can relieve orphans. If he does, he's changed his position since Blazer gave him a thrashing down in Alabama.

Now, he tells us that back in times past it was not a question of whether the gospel should be preached, it was not a question of place or arrangement. He said, "It's not an issue now, if the needy is to be taken care of, it's an issue of whether the church can take care of babies." That's an issue here tonight. He says that it's lawlessness. What I am advocating, that it's right for the church to take care of homeless children in orphan homes, that that's lawlessness. Well, Sutton, what do you recommend we do with them? Would you recommend that those twenty-five hundred that are in these homes be shot or drowned? Which do you think would be the most humane? Now, what do you think we ought to do with them? I want to know what you think, if we were to all get converted to you. What do you think we ought to do with them? Yes, I'd like to know. What about it? While you're doing it, tell us if you can have a kitchen in the basement here. I want to know what we ought to do with those children. Don't you come up here and say there was not any need for them in the first place. There's 17 agencies in Chicago alone that's looking for places for children. Over in Louisville, Kentucky they had over 300 children that were needing homes at one time over there just recently.

Now, that, friends, covers his speech item by item and statement by statement. That brings us up to some matters that I want to emphasize particularly. You remember now, that he's led you to think that the church can relieve orphan children. We're going to see whether or not he thinks that's so.

On last evening, he made the argument that what's wrong with the orphan home is that it has an in-between organization; this so called in-between organization between the church and the

130

home, the orphan home. Now, it doesn't make any difference whether that's there or not. He doesn't think it's scriptural even though we took this out. Let's pencil it out, Sutton. Tell us how you can send it to the orphans from the church and it'll still be scriptural. The truth of the business is he doesn't believe it. Now, I want to mention—do I have as much as five minutes? If I don't, I'll wait till the next speech. On last evening, I made the assertion that a deed, in order to be valid and to be an instrument by which a person can receive and sell property, must be conveyed to trustees. Sutton denied that and argued that what was wrong with the orphan home is that this in-between organization is there. I paralleled it by the trustee deal. I said, "Then do you object to trustees?" and his answer was that this congregation one time had such, but they straightened matters out. He said they straightened things out. Now, you didn't say that, Sutton? You're shaking your head as if you didn't say that. He said last night they straightened matters out. I went down today and found out how they straightened them out. They eliminated the trustees. They eliminated the incorporation, at least from the matter of holding the property, but I want to tell you this, friends. This so-called quitclaim deed that you folks have here is not worth the paper that it's written on. I want to tell you, further, that the only validity that this has, if it has any at all, would be because there were trustees, because you can't convey something that you don't hold. Unless these men have a right to this, as trustees, then this is invalid. And let me tell us this, further. Sutton has laid a premise here for a situation that will embarrass this congregation in the future. You mark my words. He told you a few nights ago that this congregation had an incorporation, but that it was arranged by those who agreed with me. Now, that's on tape. Hundreds of people heard that testimony. That means that Sutton has stated publicly that the people who were in charge at one time believe like I do. They got a hold of it. They took it down and straightened things out. They have no right to this property. He testified to that effect last night. I say that they stand in grave jeopardy of losing their property here by admission of that fact. If he runs two or three more groups off, there won't be anybody here anyway, and somebody can come in here and start a faithful New Testament church in this property. And he's laid the premise right here in this action. Now, Sutton, get busy on that when you get up here and tell us.

Another thing about it. I want to know if it's scriptural for a congregation to have trustees. Now, that's his implication. They had trustees, but they straightened things out. They eliminated the trustees. That implication is that a congregation that has trustees needs straightening out. Well, if that's true, a whole bunch of these "anti" churches need straightening out. That means that Sutton is on record that it's sinful to have trustees; that the trustees are comparable to the in-between organization that he imagines exists, but which is a figment of his imagination. Now, brother Sutton, I want to know if it's your position that the trustees arrangement is sinful; if it's parallel to your imaginary in-between organization. I want to know if there's any way by which this church can assist orphans.

I asked him some questions. We had an agreement that we would ask five questions that would be handed in early enough that they could be answered. I gave them to him nearly 35 minutes before he began to speak. He refused to answer them tonight. I'm going to read them. You can see what they are:

1. Can the Paris Street church, for which you preach, scripturally operate a kitchen in this basement? If yes, give scripture. If no, give scripture.

2. Suppose a cyclone should hit Peoria, killing a number of Christian parents and leaving a dozen orphan children. Suppose that there were no individuals so circumstanced as to be able to provide for them. Is there any way, according to your doctrine, where the church could assist these children from its treasury?

3. Can the church provide hospital care and oversight of the actual work for indigent saints? Can it supply a ball field and an umpire for the children of indigent saints?

4. Does the church have trustees? If not, is such an unscriptural organization? Do the trustees stand between the members who supply the money and the church?

132

5. Since you teach that the church cannot relieve sinners, would you forbid an alien sinner here tonight to have a drink of water from a fountain in the basement, use the restroom, wet a wash cloth from the fountain, provide shelter for accident victims, use the telephone to call a doctor or ambulance, permit use of the church building for homeless victims of a tornado, allow a baby (not old enough to obey the gospel and not related to any member of the church) to use a crib in the nursery?

Now, I insist he ought to have answered those. He had 35 minutes, approximately, to do so tonight.

Carrol R. Sutton's Second Affirmative Speech

Gentlemen moderators, brother Woods, ladies and gentlemen:

I'm glad to appear before you for the next 20 minutes in defense of the truth as stated in the proposition that I'm affirming. For fear that some of you may think that we're affirming some other proposition other than what we both signed to discuss, I want to read the proposition as follows: It is not in harmony with the scriptures for churches of Christ to build and maintain kitchens. [pause] Wait a minute. I got mixed up on that thing. It is not in harmony with the scriptures for churches of Christ to build and maintain trustees. [pause] "It is not in harmony with the scriptures for churches of Christ to build and maintain benevolent organizations, such as The Tennessee Orphan Home, Boles Home, Home for the Aged, and other such organizations for the care of the needy." That's what I'm affirming tonight, brethren, and that's exactly what I intend to stick with in this next 20 minutes, as I suggested the last two evenings and when brother Woods is in the affirmative. He tried to get away from it. I followed him wheresoever he went, and I think he wished I hadn't. I suggested, last evening, that tonight I'd show what the scriptures teach relative to these matters, so we'll proceed at this present time.

We noticed in our speech a few minutes ago, first of all, this chart that's entitled: "COMMANDS: GENERIC OR SPECIFIC." We showed how that when God specified the church in evangelism that rules out human organizations such as missionary societies. We showed further how that when He specified the church in edification, that rules out human organizations such as the Sunday school organizations. We showed further that in the field of benevolence that when God specified that the church is the organization to relieve, that rules out the benevolent organizations such as those mentioned in the proposition. That still stands untouched.

Now, last evening and the night before, I dealt with what brother Woods had to present. Now, he came over here and said something about, "What about the tools that Noah used?" That "Brother Sutton would have probably told Noah he had to use a certain kind of tool." No, I wouldn't, brother Woods. No, I wouldn't, but that wasn't even the point. The point was down here on benevolent organizations by their additions to what God said. He didn't deal with that, friends. He hasn't dealt at all with the argument I made on the diagram. He got up here and said, "Well, what about the tools?" Do you claim the benevolent organizations are tools, brother Woods? You say they are separate organizations; they're not in the category of aids. I thank you, brother Woods. That still stands untouched, brethren, and it will. That's Bible! Book, chapter, and verses have been given all of the way on it. Incidentally, I want you to note the contrast between the scriptures on the charts that show my position and the ones that he's been introducing the last two nights. For some reason, it was conspicuous by the absence of scriptures, usually.

Now, we notice this second chart also stands untouched. He didn't deal with the argument that I made at all on this chart. I showed how that here are some things that are aids and other things are additions. I showed how that in evangelism the church is the organization to do it. That missionary societies are another kind of organization; human in contrast with the divine. I showed the same thing with respect to the church relieving. That the church is the organization that God authorized to do that, and, hence, these benevolent organizations or societies are other kinds of organizations; human in origin, form, and function. Therefore, we can see how that they are additions to the word of God. He said, "Our orphan homes are not in the category of aids or additions." "They're not aids and they're not additions," he says. Well, what are they? He said they are separate organizations. That's what I've been contending for all of the time. I've been trying to show you people they are separate organizations from the church, and we know they don't constitute a family nor a home. Therefore, they are benevolent societies, and that's what I've been saying. Thank you, brother Woods. So that chart also stands untouched. It will because there are scriptures on it.

We notice also this diagram. This showed the set up that brother Woods is defending; therefore, no scripture on it. This is his proposition, actually. This is what he's defending. Therefore, there is no scripture on this chart. That describes his arrangement. Now, what about that? I couldn't find any scripture for that. That's why that I said that those things are not in harmony with the scriptures. That shows a benevolent organization, and brother Woods said, the other night, these things over here, the personnel and so forth, were no part of that Board of Directors. But yet, he tries to say that this Board of Directors is an integral part of the family. That would be about like my saying that I'm a part of you but you're not a part of me. That's brother Woods' logic. That's the way he's arguing. He says this here's no part of that, but he says that is an integral part of the family. What about it? That describes his stand, untouched.

Did you notice what he said about this down here? I asked him would this be a missionary society. He observed the "Passover" on that, didn't he? Now, do you believe in keeping the old law, brother Woods?

WOODS: Like you did about telling us whether the father is a part of his family.

SUTTON: We notice also this chart that's entitled: "IS BOLES ORPHAN HOME A BENEVOLENT SOCIETY?"

We showed how that churches are sending funds to a

benevolent organization, a body politic and corporate. It is a human organization. And notice here what the charter of incorporation says: "The name of this corporation shall be Boles Orphan Home." Now, the name of the corporation, this Board of Directors, is called that. Not the place, facilities, necessities, and personnel, but this Board is called that. "The purposes of this corporation are to provide a home." And he tries to make out like it's a home, it's a family, it's this thing and that thing, but the very purpose of it, the charter of the incorporation says, is to provide a home for destitute and dependent children, and so forth. And this corporation, it also mentions the fact: "to adopt such children or any of them as said corporation may so desire from time to time." So, we can see that here is an organization that's between the churches and the home that's provided. In this case, there are two of them provided. He said, "Well now, according to brother Sutton, since they've got 12 or 13 cottages over here, that means 12 or 13 homes." No, it doesn't, brother Woods. No, sir! I stated in my first speech the fact they had several cottages over here. All of that together is Boles Home. I stated, also down here, they have several cottages, at least two or more, and they're called the Sherwood-Myrtle Foster Home. Let's just read here from ***Potter Orphan Home Messenger***. It says 28 homes are now supported by churches of Christ. November 1961 is the date of this ***Messenger***. And then the first one listed is Boles Home, Quinlan, Texas, and the last one listed is Foster Home, Stephenville, Texas. That's 150 miles away. So, his own brethren tell him that they are two separate homes, but he says that isn't so when I say it, but it is so, anyway, because there's proof of it.

Let me show what the superintendent of Boles Home, who's also the superintendent of this home, both homes, under that Board, says in Volume 17, Number 13 of ***Boles Home News***. It says the beautiful Sherwood-Myrtle Foster Home for Children at Stephenville, Texas is to have open house at a certain time. Then it talks about the fact, also, that the manager of the home is brother James Crary, and so forth. Here is the manager of this home; there is a manager over that home. There is two separate homes involved,

136

and nobody knows it any better than brother Guy N. Woods. Then we notice, also from *Boles Home News*, Volume 18, Number 24, that we read this: It says the past year services at Boles Home and at the Foster Home at Stephenville. It was reported to the board that some 245 children receiving daily full-time care at Boles Home, and some 31 children of the Foster Home at Stephenville. That sounds like different cottages, doesn't it? Brother Woods, you deal with it when you come to the platform.

WOODS: I'll be glad to, brother Sutton.

SUTTON: When you come to the platform, brother Woods. And so, this stands untouched.

Now, notice this, brethren. If this is not a benevolent society, what would it take to make one? I want him to tell us. That's on the chart. He didn't tell us, did he? He didn't even deal with it; didn't even mention that. If this is not a benevolent society, what would it take to make one?

We notice, also, chart number 22 entitled: "THE STATE OF ALABAMA RECOGNIZES CHILDHAVEN AS A BENEVOLENT SOCIETY." You know he likes to talk a lot about legal proof, doesn't he? Incidentally, he's a lawyer. He ought to recognize this proof from the State of Alabama law. He hasn't said too much about this, has he? No, and he won't say too much about it. If he does, he'll wish he hadn't. But now, I notice here the proof: Title 10, Chapter 7, Article 3, Section 124, 1940 Code of Alabama, under which Childhaven is incorporated, provides for incorporation of churches and educational or benevolent societies. Note, since Childhaven is incorporated under this law and it is not a church, it's not an educational society, then it must be a benevolent society. Now, if it is not a benevolent society, it is either a church or educational society. Tell us which one it is when you come up here, brother Woods.

Now, yes, my opponent is defending a benevolent society, which is an addition to the word of God as we showed over here a while ago. He can't get around that. I wish he would give it up and start contending for the truth, as he did in 1946 and the principles that are suggested in 1939, as we have on the chart on the right and also the one on the left here. [Charts on pages 235-236]

Now, I want us to notice chart number 5 that's entitled: "GOD'S WAY VERSUS WAYS OF MEN." We have on one side of the chart God's ways. Here is the local congregation which is a divine organization under its elders. It engages in the works of preaching the gospel as 1 Timothy 3:14-15 says. It engages in the works of edification as Ephesians 4 shows. It is engaged in the works of relief, 1 Timothy 5; 1 Corinthians 16; and Acts 6:1-6 shows. But now, we have on this side of the chart, the ways of men. We have here the elders of the local congregation, which is a divine organization, being elders over that local congregation, and instead of simply overseeing and providing the necessaries and facilities for the work to be done in evangelism, they set up a missionary society and let it, in turn, do that work of preaching the gospel. Then in other cases there would be those that might set up an edification organization that it, in turn, might edify. Then there are those, like my opponent, who would defend churches sending to benevolent corporations. In fact, he says churches may build and maintain such. Not just send to them, but build them and establish them and let them in turn do the work of relief. Now, this is a way of men. This is not God's way. I'm contending for the way of God. Scripture, please, for this setup. This is man's wisdom, that's human; therefore, not needed. I'm asking my opponent to put the scripture up here. Tell us where in the word of God these things are authorized. I have scripture over here. There is God's wisdom, that's divine; therefore, I maintain that it's sufficient.

We notice, now, chart number 23 that's entitled: "HOW VERSUS ORGANIZATION." Brother Woods has contended that I'm trying to bind a "how," a particular method in benevolence. Such is not the case. He knows it's not so because I hold him last evening. That's the reason I know that he knows it, and if he didn't, well, I just know he does. So then, we notice here there is the command to preach the gospel as we find in 1 Timothy 3:15, Ephesians 3:10, and so forth. There is the command to edify on the part of the church, Ephesians 4, and there is the command to relieve on the part of the church in 1 Timothy 5:16. Acts 2, Acts 4, and

138

Acts 6:1-6 shows that the church engaged in relief. Now, here are three commands that the church is to carry out.

Now, notice that over here is organizations that may carry out these commands. In each case, we've got a divine organization that may perform those functions, and we've got a human organization that may do that by human authority, but not by divine. Notice, in the case of evangelism, that here's the church and the missionary society. I maintain that these verses show that the church is the organization to do it. In the case of edification, there's the church and an edification society. I maintain that the church is the organization to do it because Ephesians 4:16 shows it. In the case of relief, here's the church and benevolent organizations or societies like brother Woods is defending. I maintain that 1 Timothy 5:16 specifies the church is the divine organization to engage in that work. There is a vast difference, though, between the "organization" and the "how."

Now, I notice in the "how" there may be a place necessary, or facilities, necessaries, and personnel. Now, either the divine organization, the church, or the human organizations, may provide the "how." I'm not binding the "how"—the methods, the means, or the modes—because God's word doesn't. But since God has specified the church is the organization, that's what we're binding. God has bound such, and so there is "how" versus "organization."

We notice also with institutions, we have the same thing illustrated here. On this side the church, a divine institution, is caring for the needy. 1 Timothy 5:16 shows the church is to do that. We notice that the "how" comes in the category of expediency as to the "how" with respect to means, modes, and methods. The place where it might be built, bought, rented, etc., the necessaries, whether it's food, clothing, etc., and the supervision, the church would decide on those things, but it would be under the oversight of the church. On the other side, we have a Board of Directors, a human organization, that is going to care for the needy. It, in turn, must decide the "how"—how will we do it with and when the places involved. Will we buy the place, build it, rent it, and so forth, or will we put these needy people in private homes. You know these organizations, in many cases, have that right. Yes, they do. Surely so. So, this thing over here will decide the "how."

I'm asking you, brethren, when the Bible says the church, what do you say? Which organization? I maintain the church. My opponent suggests this Board of Directors. That's why we're discussing these matters, and that's why we're glad that brother Woods finally got us into a debate—finally. After, well, we won't go into that. Note the parallel, brethren. Note the parallel.

Here's chart number 25. Now, this again describes what brother Woods is defending in principle; therefore, no scripture on it. Down here is churches sending to missionary societies that the gospel might be preached. Here churches send to benevolent corporations or benevolent organizations, such as those mentioned in the proposition, that the needy may be cared for. Now, that's what I'm opposing in both cases. Now, brother Woods accepts this thing in relief or in benevolence. I wonder if he does in evangelism. In fact, he might just tell us whether or not he endorses churches sending funds to the organization if it has been called a missionary society that is called the Gospel Press. I kinda doubt that he'd like to answer from his seat on that one.

WOODS: What was that question?

SUTTON: Whether or not churches have a scriptural right to send to Gospel Press? Yes or no.

WOODS: Churches have a right to buy the ads that these people put in these papers, just exactly like we would if we were publishing the *Gospel Advocate*. Now, I answered your question. You answer mine: Is the father a part of the family he provides?

SUTTON: Do they have a right to send contributions to the Gospel Press, brother Woods?

WOODS: For the purpose that I set out.

SUTTON: Do they have a right to send....

WOODS: For the purpose I set out.

SUTTON: To make a contribution or buy a service?

WOODS: You see, friends. He wants me to answer, but he's not answering.

SUTTON: He's not answering the question. I asked him

whether or not make a contribution to it. He said he could buy services from it. I said contribute to it. He hasn't answered it; he's dodged. You've seen it. Can they contribute to it, brother Woods?

WOODS: Is the father...

SUTTON: Can they? He doesn't want to answer, does he?

WOODS: I already answered it.

SUTTON: He doesn't want to answer.

WOODS: I told you that the...

SUTTON: I don't blame him, either.

WOODS: I told you they could buy services from this press by putting these ads in the paper, and if they want assistance, they can send them a contribution to that end. Yes. Now, then, you answer my question.

SUTTON: You still haven't answered it directly. Can churches make contributions to these organizations and let them, in turn, oversee the expenditures of the funds?

WOODS: If I answer yes or no, will you answer about the basement and the matter of the father and his family?

SUTTON: I'll answer when I get ready to. [pause] See, he says, "*If* I answer yes or no." He's admitting he hasn't been answering, yet he contended he had answered. That's what we're confronting, brethren. Thank you, brother Woods.

WOODS: You're welcome.

SUTTON: We notice here a chart that's entitled: "YES, THE CHURCH CAN RELIEVE." In 1 Timothy 5:16, the Bible says that "If any man or woman that believeth have widows, let them relieve them, and let not the church be not charged; that it may relieve them that are widows indeed." Why can't the church provide a place, facilities, necessaries, and personnel for that? Yes, I believe the church can relieve. My opponent doesn't in the sense that the Bible uses it.

Then we notice, also, chart number 16. How much time, brother Holt? Two minutes. Chart number 16. Now, we notice here a chart entitled: "IS BROTHER WOODS CONFUSED?" We notice here that brother Woods says that "the church must supply the orphan homes," *Woods-Porter Debate* on page 254. He says,

"The church may furnish a place," *Woods-Cogdill Debate* on page 87. He says, "The church supplies the clothes," *Freed-Hardeman College Lectures*, 1960, page 10. He says, "The church may furnish the necessities of life," *Woods-Cogdill Debate*, page 87. He says, "May put them," there talking about the needy, "May put them in a home," he said in Huntsville, Alabama, September 20, 1958, second session, first speech, that's his own tape. He says that, "the church is to relieve them that are widows," *Gospel Advocate*, 10/28/54. He says, "The church arranges an orphan home," *Woods-Porter Debate*, page 255. He says, "The church operates orphanages and homes for the aged," *Woods-Porter Debate*, on page 95. We notice how that he says that the church is a "benevolent society," *Woods-Porter Debate*, page 255. And his proposition, that he contended for two nights, said the church may build and maintain benevolent organizations, and yet, brother Woods has claimed in *A Defense of Orphan Homes*, on page 14, that all the church is authorized to provide is the funds. Is he confused?

Now, here he says the church can provide all of these things, but yet he says all it's authorized to provide are the funds. That's on page 14 of his *Defense of Orphan Homes*. We read that last evening to you. I wonder if he's confused. If funds is all it can provide, how can it build and maintain these things? How can it act as a benevolent society and all of these other matters involved here? Is he confused? Now, keep this in mind, brethren.

He may talk about this thing, he may talk about that thing, and something else. He may tell you about how sorry he thinks I am, but just suppose he's right about it? What does that prove about his benevolent organizations? He signed to prove that such are scriptural. Thank you.

Guy N. Woods' Second Negative Speech

Brother moderators, brother Sutton, and ladies and gentlemen:

142

I should like for you to know that we're all in good spirits. That we are enjoying this fully. In fact, it's a pleasure to me to torment this fellow before his time. I know what he's headed for in eternity, and I'm not averse to seeing him get a little of it right here.

Now, he told you that I was lugging in matters that had nothing to do with the proposition, one of which was the matter of trustees. Who introduced the subject of trustees and when? Not only did Sutton introduce it, but he introduced it over our protests last night in his final speech when I had no reply, and now, he'd shut me up all night if he could. He not only introduced it after I had no further reply last night but tonight he wants to close the subject. Well, I don't blame him. If I were in the position that he is, I wouldn't talk about it either. But if there's a person here tonight that can't understand why he does that, don't you worry. You got a ticket up there whether there are any orphan homes or not. I wouldn't worry about it at all.

He says, "What does the kitchen have to do with it?" It has this to do with it. Sutton's argument is that the church can provide every activity that a needy person has, one of which is food, and it's better when it's heated. I asked him if this building could serve as a place to do that which he says the church can do, and I can't get any answers. Now, do any of you folks know how to get him to answer that question? If you do, I wish you'd come around and tell me.

Sutton is not famous for not stating his mind on matters when there is not anybody around to call his hand. He has the reputation for stating his mind except when he meets Woods in debate. Well, Sutton, you may live in this community a long time, but the people will never forget how that you positively refused to answer these questions, and yet, you claim to be a debater. If I couldn't do any better than that in defense of the position, I'd take down my sign. I wonder what you fellows think about this? What's the purpose of a debate anyway? Isn't it to deal with an issue and answer questions? What's a debate for? What's a debater supposed to do? If he were debating a Baptist, and he didn't do any better than he's doing in answering the arguments here tonight, we would all hang our heads in shame, and he ought to do that anyway. Sutton, what about the kitchen in the basement? What about it? I'll give you half a minute of my time to rise up on your feet and answer. Can you? Maybe you don't want to answer. Just bat your eyes a little bit. I'd get the idea. Now, why doesn't he answer, friends? You remember this, that when men defend the anti-orphan home position that's the condition they get in. I answered his questions.

He said that Woods admitted, Woods finally admitted, that what he's defending is an organization separate from the church. Can you imagine? I finally admitted it. Now, I'll tell you, he's hard put when he comes up with statements like that. I finally admitted that the family is not the church. After three nights here, he finally got me around to it. Can you imagine? I tell you Woods is hard to get around to the issue, isn't he? I finally admitted that it's a separate organization. Well, that's what makes it right. Then you don't have to argue about having a kitchen. Don't have to worry about having a kitchen in the basement. I have a kitchen in the basement where the family is. If he had my position, he wouldn't have any trouble on it.

Let's have this chart number 3. Chart number 3. Now, hold my time here while we're hunting the chart. Now, friends, I asked him two things about this, and I tried to get him to deal with it when it was obvious that he didn't intend to. I said that his idea that this is separate from the organization is a figment of the imagination, and I gave him two illustrations to deal with. I said, "If your contention is right, what about the father that provides for his family?" His argument is because this provides this. This is not this. Well, all right. Because the father provides this, the father is no part of the family which he provides for. If his argument has any merit, that's it. Why didn't he deal with that? I gave him an illustration of a man whose family was in two different places in connection with this, and no answer. Now, brother, I'd be glad if you made some attempt at answering this.

Seriously, without any attempt now to browbeat you or anything, I just want you to deal with this issue. That's what we're here for. If I'm wrong about that, show that we're wrong. Show that the two are not parallel. How about it, brother Sutton? Would you answer now,? I'll give you half a minute of my time just to tell me whether the father who provides for his family is any part of the family. This is not part of this because this provides this. That's his argument.

Then he says, "You didn't say anything about this down here.

144

Would this be a missionary society?" Well, it wouldn't be a missionary society in the sense that we speak of missionary societies, because we talk about missionary societies as being organizations which themselves operate colleges, orphan homes, missionary endeavors, papers, and a whole bunch of things. The very idea of saying that a thing is parallel to an orphan home when itself operates orphan homes as well as a bunch of schools and papers and a whole bunch of other things. There is not any parallel there. Wasn't any need for any answer to it, because it's obvious on its very face, but this requires an answer. Now, Sutton, listen to what I have to say whether you intend to answer or not.

Well, let's have now, his, oh yes, the chart about the Alabama law. Oh, yes, he doesn't use anything now but the scriptures, does he, to prove his point? But he's going to prove it by the Alabama law. I want you to see some of this marvelous logic that this theologian uses here. Hold my time. Don't make much difference. Either one of them because one is just as wrong as the other. Take them all.

Alright, here the State of Alabama recognizes Childhaven as a benevolent society. Now, that proves it, doesn't it? That proves it by the Bible. He started out with the scriptures, didn't he? He said, "I'm going to prove it by the Bible." Well, he comes up here and says, "Now, I'm going to show you that the State of Alabama says it." I'm not particularly interested in the matter of religious activities as to what the State of Alabama says. The State of Alabama says it's right to sell and drink liquor, but I don't think they're telling the truth about it. Do you, fellows?

All look at this logic now, down here. Since Childhaven is not a church or an education society, it must be a benevolent society. Isn't that a marvelous example of logic? Sutton is not a cow or a pig; therefore, he must be a monkey. There wouldn't be any other conclusion because that's his logic here. He thinks there's no alternative but this right here. Now, if this is right, then I've proved that he's a monkey tonight by the State of Alabama law, according to him. Now, Sutton, I'd be ashamed if I couldn't do any better than that.

The Catholic Church is, by the State of Alabama, recognized as a religious institution that has a right to exist and operate as a church. I don't believe it does. I don't believe it does scripturally, and he's trying to prove this thing scripturally by the State of Alabama law.

"Well," he says, "in 1946 you held a position that's contrary to your position now." I didn't do anything of the kind. That's a misrepresentation, and he knows it. He's heard it said time and again. That has a lot to do with the proposition that he's going to prove by the Bible, but he proves it by what Woods said in 1946. Woods might have said, "You ought to stand on your head" in 1946. That wouldn't have anything to do with proving his proposition.

I want to show you, friends,—move that over there against the wall—I want to show you how these fellows misrepresent me on this, and I want you to know that they know they're doing it. Sutton knows that he's doing it. Look here at what I said: "The ship of Zion has floundered more than once on the sandbar of institutionalism. The tendency to organize is characteristic of the age based on the theory that the end justifies the means. Brethren have not scrupled to form organizations in the church to do the work the church herself or itself was designed to do." What do I say there? I say that there's been a tendency to form organizations to do the work that God gave to the church to do. Have I said here that it's the work of the church to provide for orphan children? I said it was the work of the family. I'm not controverting that. I believe every word of that. It is true that you cannot establish another organization to do the work which God exclusively gave to the church, but He never gave to the church the work of being a family, and that's the point, and that fellow knows it. He knows that he's deliberately misrepresenting that when he says that.

I'm not mad at him. I'm just sorry for him. I just pity a fellow that will resort to flagrant misrepresentation in order to try to sustain his position. He knows it. All these fellows know it. They've heard me say it repeatedly. Now, just go on and keep saying it, gentlemen, but you remember that there's a judgment day coming one of these days, when Revelation 21:8 tells us that all liars will have their part in the lake of fire that burns with fire and brimstone. Now, you remember that, because that's exactly what these fellows do when they misrepresent me.

I've got this. Sutton, look up here one more time. Sutton, look here. Here, Sutton. You see what that says up there. That says,

146

"Organizations of the church to do the work that the church was designed to do." Have I argued that it's the work of the church to care for the orphan people in the sense of providing the actual work? I never did anything of the kind. Now, Sutton, I didn't do anything of the kind.

Alright, let's have now, his chart number 5: "GOD'S WAY VERSUS MAN'S." That's the value of these debates, friends. It shows you what these fellows will resort to in an effort to try to sustain their doctrine. Where is our chart? Alright, now, look here. Chart number 5: "GOD'S WAYS VERSUS MAN'S." Here is what he contends that it's the obligation of the church to preach the gospel. Nobody questions that. That it's the obligation of the church in order to edify itself, but his argument is that the church is the only organization that can edify. Now, that's not so, because the family can edify, too. So, the very premise upon which he makes this argument is false. In like fashion, it is not the function of the church to perform the actual relieving. It relieves by providing the means, but the agency that does it is the family, and he knows that, and that's what I said up here. But now, you look again at the hypocrisy involved. We're debating the orphan home question. You'd get the idea from this chart that Sutton believes that the church can take care of orphan children. He doesn't believe a word of that. He doesn't believe you can take a dime out of the church treasury and spend it for a starving orphan. He doesn't believe that. Yet, he gets up here and presents a chart that leaves the impression that the way to take care of orphan children is for the church to do it, and yet he knows that that's not what he believes. Sutton, what do you want to deceive these people for? Now, you either think the church can do this work or you don't. If you do think it does, then you have contradicted your position. If you think that it can't, then you're misrepresenting it here on the chart. Now, which is it, gentlemen? Which is it, Sutton, that you're doing? Which is it? I'll give you half a minute of my time to tell me right now. Now, friends, why did he do that? He knows that he's misrepresenting it before this congregation. He knows that he teaches that the church can't do a thing about relieving orphan children. He knows that he is telling you something that he doesn't believe. Now, why doesn't he get up here and confess that? Now, Sutton, one of two things is true. Either this

147

chart is a falsehood or you're no longer teaching what you did in the debate with Blazer. One or the other.

Let's have his chart number 23. Again, now, this will show you that he's taking the position that the church is the only organization that can perform these activities: preach, edify, or relieve. That isn't so. Not a word of truth about that. The home can preach the gospel. His argument here is the church is the only organization that can do it. That isn't so. If that were true, then it would be wrong for a parent to teach his small boy how to preach a sermon. That would be a sin because that would be done in the family. The family couldn't hold study periods for the purpose of studying the Bible. That would follow from his position. There's not a word of truth in that, because the implication is that the only organization that can preach or edify or relieve is the church, which is not so.

Again, now, in spite of the fact that I've shown you that the chart is not so, Sutton doesn't believe that the chart is so. Sutton knows that this is a flagrant misrepresentation of his position. Sutton knows that he teaches that it's sinful to take a penny out of the church treasury to spend for an orphan child. Now, do you or don't you? Just one way or the other. Just say which you do. Tell these people that I'm telling the truth about this or not, Sutton. Why wait? You say one or the other. Will you tell them whether I'm telling the truth or not?

Now, friends, you see the shape that this poor fellow's in here tonight. It's not because Sutton is not an able boy. He is. He'd do better if he'd quit trying to imitate Curtis Porter, but I tell you he has ability. Oh, he's got not only his phraseology, but he's got his method.

It just occurred to me that he says again and again, "It just so happens." Why, I've seen and heard brother Porter for years make those statements. And brother Porter was a great man; I do not reflect upon him. Brother Porter made the same miserable effort that this man is making in the same defense of the same position. But after all is said for him, if he wants to slap his hands like Roy Cogdill, it will be alright with me. But at any rate, Sutton, tell me this: Can the church spend money for orphan children whose parents are not living? I insist on that.

All right, let's have his chart number 24: "WHICH

INSTITUTION?" Now, look, friends. Here, again, we have the same situation. This man just over and over and over produces these charts that flagrantly misrepresent what he's doing—what his position is. "The church is divine; the Board of Directors is human," he tells us. I pointed out to you that the orphan home is simply the restored family. I shall not go into that, but I just want to show you that he doesn't believe a word on this. Not a word. We are debating the orphan home question tonight. The implication is that the way to do it is for the church to care for them. But how? A place: buy, build, rent, private home. The implication is that the church can buy a place or build a place or rent one or private home.

Incidentally, that private home there would get close to another institution, wouldn't it? I just wonder how far that would be from another institution if you put them in the private home and let it take care of them, Sutton? Now, you don't mean with a private home here, a house, because you already got your building there. So, you can't say the house or the home here is the same as this right here, because this is one thing and that's something else. Now, you got a private home here that the church can use. I want to know if that private home is another institution. I want to know what that is. What is that private home? Is that another institution, Sutton? Look up here, Sutton. Is that another institution? Is a private home on there another institution? At any rate, the implication here is that the church can contribute to orphan children in this way. He doesn't believe a word of it. He doesn't believe a word of that, ladies and gentlemen. He's leading you to believe that he does, but he isn't. Now, Sutton, am I telling the truth or not? Am I telling the truth about this or not, Sutton, when I say that it's your position that the church can't spend a dime of money for an orphan child whose parents are dead, which would follow necessarily? Answer.

Yes, that's right. You have to spell it out for you fellows. I learned that a long time ago. But you didn't answer, did you? Well, you're not through with it by any means.

He said he finally got me into debate. Finally, Sutton finally got me into debate. Now that he's got me in the debate, he's got a hold of me, and he doesn't know how to turn loose, does he? I'd be glad, brother Sutton, if you'd hold on just a little tighter and try to answer some of these arguments that I'm answering.

Let's see chart number 25. Chart number 25: NOTE THE PARALLEL. The church contributes to the missionary society that preaches the gospel. He says this is my position. The church contributes to benevolent corporations to care for the needy. Now, friends, you heard me deny it if there's any such thing as this. But now, then just take a look at that now. The church contributing to this, he says, for that over there. Eliminate this, call it the private home, and what difference would there be so far as his position is concerned? His position is that the church can't utilize any other institution: private home or any other. Now, that eliminates the private home. Let's see that he includes the private home. Get back to that other chart that I had just before I had that one. You see, he's even got the private home on here through which the church can act. Now, if that doesn't get him in the worse shape I've ever heard a fellow in. I don't see how a man could get in any worse shape than he's in, and yet he had the gall to tell you that Woods is confused.

Now, let's have this chart 16. Confused. Confused. You know they say that sometimes when a person loses his mind he thinks he's the only fellow that's sane in the country. Is brother Woods confused? That's a part of the scripture, isn't it? Now, he told you tonight that he'd stay with the Bible. He wouldn't take off after other things. I wonder how much the Gospel Press had to do with this proposition? How much did that have to do with, Sutton?

He says here that brother Woods says this. Now, listen, friends, you can take a man's statement and you can make him say nearly anything. That's right. He held his time there for two or three minutes while we were changing the charts. How much time? What do we say on here? About three minutes? Over a minute. Let me have half of it. We'll split the difference. Is that alright? Alright, brother Sutton?

SUTTON: You can go ahead and take five more if you want to, if you'll go ahead an answer my arguments.

WOODS: I'll be delighted. Point out the one you think I haven't answered, Sutton.

SUTTON: Start on number 1 and go through number 5 on this side first.

WOODS: I'll take up each one of those again and go over them if you'll just answer two questions: Can you build a kitchen in the basement here? That's number one and number two: Is the father part of the family? Will you answer that, sir? Learn to keep your mouth shut.

Now, here, friends, I'm going to answer this because we think these brethren can count over here, too. He says I say we must supply the orphan homes. Well, I think so. The church may do that—may furnish a place. You can take up a statement out of context and misrepresent a man, but I believe that the church can supply the clothes, may furnish them necessities, may put the needy in a home which is another institution, may relieve them of the widows, the Bible says that, arrange an orphan home. Through providing the means, may operate orphanages, that is, in the sense of supplying the means, and actually the church through its members does this. It is a benevolent society in the sense that it performs good services for mankind.

May build and maintain benevolent organizations. I affirmed that for two nights. Now, he, that is Woods, claims that the only work the church can do in relieving the needy is supply the money. I never said anything of the kind. He inserted the word "only" in the statement. It is a flagrant misrepresentation and falsehood. I thank you. I stated last night repeatedly that the church can supply both food and money, and he gets up here and says that I said the only thing they present is the money.

Carrol R. Sutton's Third Affirmative Speech

Gentlemen moderators, brother Woods, ladies and gentlemen:
I'm glad to come before you for the next 20 minutes in defense of the proposition that I've been affirming and have proven by scriptural arguments. I do appreciate the fact that you're here, and that you have a chance to see how a man flounders when he doesn't have scriptural principles.

151

We've taken up scriptural arguments tonight, and we've shown beyond a shadow of doubt that these benevolent organizations that brother Woods tried to affirm for two nights, at least he was supposed to be affirming, are thus not in harmony with the scriptures. Of course, I'm willing for you to be the judge in the matter.

If you study your Bible, you'll see that these principles that I set forth still stand unassailed. We notice that when God specified the church in evangelism, that ruled out other organizations. When God specified the church in relief, that ruled out other organizations. But brother Woods said, "Well, if that's so, then that means that it rules out the family, doesn't it?" Brother Woods, as far as church work is concerned, the church is to do its work. It can't turn its work over to some other organization. Now, from the basis that brother Woods says since the church as he contends (I don't agree with it) may contribute to a family, that justifies his benevolent organizations. Then upon the same basis he's been contending that the family can preach the gospel, which is another organization; therefore, that justifies the missionary society. No doubt, that's why that he says churches can contribute to the Gospel Press. Thank you, brother Woods.

You know, brother Woods went to Clearwater, Florida last night. He went to Newbern, Tennessee tonight. Then he even went to try to raise the dead. He talked about brother Curtis Porter. "Why would thou requite me from the dead?" It may be, though, because Hebrews 11:4 shows, "By it, he being dead yet speaketh."

WOODS: Now, Sutton, wait just a minute now. You are suggesting that I reflected on brother Curtis Porter. I spoke only in terms of how … as respectful. I complimented him, and you are out of order in charging that I reflected upon Curtis Porter. I did nothing of the kind.

SUTTON: I'll let you be the judge, since he said that you know when a fellow thought that somebody else was confused, that he himself was the one that was confused. Didn't have good sense is what it amounted to. Then he turned around and said I imitated brother Porter. You be the judge in the matter now, as to whether or not he was reflecting on him or whether or not he was commending him. He said I even imitated him, and so I followed his procedure and so forth, his method. And he even talked about his defending this doctrine that he says is going to send me to torment. Is that a compliment on brother Porter? You be the judge, brethren and neighbors and friends. You know, it may be that a fellow that's so confused as I am, it does take a fellow 24 or 25 minutes to take care of a 20-minute speech. Maybe that's why it is. Maybe it's because I'm so confused.

Then brother Woods had quite a bit to say about, finally...

WOODS: Wait a minute.

SUTTON: Is this a point of order?

WOODS: Yes. That's a reflection on these brethren over here, and I resent that. Now, they can count just as well as these fellows can, and yet he implies that these brethren are trying to give me time. Last night, this fellow ran over five minutes over there. We said, "Let him go."

SUTTON: Hold my time.

WOODS: Now, Sutton, just go ahead and speak the truth. We won't bother you. Just tell the truth.

TOTTY: Amen.

HOLT: The ones who were here last night know how many times, at least you might not know how many, brother Sutton was stopped. First, it was a matter of asking questions directly. We stopped him on that. He continued to be stopped in the last speech 25 times, every 48 seconds. Brother Sutton is not directly questioning brother Woods now. Yet, he's been stopped two times here. Now, the same things that have happened when brother Woods was speaking didn't bother us. Now, brother Woods can do as he wants to, but we want to keep it on a plane, and we appreciate the audience and your patience. So, we intend to keep it that way as far as we're concerned. That's right.

TOTTY: Brother Holt, the reason brother Woods stopped, brother Sutton reflected on the integrity of these time keepers. They've got as much sense to count minutes as you have or anybody else over there, and we won't take that. So, you can just sit down and be quiet.

HOLT: Last night the same thing was done concerning the person who kept time here. We didn't stop. We went ahead, and we gave him time. I looked at the watch back here when brother Woods

153

started, and I didn't say a thing about what time it was supposed to have started. It was exactly nine o'clock. He went to 25 after nine, but that's alright. Last night we didn't say a thing when we gave him time.

TOTTY: You couldn't do anything about it but give it to us, and if you want to give him ten minutes that's alright. We're not arguing about how much he has. We're arguing on your personal reflection on the honesty of these timekeepers. Now, that was the thing. It's not how much time he gets.

HOLT: It was done the same way last night.

TOTTY: Doesn't make any difference if it was done 40 times last night. We don't take your personal reflections like that. Now, you just as will get like you are at Corbin and be yourself. We're not going to take that, so go ahead.

HOLT: For the good of the audience, we'll go ahead and let the discussion go ahead.

WOODS: My statement is simply this: we have no desire to interrupt him at any time, if he'll state the truth. When he misrepresents us, we'll be on our feet. Now, you can just expect it. Go right ahead, brother Sutton. Give him five minutes extra to compensate for this time.

SUTTON: Are you through?

WOODS: Through.

SUTTON: Thank you, very much.

WOODS: Time him.

SUTTON: You know, brother Woods had quite a bit to say about brother Sutton saying, "He finally got me into a debate." If you'll just remember, brother Woods is the very man that said that about me, and the tape will show it. He said the night before last, or last night one, that we finally got Sutton into a debate. Yet, he comes right along here and talks about I said, "I finally got him into one." Now, maybe, somebody is confused.

Then he had quite a bit to say about tormenting me, and he enjoyed tormenting this fellow. Well, brother Woods, it just so happens I enjoy it, too.

WOODS: Good.

SUTTON: If you call it torment, what about us just staying

154

four more nights for this thing, brother Woods? Will you do it? Yes or no? Yes or no?

WOODS: Brother Sutton.

SUTTON: Yes or no?

WOODS: I just think...

SUTTON: Yes or no?

WOODS: Just hold on a minute.

SUTTON: Yes or no?

WOODS: You think you have to answer every question, yes or no.

SUTTON: Yes or no?

WOODS: Will you quit getting drunk?

SUTTON: Will you do it? Yes or no? He answers all questions, doesn't he, brethren? I'm willing for him to torment me four more nights after this one's over here, and if he don't do it, it's because he leaves without an invitation to stay. Then, I'm willing to let him torment me four more nights down at Jasper, Alabama, if he can get his brethren to back him. Also for four more nights down at Huntsville, Alabama whether he gets backing or not. Then four more nights over at Truman, Arkansas, and for four more nights over in Owensboro, Kentucky, if he gets backing. Then four more nights over at Garfield Heights, Indianapolis. What about it, brother Woods?

TOTTY: Just a minute. If he gets backing in Indianapolis. You just said if he can get backing. Now, can you get backing? What's sauce for the goose is sauce for the gander.

SUTTON: What about it, brother Woods?

TOTTY: Wait a minute. Point of order. Can you get backing in Indianapolis? If you can, I'll guarantee brother Woods will be there. Can you? I'll guarantee he'll be there.

SUTTON [to ALVIN HOLT): I'll take care of it.

TOTTY: Now, what do you say? Right in the Garfield Heights church. We'll let you lead the singing the first night, if you want to. Now, go ahead.

SUTTON: Alright, brother Woods, what about it? Yes or no? You'll stay four more nights?

WOODS: I can't stay four more nights. I've got a meeting

beginning in Memphis, Tennessee on Sunday.

SUTTON: What about staying through Saturday night, then?

WOODS: I've got to catch a train to get back down there.

SUTTON: Catch a plane on Sunday?

WOODS: Let me suggest this, friends. When a fellow is flat on his back he usually wants another chance, doesn't he?

SUTTON: Well, he enjoys tormenting me, doesn't he? He really enjoys tormenting me a lot, doesn't he? He just doesn't want another chance at it, though, does he? You be the judge, brethren. Yet, he answers all questions.

Then, of course, brother Woods said something about Acts 6, and he says, "Now, does brother Sutton mean to imply that there was only one home? There was probably hundreds. Probably hundreds," he says. Now, brother Woods, where are the homes in Acts 6 that were helped? Acts 6 shows how that there were destitute widows. Is a widow a home? Brother Woods admitted the very first evening of the debate that these contributions, he said, were made to individual members of the family rather than the family itself, and the tape will show it. I've got the quotation from the tape.

Then he had quite a bit to say on chart number 4 about Boles Home, but he didn't build with what I offered on it. I made the point here the church gives into a benevolent organization that in turn oversees two homes which includes places and families. That organization is not a place. It's not a family, and he says it's separate from the church, so it's not the church. With respect to this Tennessee Orphan Home, chart number 3, he said, "Well, now, this part down here about the missionary society, well," he says, "now, this isn't like the thing that we generally refer to as the missionary society." Well, brother Woods, I asked you if this would be one, and if it isn't, would you endorse this arrangement? Did he answer? No, he evaded it. I don't blame him; I would, too, if I was in his position.

Then on chart number 2, he said, "Now, this orphan home is neither an aid or addition, but a separate institution or organization." But you note in the **Woods-Porter Debate** on pages 35 and 36, he said, "The orphanages, the homes for the aged, the Sunday schools ... are the means by which the church uses to accomplish its work." He put

156

the orphanages, homes for the aged in the same category with the Sunday schools, and he meant by that Bible classes. Are Bible classes separate organizations, brother Woods, under a Board of Directors with a president and vice-president? We'll see if he answers that one. He answers all questions, you know.

We notice also that he said concerning Psalms 68 and verses 5 and 6, that God said, "solitary in families." I've shown for two nights, brethren, that that doesn't mention a benevolent organization. That this benevolent organization, such as Tennessee Orphan Home, is not a family. Why does he want to put them under the direction of that thing when God puts them in families? That's my position, not his. Thank you, brother Woods.

He also had quite a lot to say about the church would furnish the money, supply the means, and then, but it says it doesn't do the actual care or relief. That's what he opposed in my chart entitled "GOD'S WAY VERSUS THE WAYS OF MEN." He said I didn't correctly represent the situation because he says the church doesn't actually relieve or actually do the caring for. That's what I've said all the time: that he didn't believe the church could do it.

Brethren, on page 14 of this book that he put out called, **Defense of Orphan Homes**, it says, "When the church, in its organized capacity, does all that it's authorized to do, that is, supplies the money for the needy." "That's *all* it's authorized to do," he says. And what about this little child that gets run over out here. There's a wreck, you know, and gets run over, and he's bloody. Could you come into the church building and get some water and wash his face off, the blood off him? He says, "Sutton doesn't believe that you can." According to him, he doesn't believe it, because all the church can do is send money for the child. He's the man that doesn't believe that! He'd let him lay there. You couldn't take anything but money out of the treasury, and that wouldn't wash the blood off his face, brother Woods. And he talks about me. No, I wouldn't have to send the benevolent organization to get his face washed, either, not if I had to wait to get money out of the treasury to do it. Would you, brethren? Now, he might leave him out there and wait for some benevolent organization to come along and get him. I don't know.

157

Incidentally, if the church did that, the church would actually, according to him, be engaging in child care, and that's the work of the family. That would make a home out of the church, according to him. That's what he's been accusing me of. Thank you, brother Woods.

Incidentally, in the **Gospel Advocate** he says the early church operated the home for destitute widows. He said, "The church operated a home for destitute widows." But now, he says all the church is authorized to do is supply the means or the funds. He also said in 1946 that the seven deacons had the supervision of feeding the widows. That's more than supplying for, that's supervision of something. "Dispensing food," he said.

He talked about Blazer giving me a thrashing down in Alabama. Yeah, he went to Alabama, too, didn't he? For some reason, brother Woods, he wasn't too anxious to give me another thrashing either. Just like you're not too anxious to. You be the judge as to why he's not, brethren.

He said that brother Sutton introduced the subject of the trustees. That isn't so, brother Woods. That isn't so, brethren. With respect to the subject of trustees of church buildings, brother Woods is the man that introduced that subject, and the tapes will show that, too, when they're played. Yet, he accuses me of it and says I misrepresented him. Then he said that brother Sutton said they had trustees here and they straightened it out. I said no such of a thing, and I demand the proof of it. That's another false misrepresentation. It isn't so. I didn't do no such of a thing. Those here last night know that I mentioned the incorporation. I didn't mention the trustees of this church building or of this congregation. I said the incorporation was dissolved. I didn't say anything about whether we had trustees or didn't have trustees, but what I introduced was a copy of two deeds. One from the Washington congregation over here in Illinois and the other from Alabama, and he didn't even mention either one of them, because he saw them and that shows that what he said isn't so. Then what I didn't introduce, he said I did. You be the judge.

Why didn't he deal with what I offered him? He said last night a church could not own property without trustees. Yet, he saw a copy of two deeds where they could. That shows he's wrong even about the law. Just as wrong as he is about the word of God. That doesn't surprise me, though. Does it you?

Then he asked me a question, and he had quite a bit to say about "Is the father a part of the family?" He said, "Would you answer it?" I said I would when I came up here, and that's what I intend to do. If he means an ordinary family, then a father would be a part of that family. There are some cases where there are fathers, men who have begat children, and yet all of their family is dead. So, they are no part of a family then. But I am a part of my family, and I'm a father. But brother Woods is contending for a benevolent organization that he claims is the father, that stands in place of the father, so they are the fathers. Yet those fathers will turn their funds over to some other men for them to expend for their children. I don't do that, brother Woods. No, I don't do that. Thank you, again.

You know, he said now, and when the father provides a family, he said, is he a part of that family. He said, "Now, or for homes provided, is that a, is he a part of the home?" He said, "I stayed with brother Keplinger and so forth last night." Well, I just wonder, since brother Keplinger provided brother Woods a home, is brother Woods a part of brother Keplinger's family? According to him, he is. "Now," he said, "if you, if something provided something, that was a part of it." So, therefore, he's become a part of brother Keplinger's family.

I maintain these organizations provide the home. They're separate from that which they provide. Just as much so as brother Woods is separate from the family that brother Keplinger has, although, brother Keplinger has provided him a home this week. Thank you, brother Woods.

Incidentally, brother Brock, down at Childhaven, says he's the daddy, and brother Woods says that the Board of Directors are the daddies. Who are the daddies? They don't know whose daddies are whose. Incidentally, he's going to have somebody over several families in a little bit if he's not careful; going to have too many daddies. Better watch it, brother Woods. On the same basis, I wonder if in these homes for the aged when there are widows, does the Board of Directors stand in place of their husbands, brother Woods? If not, why not? Had they been in the place of the husband? Oh, well. We'll just drop it there.

Brother Woods says Sutton is on record as saying it is sinful to have trustees. Not so. I haven't said any such of a thing. I simply showed that you were wrong when you said the church could not own property without trustees. I proved it, and you should have to apologize for being wrong.

Yes, I believe he said something about the kitchen, didn't he? You know it just so happens that last evening I answered brother Woods' question about the kitchen. Yet, he's come over, over and over and over, and says, "Why doesn't he answer? Why doesn't he answer?" I even wrote it out for him, friends, on the questions that he had in his possession last night and tonight. Yet, he gets over here and chides me: "What about the kitchen? What about the kitchen?" Well, now, if he can't understand plain simple English, I don't believe he'd understand if I read it to him, but I'm going to read it anyway. But he's liable to come back and say, "Well, he didn't say a word about the kitchen." Well, just let him do it if he wants to. If that's his tactics, he's welcome to them.

Now, with regard to the question that he asked me about a soup kitchen in the basement for destitute saints, here's what I said. Quote (and he's got it in his possession, too): "If such were to happen, the congregation would decide on the method of administering the relief that was essential." He read that much, made fun of it, and stopped. But here's what the rest of the question said that's in his possession. "If the church deemed it expedient to use the basement for such, it would have that right." The scriptures which authorize such are Acts 6:1-6, and I gave three or four others. He didn't read that last evening or tonight, either. It has been in his possession both times. He read part of it, left the rest of it off where I answered his question, and he's chided me over and over for not doing what I did do. Is that fairness, honesty, integrity? What about it? You be the judge.

I'd like to mention also a thing or two, now, with respect to the chart over here about Alabama recognizing Childhaven as a benevolent society. He said, this is really rich, isn't it? He said, "Now, if brother Sutton's not a pig or a cow, he'd be a monkey." Brother Woods, this chart said, notice what it says, friends: "That it provides for incorporation of churches, educational or benevolent societies."

160

There's only three choices here. So, this thing must either be a church, educational or benevolent society. Now, if there are only three choices that I could be, a cow or pig or monkey, I'd have to be one of the three. But there are more choices involved there but there's not here. He said, "Yes," he understood that. He knew it all of the time, brethren. He knew that.

WOODS: I said there were more than three choices here.

SUTTON: There isn't, friend. You can see it for yourself. The Code of Alabama provides only in this particular title, chapter, article, and section, and I challenge him to show otherwise. "For the incorporation of churches, educational or benevolent societies." I demand the proof of it, brother Woods. There is only three things involved here, and he knows that it's so. He won't show otherwise. He may assert it, but he won't prove it. Thank you, brother Woods.

Then he had something to say about this chart over here. He said, "These fellows misrepresent me" and says, "They know that they do it while they're doing it." It just so happens that I've got exactly word for word what brother Woods said. I didn't leave out one sentence from the time I began until I ended. Is that a misrepresentation, friends? If it is, he misrepresented himself. What about that? That's exactly what he said. If he's ashamed of it, he ought to apologize for having spoken it back in 1939. Now, notice what he said. That sounds kind of like me preaching sometimes, doesn't it, about "the ship of Zion has floundered more than once on the sandbar of institutionalism"? That wasn't me, though, that was brother Woods.

We notice also that he says on the theory that the end justifies the means: "Brethren have not scrupled to form organizations in the church to do the work the church itself was designed to do. All such organizations usurp the work of the church, are unnecessary and sinful." Then he says, "This writer has ever been unable to appreciate the logic of those who do see grave danger in missionary societies, but also we're not to form similar organizations for the purposes of caring for orphans." Was he just opposing missionary societies? He said organizations that were similar to missionary societies to care for orphans is what he was opposing back then. Thank you, brother Woods. I wish you would still oppose them as you did back in 1939.

Of course, we notice how that he went on to show that he recommended Tipton Orphan Home at the time because he said it was entirely scriptural "being managed and conducted by the elders of the church in Tipton, Oklahoma; aided by funds sent to them by elders of other congregations round about. We, here and now, deny or protest against any other method or arrangement to accomplishing this work." But, now, he says you can't put these homes under elders, as elders, but back then he said anything else besides that was sinful. Who is confused, brother Woods?

Incidentally, these questions I asked brother Woods, tonight, he didn't answer. Now, he wrote something out, but he didn't answer my questions. I asked him one question concerning whether or not churches may scripturally contribute funds out of the treasury of the church to assist and care for the needy. He talked a while, but never did say whether they could or not. Yet he gets direct to the point. I said, "Since you contended Tuesday evening that the church could send money to Tennessee Orphan Home and let it buy a pig for a child, please give the scripture that authorizes such." He's got about 15 or 20 scriptures here, and the first one was James 1:27. Now, if he can get a pig out of James 1:27 for an orphan child, I guess he can get his benevolent organization in the same verse. He's got a pig out of that verse. Is a pig necessary for the relief of that destitute orphan? To buy him a pig? What would he do with it if he had it, brother Woods? Could he kill his own pig? He might get by just about as well with that dirt he was talking about last night as the pig. That little infant; he couldn't kill him, could he?

But keep this in mind, brethren, that we're discussing whether or not it's scriptural for churches of Christ to build and maintain benevolent organizations for the care of the needy. I maintain that it's not. Thank you.

Guy N. Woods' Third Negative Speech

Brethren moderators, brother Sutton, ladies and gentlemen:

I am before you now, for the final 20-minute speech of the evening. I sincerely hope that it will pass rapidly and pleasantly for you.

May I call attention to the last thing that brother Sutton said. He said … May I have those questions, please?

SUTTON: Will you give them back to me?

WOODS: I'll give them back to you. I want you to answer them. Read the answers.

Well now, while he's finding them, on this matter of the pig. He asked me a question: "Since you contended Tuesday evening that the church could send money to Tennessee Orphan Home and let it buy a child a pig, please give the scripture that authorizes such." I put down a number of scriptures here that authorizes the church to assist in benevolence. Now, he came back and tried to make fun of it. He said that whoever heard of a child receiving a pig, and, besides, could the child kill the pig? Well now, you could eat a pig if you got real hungry. You'd have to cook it, I'd say. Maybe we could borrow the basement here to do the cooking of the pig. Let me suggest this. I've got a plan by which to, at least, get a pig to a child. I think that you could, at least, give it a pig. He doesn't think that you could give. You could supply feed for the pigs if the preacher owned the pigs, but you can't if the orphan had them. You can't supply it according to Sutton. He said, "Who kills the pig?" Now, his idea on these charts is, of course, he doesn't believe a word of it, is that the church is the one that supplies all that the child needs. Well, if the child needed the pig, the church could supply it. I guess he could have the preacher to kill the pig. Would have the rabbi system of kosher meat, wouldn't it? Sutton, are you the pig killer of this congregation? They don't even do as much as the Jews along that line.

Now, he didn't want to read the answers to these questions. I answered them. I want to read his questions and my answers: Since you contended here tonight in this debate that an orphan home is simply a means by way of which the church accomplishes its work, please tell me who has control over the means that is the orphan home? The answer: An orphan home is the means by which the church relieves, 1 Timothy 5:16, just like the private home is a means to the same end. But, in either case, does the church take over the home and operate it? Parents or their equivalent to operate homes. The church and the home are separate institutions.

Now, his second question: What scriptural principle is violated if churches send contributions to an organization, benevolent society, which in turn establishes orphanages? My answer: If by the word "orphanages," you mean legal families, and by benevolent societies, an organization that is no part of the family which provides the child care, such an arrangement is unnecessary and does not today exist among us. Being neither a church nor a home such would add to the word of God. Deuteronomy 4:2 and Proverbs 30:6.

Third question: Please name one essential thing in relieving destitute saints that the benevolent organization, such as the Tennessee Orphan Home, can provide that the church can't provide? Well, among the things that I mention here are, I mention first the kitchen. He's finally admitted that the church can provide a kitchen. We'll have some more to say about that a little later. Number two: tables. I say it figuratively for the purpose of serving food. Hospitalization, nursing care, physical therapy, and, in the case of children, recreation, manual training, and discipline. These are some of the things that a child needs that the church can't engage in.

I ask him the question: Can the church provide, that is participate in such? Is anything wrong, fellows? Beg pardon. They've been bothering me over here just a little bit. I want them to hear what I'm saying, and if there's anything wrong, out with it. Let us all know about it.

Number four: May churches scripturally contribute funds out of their treasuries to the State to assist it in caring for the needy? Here's my answer: The State, though existing by divine right, was not set up as an agency through which child care is to be done as the family was. Hitler thought it was and so do you. Both of you are wrong. Hitler now, knows it and so will you, one of these days, if you don't repent and cease teaching such grave error. It's not surprising then, is it?

164

Number five: I already dealt with that. That's the matter of the pig. Who kills the pig here? Who's the official pig killer and what are his qualifications set out in the Bible?

Well, alright now, let's take up his speech. "In 1946 he says." Well, you didn't do a thing but put it on the board. That's right, and I endorsed every statement up there. But let me tell you this. He told you that I taught things now that I didn't teach back then. He knew that was a falsehood when he said it, because I pointed that out to him. Now, you watch here, friends. When I penned this statement, I wrote this out as a speech which I delivered to Abilene Christian College. Back in those days nobody ever thought about opposing an orphan home in the South. So far as those who stood with us, nobody on that day thought about it, because we all believed in and supported the orphan homes. This thing started about 14 or 15 years ago, and I can tell you, maybe tomorrow night, how it started and why it started.

At any rate, all of us were against missionary societies in that day, and in our efforts to oppose missionary societies we penned statements which these fellows will take out of their context and apply to the orphan home. I made no such application here. I was talking about work which the church does.

He says, "Down here now, you say you recommend the way that it's done out at Tipton." Well, I believe it's eminently scriptural. My purpose in that was to show how the money was received. I said, "It's sent to the elders of the church out there." Those men receive the money. These men are not elders over that home. They say they're trustees over the home. I believe they are. I think they're telling the truth. I have no objection to men who are elders being legal parents. Of course, the elders of a congregation may operate a home, but they are not operating it as elders any more than they are operating their own home as elders. A man may be the president of a bank, the head of his family, a member of a legal family, and an elder of the church, but he's not any one of those because he's the others, necessarily. This is it. There's the difference, and these fellows will continue, of course, to misrepresent me.

Now, he said he'd answered the question about the kitchen. Read these over tonight before you go to bed. He said he'd answered that. Now, he hadn't answered it forthrightly. He hadn't answered the question in a way that made it clear. He said that "if they deemed it expedient" they might do this. I asked him if he believed that it was scriptural to have a kitchen in the basement.

Now, you listen, ladies and gentlemen, these fellows have gone all over this country. I'm glad we finally have smoked him out on it. These fellows have gone all over this country condemning the congregations that have fellowship meetings in the basement because they've got a kitchen down there, in some instances. They've gone all over the country telling us that it was sinful to have a kitchen in the church building. You know that? Sutton has preached it all over this country. There isn't a person here tonight that doesn't know that I'm telling the truth about that, and yet, now, he tells us that that's right. That it's right to have a kitchen in the basement. He says he's answered it, and he answered it in the affirmative.

Well now, if it's right to have the kitchen down there, why was it that you fellows forbade a bunch of little girls, or little children, in a vacation Bible school here to even eat a cookie down in the basement? What did you do that for? Now, don't look surprised. What did you do that for? Wrong for little children to eat cookies in the basement. Why, maybe this kitchen is just for the saints, the adult saints. Sutton, you still haven't answered the argument. You haven't answered the question. I maintain that he hasn't answered my question about the kitchen in the basement because, you get it now, he took a question that I asked about needy saints and he answered it about needy saints. I asked it about taking care of orphan children. That's what we're discussing here tonight. Can the church operate a kitchen in the basement for the purpose of caring for orphan children? That was my question. He hasn't answered it yet, ladies and gentlemen. He dodged that question and took one that I asked him about needy saints and said they might put one down there for them. Now, he still hasn't answered it. Sutton, can the church operate a kitchen in the basement for orphans?

Why, if he's so glad to answer these questions, why doesn't he? Get up a minute and answer that. Just get up and answer it, Sutton. Help him up. Answer those, Sutton; please do. Please answer those.

166

How about it? Brother Holt, tell him to answer it. Say you already answered it? You answered it, let's say about saints. Now, can it help orphans? He makes a distinction between orphans and saints. Can you put a kitchen in the basement for orphans? Any of you folks know how to get him aroused? I wish we could get an answer from him on that.

He said I misrepresented him when I said that the trustees were wrong. Well, now, in straightening out the thing (he said they went down and straightened matters out), they eliminated the trustees in this quitclaim deed, a copy of which I have over here. So, they've eliminated that arrangement. But let me tell you this: You can't sell this property without having trustees. You can't even receive it and hold it legally, that is, in the sense of having a document that's valid. I could make you a deed to this property. It would be as good as this thing right here. The truth of the business is that you cannot convey property held by the church or owned by the church except by means of or through trustees. Who's gonna sign the deed? The church? What part of the church signs the deed when you convey it? Now, these fellows ought to know that.

Well now, he says the trustees are not wrong. Alright, that gets us right back where we started then. We've got an in-between organization between the preacher and his family. What have we got? We've got the church giving to what he calls an organization made up of trustees. Money and these trustees then furnish a home for the preacher. Now, he objects to that when we put orphans here, but he's not adverse to it when the preacher's on the receiving end of it. That's his position exactly.

He wants to know who the daddies are in the orphan homes. I've had two or three meetings in Cullman, Alabama. I stayed in Childhaven during one of those meetings in the guest room there. Then the other meeting I stayed in the home of brother Brock and it amazed me at the manifestation of love that those children exhibited toward him. Many of them called him Daddy. That's right. They did that, of course, in the sense that he was their foster parent. He wants to know who the daddies are and how many they got. Well, I'm inclined to think that it's a whole lot better, and I'm using the word figuratively, to have more than one daddy than to have none at all. I'm kind of inclined to feel that the more daddies the better under those circumstances, for a child. Sutton, how many of those children is this, are the elders of this congregation the daddies of? You say that's the way to do it. The church can do it. You put it on these charts that the church is the organization to do it, though you don't believe a word of it. How many daddies do you have in this congregation among your elders and your leaders? Do you have elders at all, and besides that, Sutton, you said that before men could serve as foster parents they'd have to exhaust their own means. You said these men were rich men, some of them. I don't know any of them are especially rich, but I don't believe that these foster parents have to exhaust their means before they can receive help. If that be true, then the elders of the church could have supervision of what you call the same thing, would have to spend all the money they've got before they could let the congregation help them. If not, why not? Why wouldn't it apply just the same? It would, of course. We don't believe that. He doesn't believe it. He misrepresents it when he says that the church can do that. He doesn't believe a word of it.

Now, he says with reference to this providing the family, "I'll answer that," said, "yes, the father is part of the family." Alright, then he contradicts his position. He says, "Well, you're staying in the Keplinger home; therefore, you are a part of it." That was his argument. I am a part of the Keplinger family while I'm there, that's very true. That's very true. They share with me the things of their family. Alright, help him out there. While you're doing it, tell him to tell us a little more about this matter of the basement. You should do that, sir. But now, get this. (No, brother Keplinger is not my daddy.) But if I didn't have anybody to provide for me more in Peoria than Sutton and his outfit has provision for the church to provide for the orphan children, I'd be mighty hungry while I'm here, I'll tell you.

Here is the thing about it. Sutton is the fellow that made that argument. Sutton had on the chart here that this over here provides this; therefore, that's not this. I just took his argument and made an application of it. Now, Sutton, have at it. Do all you want to do with it. You still haven't met the issue.

He said I have made the statement in my tract that the only

thing the church could supply is the money. I said that was a flagrant misrepresentation. He read from me when I said the church has done all that it could do, the actual child care remained to be done. When I mentioned the money, I used that as the means that the church supplies. Whether it was money or food would be immaterial. My point was this: That you might move a bunch of children in the basement of this church building. You might move in beds and clothes and provide for them. That wouldn't be a church operating down there. That would be a home operating in the basement. It would still be a home, and that's our contention exactly regarding this. But he says, "Looks like now, that you don't have any provision for the bloody child because all the thing you could supply them was money and all." That's a misrepresentation. I say that the church could make provision for him even though he's not a member of the church.

I despise and detest a doctrine that would say that the church of the Lord must bar the door to people, and that it cannot minister to the needy round about it, if it has the means to do so. Do you mean to tell me that there are people here that believe that if there were a sinner who had an automobile accident out here in the street and was suffering great need, and there were means here in this building provided by the church, that the church of our Lord couldn't come to his aid? Do you mean to tell me there are people who claim to believe that? Why I'd repudiate such a doctrine, and I'd walk out of here and never darken the door as long as the preacher talked that way. Thank you.

That's exactly what Sutton believes. He said Psalms 68:5-6 says that the Lord puts them in families. That's exactly what I say and what I believe and what Sutton denies, unless he thinks the family and the church are the same thing. Now, Sutton, is the family the church?

He said the widows in Acts 6, that these were just widows. That that's all that received any assistance and that the widows were not homes. Now, that shows how little the fellow knows about the text itself. I want you to see, friends, what actually happened over there. Let's take the statement first here found in the fourth chapter. Well, let's begin with the second chapter here and verse 44. "And all that believed." Now, that means more than the widows, doesn't it? "All that believed were together and had all things common, and sold their possessions and goods and parted them to all men." The word "men" there is in italics, and so as a matter of fact that just means that all of them did this "as every man had need and they continued daily with one accord," and so on.

Now, turn over to the fourth chapter. Look at the fourth chapter here, verse 32. "And the multitude of them that believed were of one heart and one soul. Neither said any of them that all of the things which he possessed were his own, but they had all things common." Every member of the church participated in that common fund, and when this man tries to leave the impression here that the widows were the only ones that participated in that fund, that shows either he doesn't know what the text says or else he's trying to deceive you.

He wants to meet me again in debates. Now, I'm not adverse to debating, as my brethren well know. I have one just one month from now, in Reform, Alabama with a Baptist preacher. At least the Baptist preachers will try to answer your questions. I'm always glad to debate, but I tell you frankly if I didn't have more to do than I've had in this one, I don't think I'd even stay in practice. Sutton is undoubtedly one of the poorest speakers that I've yet run into. I think every one of them gets a little worse, but he takes the cake. He's something entirely less than sensational. Any of these brethren over here could tie their hands behind their back and meet him. Sutton, I wouldn't say any more about that or I'll tell you what I think of your abilities as a debater one of these nights.

He wants another debate. I never saw a fellow who got a licking and didn't want another chance. I'm perfectly satisfied with this one. I'm entirely satisfied with it. Yes, sir. It will take him six months to recover from this one.

Now, he said that the church, how much time I got? [TOTTY: Two minutes.]

Alright. The church, God specified the church as the only organization. What's the matter, Sutton? Time is up? Now, you fellows took about three minutes over. Friends, I have no disposition to want to take any more time than that which belongs to me. We don't need to. We've already clearly routed this fellow out here. He won't answer our questions. He can't answer our demands. Let me just take the final moment to ask this: Now, Sutton, will you tell us, can you put the kitchen in the basement for the orphans? We've got to take the half minute that's remaining of my time and answer it, will you? Will you get up? Thank you, friends.

TOTTY: Brother Sutton mentions Garfield Heights in Indianapolis. Brother Woods has an invitation, which he's carried or had in his possession for a number of years, inviting him to Indianapolis to meet any preacher of that persuasion who can get endorsement in Indianapolis from one of their churches. That includes brother Holt, brother Sutton, or any of the rest of them who want to come. But brother Woods has a meeting, as he said, Sunday so he couldn't be there next week, but we'll fix the time for him.

Now, if any of you preachers, or you know any who'll come, he's welcome to Garfield Heights, providing he can get a church in Indianapolis that believes what Sutton just endorsed. The reason I'm saying that is he put that stipulation in when he said if brother Woods can get backing. That's what he meant, endorsement. So now, if you can get backing you come on over there. Will you do it?

WOODS: You might tell him, brother Totty, some of the churches up there that are on his side of it.

TOTTY: Yeah, there's Belmont, Lafayette Heights. Get your endorsement from either one of them or we'll take the whole county in. We won't put it only in Indianapolis, we'll take Marion County. Now, if any one of them or they know one can get endorsement from any one of those churches—and if he hadn't added backing, we wouldn't even have asked him to do that. I just say that to let you know that he's only whistling by the graveyard, and we'll meet him any time. Brother Woods has had the invitation and has had it and will keep it.

HOLT: We don't want to keep you much longer. You've been wonderful in your attention again tonight. We have with us brother Cecil Sawyer also from Indianapolis. There seems to be just several people from Indianapolis. We're going to ask him, after a few statements and announcements, to come to the microphone and dismiss us.

I thought this would be in order, since it's been referred to all three nights, concerning the congregation here and the devotional service. I believe this explanation, the people in the congregation here realize this, but those who are visiting, they appreciate your being here, some of you don't know the reason for the decision. Of course, it's a matter of judgment, and you can judge whether they made the right decision. But I think that this ought to be passed on since it was referred to again tonight.

They've had other discussions here, and it's been their policy to where they furnish the building, the facilities, and the people to park the cars and so forth, to lead the singing and the prayer. So, you visitors, it's a matter of judgment as to whether their policy in the past has been the right policy or not, but I think that, knowing the congregation here, they had no intention of being unfair, but only standing by that which was their conviction. Since that's been referred to all three nights, I thought that was only fair to the congregation here.

Another thing that I'd like to announce is that in the morning at 10 o'clock beginning, we'll look forward to another good service. Brother Tom O'Neal, who led the singing, will bring a 30-minute lesson and brother A. C. Belue, who is here from Gary, will also bring a lesson. You're invited to be present for that service in the morning. Two wonderful lessons this morning. Then tomorrow evening be back for the discussion. I believe all can see the good that's being done and the reason that discussions like this should be conducted, and we hope others will be.

TOTTY: He sugar-coated that statement about the parking lot and the house. That is not the custom. It may be the custom of you brethren here to be that discourteous to visitors, but it isn't to churches all over the country. I never saw it nor heard of it before. Now, I'd be willing to pay for parking my car out there if you're running a parking lot for that purpose. I don't want to impose on anybody, but that wasn't what they told us. Brother Sutton said we agreed that you fellows can't take any part in that. Now, that's the point: That we couldn't do it, and the point was they're so bitter against us they want to quarantine us and yet cry that somebody's quarantining them. Brother Holt, don't try to sugar-coat the thing. Make a confession if you want to, and if you don't, just let it go because we know what you told us that they wouldn't let us take any part in leading the singing in this house and they referred to "our house." "This is our house." "This is our parking lot." Like a little boy playing ball that owns the bat. "If you don't do what I say, I'll take my bat and go home." Now, that's the way they put it out. Now, I'll stay here all night. You, the people, go home if you want to, but you are not going to put that over, Holt.

HOLT: As I said a while ago, I gave the reason for the congregation here as in the past, as had been their policy, and as I suggested you can. It's a matter of judgment. You can judge as to whether you think that was alright, as the way you saw it or not. That's what I said about it, and that's the truth about it, and it still stands.

If brother Sawyer will, we just want to thank the Lord for the word and for His people who are willing to come together as neighbors and listen and show the wonderful Christian attitude that this congregation has these three nights. Certainly, it shows the good that can be done when the word of the Lord is talked and discussed in services like this. Brother Sawyer.

Fourth Session
June 1, 1962
7:30 p.m.

Alvin Holt's Preliminary Remarks

For the congregation here at Paris Avenue, again tonight, I'd like to express appreciation for your coming, also for the splendid attention that's been given, and for the good conduct of the audience throughout these past three nights. Of course, we anticipate nothing but that tonight and, as brother Robertson has led us in the prayer, we want to consider that we're in the presence of the Lord and will meet Him to give an answer as to the way that we use the time He gives us, which is to be used in the discussion of this proposition. "It is not in harmony with the scriptures for churches of Christ to build and maintain benevolent organizations such as the Tennessee Orphan Home, Boles Home, Home for the Aged, and other such organizations for the care of the needy." Brother Carrol R. Sutton is affirming and brother Guy N. Woods denying.

There are four rules stated and signed by these speakers to govern in this discussion. The discussion shall be conducted at a time and place acceptable to all parties participating. It shall continue for four evenings. The speakers shall divide time equally and each shall make three 20-minute speeches each evening. Each speaker shall be permitted to submit five written questions to his opponent and the answers shall be in writing. The questions shall be submitted early enough for the answers to be written before the session begins each evening. Each speaker may submit five questions each evening of the debate. The speakers agree to conduct themselves as Christians.

Brother Sutton will now speak 20 minutes, followed by brother Woods.

174

Carrol R. Sutton's Fourth Affirmative Speech

Gentlemen moderators, brother Woods, ladies and gentlemen:

I'm glad to appear before you this afternoon for the purpose of discussing the proposition that you've heard read in your hearing. We certainly are grateful for this occasion. The very fact that you're here is indicative of your interest in these matters and, certainly, it's always good for those who differ to meet in such capacities as this that they might thus discuss their differences. All of us ought to recognize that truth is important. Our Lord said in John 8:32, "And ye shall know the truth and the truth shall make you free." In John 17, in verse 17, our Lord also said, "Thy word is truth." We notice in John 12:48, Jesus said, "He that rejecteth me and receiveth not my words hath one that judgeth him. The words which I have spoken, the same shall judge him in the last day." In view of the fact that we'll be judged by the words of Christ, we ought to recognize the very serious and fearful responsibility that is upon us tonight. Upon those of us who are speakers, that we might speak the truth. Upon you as a hearer, that you might discern between truth and error.

In 2 Peter 1:3, the apostle Peter says, "According as His divine power hath given to us all things that pertain to life and godliness." We're concerned about those things that pertain to life and godliness. If these things that we're discussing, these benevolent organizations, pertain thereto, of course we'll find them in the word of God. If we do not find them in the word of God, then they do not thus pertain to life and to godliness.

In 2 Timothy 3, verses 16 and 17, the apostle Paul says, "All scripture is given by inspiration of God, and is profitable for doctrine, for reproof, for correction, for instruction in righteousness: That the man of God may be perfect, thoroughly furnished unto all good works." Now, if these things that we're discussing are good works, then we'll find them in the pages of God's book.

In 1 Peter 4:11, the apostle Peter says, "If any man speak, let him speak as the oracles of God." We notice also that in 2 John 9 that John says, "Whosoever transgresseth, and abideth not in the doctrine of

Christ, hath not God. He that abideth in the doctrine of Christ, he hath both the Father and the Son." In view of that, we ought to abide in the doctrine of Christ, within the pages of God's inspired book, realizing that we'll be judged by the contents thereof.

In Ephesians 5, in verse 10, Paul says, "Proving what is acceptable unto the Lord." You and I ought not to have a disposition of heart that unless the Bible says, "Do not do this," that it's right in the sight of God. We ought to prove what God accepts. We ought to test and try things that people would originate or things that people would advocate and see if they're found on the pages of God's book.

If I know my heart tonight, I'm here again tonight in interest of truth and truth only. Now, I'm not here to please man, but God, Galatians 1 and verse 10. I'm not here to win a personal victory over brother Woods but a victory for truth. I'm not here to defend human organizations such as those mentioned in the proposition, but I'm here to defend the church of the living God, a divine organization, as being all-sufficient in organization to do all that God requires of his people in organized capacity. I'm thus here to oppose benevolent societies such as those mentioned in the proposition. I'm here to defend and "contend for the faith which was once delivered unto the saints," Jude 3.

Now, let's read the proposition again. It's before each of you on the chart back of me so that you might see, as the discussion progresses tonight, what the proposition of difference is. Actually, what we're supposed to be discussing. The proposition that I'm affirming says, "It is not in harmony with the scriptures for churches of Christ to build and maintain benevolent organizations such as the Tennessee Orphan Home, Boles Home, Home for the Aged, and other such organizations for the care of the needy."

Now, last evening I defined the terms of the proposition and evidently my opponent accepted my definitions. I see no point in discussing them further at this particular time. In denying the proposition last evening, as I defined it, my opponent is admitting that the benevolent organizations that he's defending thus constitute benevolent associations, or benevolent societies, because I defined them as such in the course of the study last evening.

Now, before considering some more scriptural arguments in

176

addition to the ones that we considered last evening in the defense of the proposition, I'd like for us to consider just a few things now, that we might see really what the issue of difference is. The issue of difference is not "Should the needy be cared for?" We agree on that. It is not "Can a home be maintained or provided for the needy?" It is not a matter of systematic arrangement. It is not a question or matter of how with respect to means, modes, or methods. The issue of difference is: "Is it scriptural for churches of Christ to build and maintain benevolent organizations" such as those mentioned in the proposition?

Now, last evening, I introduced at least 11 charts setting forth the fallacy of my opponent's position. Those who were present last evening, no doubt, realize that those arguments were not answered although some references, in some cases, were made to some of the charts. But I want us to notice what we considered last evening very briefly.

We showed first of all chart number 1, and showed how that God gave commands to the church to evangelize, to edify, and to relieve. We showed how that God did not give a generic term, "organizations," but God specified the "church." In each particular case, when we suggested that when God specified the church, that ruled out other organizations from doing the work of the church. Now, we're not discussing individual work but the work of the church.

Then we showed further last evening that when God gave the command to the church to evangelize, to edify, and to relieve, that there were some things that came in the category of aids. Then we showed how that societies of human origin such as the missionary societies, Sunday school societies, and benevolent organizations are another kind of organization. That they're human in origin, they're human in form, and human in function. Therefore, we showed how they are additions to the word of God, and, hence, we claimed last evening that, in view of that, they're not in harmony with the scriptures.

We further showed, last evening, the fact that Tennessee Orphan Home is a benevolent organization. A benevolent organization that my opponent is defending—the one which he hasn't found one passage of scripture for in three evenings. We showed how that this

177

benevolent society consists of a Board of Directors, nine in number, and they provide a home, necessaries, and personnel for the care of the destitute at Spring Hill, Tennessee. The charter of the corporation says that they may do the same thing—they may establish branches in any county in the State of Tennessee, showing there's a difference between this Board of Directors and those things that may be established by them.

We asked him last evening if it had the same set-up in evangelism, if that would be a missionary society, and if so would he endorse it? But he failed to tell us whether or not he would endorse such or whether or not it would constitute a missionary society.

Then we further showed last evening that the same set-up is involved in Boles Orphan Home. There's a Board of Directors who in turn supervises two homes. We read, last evening, proof from the **Boles Home News** and from the **Potter Messenger** and we gave quotation after quotation that show that there are two homes being operated by the same board. One of these homes is known as Boles Home at Quinlan, Texas. The other one is known as the Sherwood-Myrtle Foster Home, 150 miles away down at Stephenville, Texas. We asked our opponent to point out if this is not a benevolent society, what would it take to make one? Yet, he failed to do so.

So then, we showed further last evening GOD'S WAY VERSUS THE WAYS OF MEN. We showed how that in 1 Timothy 3, verses 14 and 15, Ephesians 3:10, etc., that God tells the local congregation (the church) to evangelize. That God in Ephesians 4 tells the church to edify. That God in 1 Timothy 5 tells the church to relieve. That these works ought to be done by and through the church as the organization that God has specified. Then we showed on this side of the chart some of the ways of men and showed that our opponent is affirming that the local congregation can work through another organization that it might thus accomplish its work of benevolence. He said the other evening that when the congregation provided means, when it provided a place and facilities necessary in evangelism, that did not constitute another organization. But he says when the same thing is provided in benevolence, that's another organization. What makes the difference? They are the same organizationally speaking. There's only

178

difference in the work involved, and, so then, if one constitutes another organization then so would the other. So, we showed last evening these principles and thus showed how that these societies are additions to the word of God. We maintained last evening that this is God's wisdom, that it's divine, therefore, sufficient. That these are the ways of men. We asked for the scripture for this set-up, but none was forthcoming. We suggested, last evening, that this is man's wisdom—that is, human; therefore, not needed.

Now, let's go further this evening in defense of the proposition. Not that it needs any more proof, but that we might further show ample proof that you might thus see that the Bible is sufficient to guide us, and that there's no authority for these human organizations.

I have here chart number 20, that says PLEASE CONSIDER THESE PASSAGES VERY CAREFULLY.

We notice, for example, Acts 2, verses 44 and 45, that the word of God says, "And all that believed were together, and had all things common and sold their possessions and goods and parted them to all men, as every man had need." We notice also in Acts 4, verses 34 and 35, this reading. The word of God says, "Neither was there any among them that lacked: for as many as were possessors of lands or houses sold them and brought the prices of the things that were sold and laid them down at the apostles' feet: and distribution was made unto every man according as he had need." We notice in Acts 6, verse 1 beginning, this reading: "And in those days, when the number of the disciples was multiplied, there arose a murmuring of the Grecians against the Hebrews, because their widows were neglected in the daily ministration. Then the twelve called the multitude of the disciples unto them, and said, It is not reason that we should leave the word of God and serve tables. Wherefore, brethren, look ye out among you seven men of honest report, full of the Holy Ghost and wisdom, whom we may appoint over this business." And so, the word of God shows they did that.

We notice also in Acts 11 and verses 27-30 that, "And in those days came prophets from Jerusalem unto Antioch. And there stood up one of them named Agabus and signified by the Spirit that there should be great dearth throughout all the world: which came to pass in the days of Claudius Caesar. Then the disciples, every man according to his ability, determined to send relief unto the brethren which dwelt in Judea: which also they did, and sent it to the elders by the hands of Barnabas and Saul."

We notice also in Romans 15, verses 25 and 26, Paul says, "But now, I go unto Jerusalem to minister unto the saints. For it hath pleased them of Macedonia and Achaia to make a certain contribution for the poor saints which are at Jerusalem."

In 1 Corinthians 16, in verse 1 beginning, we have this reading: "Now, concerning the collection for the saints, as I have given orders to the churches of Galatia, even so do ye." We notice also in chapters 8 and 9 of Second Corinthians, that it mentions the ministering to the saints.

Then in 1 Timothy 5, in verse 16, the apostle Paul says, "If any man or woman that believeth have widows, let them relieve them, and let not the church be charged; that it." That *it* what? That *the church* "may relieve them that are widows indeed."

Now, notice this, brethren. Here's my position tonight. I've showed passage after passage that shows that the church can relieve those for whom it's responsible. I've showed passage after passage where the work was engaged in. And note this: There's not the slightest hint of a benevolent organization such as my opponent is defending in the proposition, the Tennessee Orphan Home and Home for the Aged, in any of these passages through which the churches did their works of benevolence.

Now, notice this. We read most of the passages. There wasn't anything about benevolent organizations in any of them. Now, a question please. Are the scriptures sufficient to guide us? Do we need something else, brethren, neighbors, and friends, or should we abide in the doctrine of Christ? I've shown what the doctrine of Christ says. If my opponent cannot find within the bounds of the doctrine of Christ his benevolent organizations, they thus stand without authority in the book of God. I maintained for three nights now, that he hasn't produced the passage of scripture that thus authorizes his benevolent organizations. He may talk about the family, he may talk about something else, but he hasn't produced the passage of scripture that shows his benevolent organizations, and that's the point of difference here tonight.

Now, we want to notice Chart number 32. This chart is entitled, "Authority for Buildings and Organizations."

We notice in one column that we have "Commands." We have the passages of scriptures given. We show how there is divine authority for these things and on this other side, "Human Authority" for these.

In Ephesians 3, in verse 10, and 1 Timothy 3:14-15, the church is to teach. Then within the bounds of the command would be a place to preach. So, that's divinely authorized. But there's only human authority for the missionary society, because it's not found in the bounds of God's book.

In Matthew 28, in verse 19, the command to baptize. The command to baptize necessitates the place to baptize, but these baptismal associations would be humanly authorized because they are not found in God's book.

We notice also in the case to teach, that a place to teach is required, and, hence, authorized, but Sunday school organizations would be additions to the word of God and thus only humanly authorized.

We notice also in the case of assembling that Hebrews 10, in verse 25, that a place to assemble is inherent within the command to assemble. There's the authority for the place to assemble, but a church building society is not authorized in God's book. There's another organization involved besides the church in that case.

We notice also in 1 Corinthians 9, verses 1 through 14, that the preachers are to be supported, and within the bounds of support would be a place to live. But suppose there was a preacher's supporting corporation? They're not authorized, neighbors and friends, to which the church might send funds and let it in turn hire the preachers.

We notice the same thing with respect to relief. In 1 Timothy 5:16 Paul tells the church to relieve, and so the place for the needy to be relieved is inherent within the command. That's divinely authorized, but there's not divine authority for the benevolent corporations or organizations like my opponent is defending. Now, both are authorized. These things divinely and those things humanly and so notice this. Are human organizations necessary? They violate the principle of the sufficiency of the church, and so I maintain that these human organizations being built and maintained by churches of Christ are thus without divine authority.

Now, chart number 15. We notice here chart number 15 that says BROTHER WOODS SAYS, "NO AUTHORITY." Now, I've shown from scriptural principles that my position is true. I showed that last evening. I've shown that again this evening, but I want to go beyond that now. I want to let brother Woods testify in behalf of my proposition. We notice, for example, in Huntsville, Alabama, September 28, 1958, second session, second speech, according to the tape, that brother Woods said this, "And besides that, there isn't any authority in the scriptures for the church to serve, or even Christians by support of the church, to serve as an adoption agency. No authority." Now, brother Woods said then there's no authority for Christians to serve by support of the church as an adoption agency. But the following institutions serve as adoption agencies: The Tennessee Orphan Home (Spring Hill, Tennessee), Potter Orphan Home and School, Childhaven for Children, The Children's Home in Lubbock, Texas. Now, according to brother Woods' statement, churches have no authority to support the above institutions, yet he's been defending them for three nights. I'm asking brother Woods to repudiate either the statement that he made or these institutions, one of the two. I believe you can see that, brethren. He's on my side of the thing here. He's either wrong then or he's wrong tonight. I'm asking him to accept what the word of God says, and when the word of God shows the church is to do its work, then let the church do that without these human organizations being built and maintained by the church. You keep that issue in mind: that it is whether or not churches may build and maintain these benevolent organizations. If brother Woods told the truth here, then these institutions that serve as adoption agencies thus operate without divine authority when supported by churches of Christ. Now, let's keep that in mind. That's what brother Woods says, and so brother Woods is testifying in this particular case on behalf of my proposition. I've shown it from the scriptures that my proposition is so, and now, I've shown it by my opponent's speeches in the past. Thank you.

Guy N. Woods' Fourth Negative Speech

Brethren moderators, brother Sutton, ladies, and gentlemen:

I should like to take just one moment to express the appreciation that I feel to those with whom I stand on these matters for the invitation to come this way and the opportunity to be associated with you in the support and defense of that which we believe to be in harmony with the word of God. I have enjoyed fully my association with you. I regret that I could not, because of limited time and opportunity, accept the many invitations that I've had.

I would like to express appreciation to brother W. L. Totty, who preaches for the Garfield Heights congregation in Indianapolis, for being with me in the capacity of moderator, and to the Garfield Heights church for allowing him to come and be with us in this effort. It may interest you to know that brother Totty has preached for that congregation for about a quarter of a century. He went there when there was a mere handful of people, and now, it's more than twice as large as any church, that is, any church of Christ in the state of Indiana. So, I'm grateful to him and to all of you for all the many favors that have come my way since I've been in your midst.

Now, for half of brother Sutton's speech, we listened to a rehash of matters presented on last night and which we answered twice, or maybe three times, some of it last evening, and interposed objections to which he made no reply whatsoever. But, in view of the fact that it's my practice to answer everything that's presented, I shall deal with it again and again, just as he pleases to take up his time in presenting it. I might say, with reference to brother Holt's complaint last night regarding interruptions, that we interrupt only when Sutton misrepresents. Now, if he'll quit misrepresenting, we'll quit interrupting, but I assure you that I shall be on the floor the very moment that such misrepresentation occurs.

We had an agreement with reference to some questions, and this agreement specified no time other than that sufficient time would be given to allow answering before the session started. Both last evening and tonight, I had questions over here 35 minutes before time to start. He made no effort tonight to answer the questions, but I have his, and while I'm not going to give them to him until he answers mine, I'm going to read the answers because I answer all questions.

1. "What do you mean by charitable organizations when you wrote it on page 340 of the *Annual Lesson Commentary*, 1946?"

Can't you read? See the context. I was condemning organizations comparable to the missionary society.

2. "Are elders serving as elders over the children's home of Lubbock, the Maude Carpenter Children's Home, Tipton Home, Sunny Glen Home, Turner Children's Home which, you say, have been built and maintained by churches of Christ?"

Answer: Their publications say that they're trustees; the Department of Public Welfare in various states say this is what they are.

3. "Does the word 'relieve' in 1 Timothy 5:16 mean money only or may it include such things as food, clothing, shelter, medical care, and supervision?"

Answer: It includes means or whatever nature requires, but it does not include functions outside the proper church activity such as supervision, recreation, discipline. I asked him, "Does it include care of children?" But don't you look for an answer.

4. "Why do you oppose churches sending donations to denominational orphanages such as Buckner Orphan Home?"

Answer: Because false doctrine is taught there. Why do you oppose supporting a Baptist preacher's home?

5. "Did the seven men chosen in Acts 6:1-6 to serve tables constitute a Board of Directors such as Tennessee Orphan Home, Childhaven, or are they simply servants chosen by the church to care for the needy?"

The Seven were chosen, so the Bible says, to take care of business. In this sense, they performed duties comparable to the Board of Directors of Tennessee Orphan Home. Remember, there was but one congregation. Hence, they were selected from the church universal just as many members of such boards are selected today.

184

That, friends, answers his questions. All of them presented. We'll see whether or not he answers mine. If he doesn't, I'll read the questions to you in just a few minutes. He said that he's not here for the purpose of gaining a personal victory. Well, if he isn't, then why doesn't he answer my questions? If he doesn't care what it does to him, if he's interested in the issues, why doesn't he answer my questions? I'm going to show you that it's simply because he's afraid that he will lose, and he's already lost it. So, he might as well go ahead and answer.

Now, he says he is attacking benevolent societies. I told you from the outset that he uses that phrase in prejudicial fashion. He means something entirely different from what we mean. It's comparable to a denominational preacher shouting, "Campbellite." You just remember that every time he says it. In the connotation that he has, he's practicing the same thing that a denominational preacher does when he shouts, "Campbellite."

Now, let's have ... well first though, he again cited John 8:32, John 17:17, and John 12:48 to show we ought to go by the truth. Well, I insist upon that. That's the reason I insist upon answers to my arguments and questions, to see who has the truth. He called attention to 2 Peter 1:3. We mention these matters two or three times already. "All things that pertain to life and godliness." I remember the scriptures. We believe that as we do the inspiration suggested in 2 Timothy 3:16-17. We're agreed upon this. We're not agreed upon their application, however, because he's advocating things contrary to the scriptures.

He called attention to 2 John 9, "Whosoever transgresseth and goes beyond, hath not God." The Greek work there is *proagō*, which means literally, "who goes beyond that which is taught." He's doing exactly that when he refuses to admit the place of the home in God's benevolent plan.

Then he cites to us Ephesians 5:10 that admonishes us to prove all things that are acceptable. But the very next verse reads, "Have no fellowship with the unfruitful works of darkness, but rather reprove them." That's what we are trying to do in this debate. Those matters we've dealt with repeatedly.

Now, let's have his chart number 1. Chart number 1. This,

friends, we answered three times last evening, but we are glad to give our attention to it tonight. Observe here that he has COMMANDS— GENERIC AND SPECIFIC." Brother Sutton implies that the word 'relieve,' here, is specific. I deny it. I believe that the church is to relieve. I believe the church is to relieve needy saints. I believe the church is to relieve orphans. I believe the church is to relieve, as far as it can, people who are not Christians, if they're deserving people. I believe in relieving. The only difference is that word "specific" and "generic." Now, if it's specific, that is, if it specifies, and this passage is itself specific, then where's the authority for providing for a bachelor? This mentions the widow, Sutton. Where is the scripture that authorizes the church to help a bachelor? Now, you remember that he's insisting upon specific authority here.

Now, don't cite me to Acts 6 because that doesn't say a word about a bachelor. The word *bachelor* is not in that passage. Oh, he'll come over there and say, "Yeah, but there must have been some in there." You prove there were. Prove there were bachelors in that group. It just says widows over there.

Don't cite me to Acts 11:27-30. That doesn't say anything about bachelors. 1 Corinthians 16:1-2 doesn't. Tell me the passage that justifies the helping of a bachelor. Now, he couldn't do it if his life depended upon it, because the term is not found here. That shows the fallacy of this.

Now, you look at the hypocrisy involved in this, friends. What are we debating? The orphan home question. What is the implication? That I am wrong because I'm urging this to be done by orphan homes. What's the right way to care for orphans? The implication is that the way is for the church to do it, but he doesn't believe that the church can spend a dime out of its treasury for an orphan child. I challenge him to deny that. He doesn't believe a word of it. That statement right here, friends, put on this chart by him, involves insincerity and hypocrisy. Now, I'm either right about that or I'm wrong. I charged that time and again last evening. Why doesn't he make some reply to it?

Let's have his next chart, chart number … well, the Tennessee Orphan Home chart. He gave no number on two or three of them. I don't think it was, but that's all right because that is the number here.

186

Remember last night, friends, that I pointed out to him that this chart doesn't fit the case because we don't claim that the orphan homes are either aids or additions to the church. Our contention is that the orphan home is a home, not a church. It's not a part of a church as a church and the orphan home is a family arrangement, not a church arrangement, and, hence, it's neither an aid nor addition. If you remember again, why has he got this up here for? Why, the purpose of showing us how I am wrong and how it ought to be done. Well, how is it? By the church. Doing what? Care for orphan children. But he has preached all over this country and debated it in the past that it's sinful for the church to spend a dime for any person who is not a needy saint.

Now, he has a little dodge on that so far as orphan children are children whose parents are still living. Not orphan children, but for children whose parents are still living. He's got a little dodge on that, and he'd try to deceive you with it. Here's his dodge: That the church can help the parents, and the parents then can use that to help the children. Now, he's shown us an indirect way of doing what he says the church can't do. That's what it amounts to. That's telling us that it can do what it can't do. What is it that it can't do? It can't help anybody that's not a member of the church. That's the basic premise, but he comes back and says, "Well, but it can help the parents and the parents can help the children." Well, all right, if he can do that, if he can help the natural parents, why can't you help legal parents? That's all we're doing at Boles Home and Childhaven and so on. We're just helping people to help somebody else. Now, Sutton, this statement here is hypocritical, and you know it. You know that you, in putting this on this chart here, that your statement is hypocritical in leaving this audience with the impression that you believe the church can do it that way. You don't do anything of the kind, do you? I'll apologize to you for making this statement if you'll get up and say you do believe the church can help an orphan child with money out of its treasury. He didn't say it, friends.

Let's have next the Boles Home chart, or maybe the next one in the notes is the Tennessee Orphan Home chart. Yes, this is it. Now, ladies and gentlemen, listen. We've already answered this time and time again. We've gone over it repeatedly. He said that I take the position that because *this* provides *this*, that, therefore, *this* has to be a part of *this*. No, I didn't say that. I said that your argument is that because this supplies this, that this cannot be the same as that. But I showed that I believe that the organization is itself the home and that all of it constitutes an integral part of it. I believe that, but that's not his argument, and that's not the thing that I was answering. Now, you listen. I'm going to show you that there is absolutely essential what he calls a so-called in-between organization.

I have here, and I introduced this once before, but he paid no attention to it, the minimum standards for child placing agencies and institutions of the State of Kentucky, Department of Economic Security, Division of Children's Services, Frankfurt. Here under point number two, and I'll be glad for him to have this and examine it, this is actually a regulation adopted pursuant to authority KRS 199640, as amended by Section 9, House Bill 362, regular session 1956 General Assembly. "Institutional Management and Operating Personnel: Each institution shall have an organized Board of Directors with at least five members who live in Kentucky within commuting distance of the institution. The names and addresses of the board members shall be forwarded to the Department of Economic Security. Board meetings shall be held regularly. The Board shall include at least five members who are or have served in any one of the following positions: county judge, school superintendent, banker, merchant, president of PTA, minister or priest, county health nurse, or physician." Now, it goes on and gives great detail with reference to how the housekeeping must be, how many children there may be to a certain square feet, the physical standards of the home, the water supply, the home providing play space, the home reasonably accessible to such community facilities as schools, church and neighbors, and so on. All of it detailed information. Now, listen. If brother Sutton were telling the truth about the church here, that is, if he were actually saying that the church could do it, which he says he can't, he'd get put in jail if he tried to do it like he says on these charts it can be. Now, that's right, isn't it? It's right that you've got to go by the law, haven't you, brother Holt? You live in Kentucky, don't you? You've got to go by the law or you get in trouble with reference to it. Now, Sutton, you know that, yet he's

188

telling you that you can follow a course that, if you followed it all, which you're not going to, but if you did, you'd get put in jail. Now, I can prove that more definitely if you want me to do so. Now, do something with this. Say something about this when you get up here, if you will.

Let's have next the Boles Home chart. All right. Now, this, too, friends, we've answered. I asked him last night to tell us, with reference to this, whether or not there were several homes involved in that distribution of funds in Acts 6. We had no mention made of it whatsoever. Hence, I'm going to wait until he answers what I've said about it last night.

Again, this chart GOD'S WAY [Chart Number 5]. I answered it last night. Let's have it right quickly. I went over that in detail. I showed you he makes it appear here that the church can preach, edify, relieve. What's his implication? That that's the only way it can be done. I don't believe a word of that. I don't believe that's the only way it can be done. I think a family can preach or edify, and I know that the family can relieve, and yet he's leaving the impression that the church here can relieve orphan children here. He doesn't believe a word of it. He doesn't believe a word of it. No, that I pointed that out last night.

Let's have his chart number 20 now. Hold my time now, because we're losing some valuable time. Chart number 20. Is that it? Now, friends, we have no question whatever to raise with reference to these passages of scripture. We believe Acts 2, Acts 4, Acts 6 and 11 and 15 and these passages. We believe that the church did supply the means. That's not the question. Here, for example, in Acts 2, did they take this money and take these people into the congregation and make them a part of the church before they could spend this money, or did they give it to the home? In this case, in Acts 4 when distribution was made for all, did those people become church members simply because they received a donation, or did they give it for the family to spend? And for this, and this, and this. We believe all of this, but we say that the money was supplied by the church and turned over to the family to spend.

All right, let's have now, chart number 32. I demand an answer to that. I pointed that out repeatedly. Chart number 32. Now, you observe this, friends: AUTHORITY FOR BUILDINGS AND ORGANIZATIONS. He says we have divine authority for preaching the gospel. I believe that, and to baptize and to teach and to assemble and so on. Yet he believes there may be, and he said in answer to one of these questions tonight, that it is scriptural to have trustees. All right. Do trustees constitute a church building society? Let him answer that. We'll have more to say about it. We believe in supporting the preacher, but what about supporting a preacher's home that has trustees over it? The church gives the money to the trustees and the trustees furnish the house. Let him answer that. We'll have more to say about it. Now, as to relieving here, we believe that. He doesn't. Again, here is hypocrisy evident. He leaves the impression that's the way to do it when he doesn't believe the church can do it that way.

Let's have chart 15. This is the last chart that he introduced: BROTHER WOODS SAYS, "NO AUTHORITY."—"Besides that, there isn't any authority in the scriptures for the church to serve even Christians by support of the church, to serve as an adoption agency." Here is the context in which that statement was made, and it states it even here. "That the church itself is not an adoption agency. The church is not a family if families adopt and, hence, the church not being an adoption agency, is itself not, of course, authorized to adopt. I believe in the adoption of children. I urge it not only by private families but by these homes, to urge other people to adopt children. I'm glad that they do and glad that they can when it's feasible and when it's good for the child." Now, that, friends, is the statement. To apply this to the adoption of children is to misrepresent what I said. I assume that he knew no better. He does now. Let me tell you, have I got a half a minute? [TOTTY: You have one minute.]

Alright. Now, here, friends, is our argument, and again I say it stands like the Rock of Gibraltar. He's never made any attempt to answer it. Never referred to it for that matter. That the church has an obligation to needy families. That the church may come to the aid of families, but sometimes the whole structure of that family is destroyed through no fault of the child. Then somebody reestablishes the family relationship. That's exactly what the orphan home is. It is the home that the child had lost and has been restored. The child had a right to a

190

home to begin with. It has a right to a home to end with. The home is not in conflict with the church because it's not doing the work of the church as a church. It's not in conflict with the home because that home is gone. What is the orphan home? It's the home the child had lost and has been restored, and it has just as much right to that home as you have to yours. This is not a human institution. It is a divine one, but you've got to go by the law. Now, tell us if we have to go by the law, Sutton.

Carrol R. Sutton's Fifth Affirmative Speech

Brethren, get me chart number 7.

Gentlemen moderators, brother Woods, ladies and gentlemen:

I'm glad to come before you for the next 20 minutes in defense of the proposition that I'm affirming this evening. The proposition reads as follows: "It is not in harmony with the scriptures for churches of Christ to build and maintain benevolent organizations such as the Tennessee Orphan Home, Boles Home, Home for the Aged, and other such organizations for the care of the needy.

Now, brother Woods says that we're debating orphan homes. That isn't so. We're debating benevolent organizations. Now, those benevolent organizations may in turn provide a home for orphans or they may in turn provide a home for the aged. What has he been saying about the homes for the aged provided by these benevolent organizations? He's trying to sidetrack the issue. He's trying to make like we're discussing caring only for orphans. We're not even discussing, actually, caring for orphans proper. We're discussing these benevolent organizations. That's the very thing that he's getting away from, but I don't intend to let him get by with it.

I want us to notice further in my affirmative, chart number 7 that's entitled WHERE WILL MY OPPONENT DRAW THE LINE? Now, does the word "visit the fatherless" in James 1:27 authorize churches to make contributions to benevolent institutions such as

Childhaven? If so, think about this. Does "visit the sick" in Matthew 25:36 authorize churches to make contributions to hospitals, or we might say, build and maintain such? Brother Woods believes that it does, as long as the hospital is set up on a non-profit basis, to care only for saints. He said so in the ***Porter-Woods Debate*** in Indianapolis. I wonder if that hospital is a divine institution. He's trying to defend these benevolent organizations here as divine institutions. Is that hospital a divine institution?

Then does "feed the hungry" in Romans 12:20 authorize churches to make contributions to grocery companies or to build and maintain grocery companies. If not, why not, on the same basis that he applies to these others?

Then does the words "entertain strangers" in Hebrews 13 authorize churches to build and maintain or make contributions to hotels? Are hotels divine institutions? You know, brother Gayle Oler, Superintendent of Boles Home, put the Boles Orphan Home in the same category with hotels and radio stations. Yet, brother Woods says that he believes the same thing about these matters as he does. Therefore, brother Woods believes, if he believes what brother Oler says, that these things, such as the hotels, are divine institutions. Either that or he's saying that brother Oler does not say that the benevolent organizations are divine institutions, and if he says they're human, that's exactly what I'm contending for.

Then we notice also, does "clothe the naked" in Matthew 25:36 authorize churches to build and maintain or make contributions to clothing companies? If one is authorized, why not all? Now, will my opponent tell us? Wait and see. Now, think about that, brethren. Think about it, neighbors and friends. So then, if not, why not? Where will he draw the line?

We also have here a chart that's entitled IF CHURCHES CAN CONTRIBUTE TO ONE, WHY NOT ALL? Chart number 8. Now, if churches of Christ can contribute to a human organization that's called the orphan home or home for the aged, to care for orphans and relieve the aged, and if they can contribute to human organizations called the Gospel Press, like he said the other night that it might in turn advertise the church or advertise the gospel, then upon the same basis, why can't

192

churches send to a human organization called the Christian College that it might train preachers, to a human organization called the Sunday School that it might edify the church. Now, I'm not talking about Bible classes. I'm talking about organized Sunday school societies, or even an organization called a hospital that it might care for the sick, and he's on record as saying that it can, then why can't it do the same thing with respect to human organizations that are called a grocery company that it might feed the hungry, and a human organization called the missionary society that it might preach the gospel? Now, he's got one human organization called the Gospel Press, and he says churches can contribute to that so that it in turn might advertise the gospel. Why not one called the missionary society? Now, think about it. If churches can contribute to one, why not all of them? I maintain upon the same basis it can to one it can to the others. Now, please give the scriptural authority for this set up. Remember 2 John 9 says we're to abide in the doctrine. Brother Woods says that the word "transgresseth" means "go beyond the teaching." That's what I'm contending for, and I showed from chart number 20 the passages of scripture that show the teaching about the church relieving. Brother Woods has gone beyond that to get these benevolent organizations. He says if you go beyond the teaching, you've gone beyond the doctrine and you don't have God. I agree with him. Thank you, brother Woods. Come back inside the teaching and leave these organizations outside where they are. So then, if churches can contribute to one, why not all?

Now, chart number 11. This one's entitled MISSIONARY AND BENEVOLENT SOCIETIES PARALLEL. I want you to see some things, brethren. Now, both originated in the minds of man. Both are human organizations. Both are designed to do the work of the church. Both perform the work of the church. Both have a Board of Directors. Both have their own constitution, by-laws, etc. Both solicit and accept contributions from churches. Both are organizations to activate the universal church. Both have to employ means and methods. They're organizations; they're not means, methods. They're organizations that employ means and methods and both are operated by those who claim to be Christians. Both are justified, quotation marks, in the eyes of some as an expediency. I wonder if our opponent would tell us whether or not he justifies these benevolent organizations on the grounds of expediency. I don't believe he'll tell us. I wonder if he will.

We notice also that both are doing what some brethren call "a good work." Both have caused division in the church because they were introduced without divine authority. The introduction of these things caused division. The opposition to them do not cause division in the sight of God, but those that introduce unscriptural innovations certainly are guilty of causing division. Now, both exist. Neither exists by divine authority to do the work of the church. Now, how can we reject one and accept the other? I want him to tell us.

Now, we'll notice chart number 31: NO, THE "HOW" ISN'T, BUT THE "WHO" IS. Now, if he's talking about, "That Sutton tries to tell us how to do it," I told you to begin with it's not a question of "how" with respect to means, modes, or methods. The issue is a question of organizations. There's a vast difference between organizations and the methods or means employed by the organizations. No, the "how" isn't told, but the "who" is. We have on this side the "who." Here's the local church, which is a divine organization. Here's the benevolent society, such as Tennessee Orphan Home, which is a human organization. The Superintendent of it says it's human; I say it's human; and so, we have a human organization in this benevolent society, this Tennessee Orphan Home, and we have the church. Both of them could provide a "how." One with divine authority, the other with human authority. Now, the "how" provided would be a place, facilities, necessaries, and personnel for the care of the needy.

Now, 1 Timothy 5:16 specifies that the church is to relieve widows indeed. Now, he may say, "We're not discussing that. We're discussing orphans." Now, keep in mind the home for the aged. He tries to get around that, brethren. He doesn't want to talk about that because when he thinks about that, he'll think about the fact that if they restore the parents in the case of the children, they'll have the same set up in the case of the widows. So, they restore the husbands, and the board members would be husbands to the widows, and they'd be guilty … oh well. I'll just stop there. But anyway, we notice here that the

194

"how" isn't told, but the "who" is. I maintain God has bound or has specified the "who."

Now, chart number 9 entitled SOME "HOWS" IN CARING FOR THE NEEDY. Now, he's talked a lot about "Sutton won't tell us how that it could be done." Now, keep this in mind, brethren. I can't bind one of these "hows" because the Bible doesn't bind them. But the Bible does bind the organization, the church, a divine organization. But I'm just simply showing some ways that it may be done. We notice in view of the fact that 1 Timothy 5 shows that the church is to relieve destitute widows, Acts 6:1-6 shows that the church did do it, the church did relieve some neglected widows, then here's some ways that it could be done. That the needy could be placed in a private home, and I don't mean what he calls an institution or organization. I mean a private place, a place owned by individuals. Then, of course, there could be personnel employed. They'd be paid as they carried out whatever might be necessary, but they'd do it under the supervision of the congregation.

Another way that it could be done, if it was feasible to do so, the church might build a home, provide facilities, and when I say build a home, I mean build a house.

WOODS: Sutton, I want to ask you a question. It's not interrupting you. I'm just trying to get a clear statement.

SUTTON: You can hold my time.

WOODS: I don't understand where you said that the church could supply a private home, and you didn't mean by that an institution. I don't know whether you're talking about widows or whether you're talking about orphan children. Would you clarify that, please?

SUTTON: If brother Woods wants to discuss that, I'll be glad to sign a proposition with him, and we'll discuss for whom the church is responsible, but that's not involved in this proposition.

TOTTY: Point of order, please. I appeal to brother Holt. You clarify that. You know, we don't know what you're talking about unless you say. Do you mean orphan children are included in that? Just say yes or no. That would be enough.

WOODS: What do you think, brother Holt?

HOLT: The audience, the thing that's being discussed is building and maintaining benevolent organizations, and since that's not a question in the proposition, then it's for brother Sutton to deal with the proposition and not some other issues.

TOTTY: Then he won't tell who's included in that for whom the church may be responsible for.

SUTTON: If they want to debate it, we will.

TOTTY: Can the church put orphan children in that private home or not? We just want to know.

HOLT: It's not a matter of who they could but in there. It's not in the issue, but brother Sutton says if you want to discuss that he'll be glad to sign the proposition.

WOODS: I beg your pardon. It is the question, because we're discussing how can you care for orphan children. He's told us that somebody can be put in a private home and be supported by the church. I'm trying to find out if that includes orphan children. That's the question whether it's widows or orphan children or both.

SUTTON: Ask him if he'll let me go ahead with my speech.

HOLT: The proposition is for the churches of Christ to build and maintain benevolent organizations, and I would rule that we go ahead with this.

WOODS: You would rule that he doesn't answer. OK, thank you.

SUTTON: Now, brethren, you can see that was an effort to get me off of the proposition.

WOODS: I beg your pardon, sir. It was not.

SUTTON: Because the proposition says, "It is not in harmony with the scriptures for churches of Christ to build and maintain benevolent organizations."

WOODS: I'd like to get him on the subject.

HOLT: We have had good order during the discussion as far as the audience is concerned. The night before last, brother Sutton was stopped in his last speech every 48 seconds. We do not want anything except the proposition discussed in the time allowed for that. Brother Sutton was supposed to have 20 minutes. The audience has known that we have not stopped brother Woods one time during the discussion

196

thus far, neither do we intend to. We intend to respect, in the sense of listening to him, when he's before you.

WOODS: Now, brother Holt, may I say this? If I know my heart I had only one purpose. I didn't understand whether orphan children were to be put in that private home that he said the church could support, and I just wanted to find out. I'm perfectly willing for him to proceed.

HOLT: Well, that's fine. We appreciate your patience in it, and we just want you to listen and notice the proposition, and it's for you to judge whether he stays with the proposition.

TOTTY: All right, if that's the case, then in all that scripture that he said he wants the truth amounts to nothing to him because if he wanted the truth, he wouldn't be afraid to say whether orphan children are included in that or not. Now, that's the point.

HOLT: If a person wanted the truth, they might say whether baptism is essential, but that's not the proposition here, friend. You see it, and so it's time for us to go on.

WOODS: No, it isn't. Since you brought in baptism, if someone will raise up from the audience and say, "Brother Sutton, is sprinkling baptism?" would he refuse to answer? No. That shows he's afraid to answer this. He wouldn't be afraid to say sprinkling isn't baptism. Now, you introduced baptism.

HOLT: If it's in the proposition, it would be right for him to answer, but as far as running all over the country on how the proposition, that we're supposed to be discussing, we're not supposed to do it, and we will stay with the proposition.

SUTTON: Thank you, brother Holt. Now, I was showing, when I was interrupted a while ago, some "hows" in caring for the needy, whomever the church may be responsible to care for. That, of course, is the subject that if brother Woods wants to discuss it under separate proposition, I'll be glad to do so with him. But we're discussing now these benevolent organizations—whether or not churches of Christ may build and maintain such. So, then we showed one "how." We were showing a second "how." The church may build a home, provide facilities, buy necessaries, employ personnel or it may buy or rent a home or house, provide facilities, buy necessaries, and employ personnel. Now, I suggest to you these are some of the "hows" that the church may use.

On this side, here is a benevolent organization such as Tennessee Orphan Home, Boles Home, Childhaven, Home for the Aged, and so forth that are human organizations. Now, they, in turn, could do the same thing over here that the church could do over there. So, you can see then that it's not a question of "how" should it be done, but whether or not the church, a divine institution, ought to provide the "how," oversee the "how," or should it send funds to a benevolent organization, a human institution, and let it in turn provide the "how." I have scriptures for this. Where is the scripture for this set up? This human institution? This benevolent corporation? Now, notice this: The issue is not a question of methods, but organizations. The issue is which organization is authorized to provide the "how." Is it the church or a human organization? Now, that's the issue, friends. That's what we're discussing. So, there are some "hows" that could be followed. I don't bind the "hows." I said over here, "No, The 'How' Isn't Told, But The "Who" Is." It's a matter of organization, a matter of societies, if you please. It is not a question of methods or means or modes.

Now, I'd like to have chart number 17, please. On this side. The large one.

We have here chart number 17 that's entitled CONTRADICTIONS OF BROTHER WOODS. Now, I've already shown, by the scriptures, principles that condemn these benevolent organizations. I want us to notice some things that my opponent has stated in times past, not to prove my proposition, but simply to prove the fact that he's confused, because he speaks one way one time, another way another time, and expects you to believe him both times.

Now, notice this, for example. We have here contradictions. Chart number 17.

WOODS: May I rise to a point of order and ask what this has to do with the proposition, or what Woods has said on one occasion or the other? Is Woods in the proposition? Are we … are you affirming, in the proposition, that Woods is inconsistent? Think about that a little, if you fellows are so anxious to insist on the proposition.

198

SUTTON: I've already shown the very purpose of it. I've already shown that. Now, notice number one. In *Annual Lesson Commentary*, page 340, 1946, brother Woods said the church "is the only charitable organization that the Lord authorizes or that is needed to do the work the Lord expects his people today to do." Yet, in the Porter-Woods debate in Paragould, the second session and second speech, he said, "and yet he censors me for arguing for an additional organization or a different body apart from the church to perform that function." One time he says the church is the only organization, the next time he says that he's arguing for an additional organization.

We notice in the *Gospel Advocate*, 10/28/54, that he said, "The early church operated a home for destitute widows." In Huntsville, Alabama, 9/28/58, second session, first speech, his own tape, he said, "Well, but didn't the church in Jerusalem operate a needy home? No, sir. There was never a more absurd conclusion drawn than some draw from that." In the *Porter-Woods Debate*, on page 93, he had this to say: "When we come to the question of benevolence, we still have the same organization, the church." But in the *Cogdill-Woods Debate*, on page 97, he says, "Here are the essential items. An organization apart from the church and operating as a home, not as a church." We have on page 100 and page 217, *Annual Lesson Commentary*, 1946, that brother Woods said this: "Stephen was one of the seven selected to dispense food for the Grecian widows." Then further: "Their work, in this instance, was the supervision of the tables of the poor."

In the *Gospel Advocate*, 3/27/58, he had this to say: "The apostles appointed the seven, not to supervise the feeding of the widows, but to administer the fund out of which their support was taken." We notice also that in the *Woods-Garrett Debate* in Stockton, California, 1954. This is contained in the *Porter-Woods Debate*, page 196 and also 211: "I deny it's a separate body. It is not a separate body. It is the church functioning through the only divine body that God has authorized." Yet, in the Porter-Woods debate in Paragould, Arkansas, 1957, first session, third speech, he says, "Benevolent corporations. These are other bodies. Well, of course, they are. That's what makes them right. The church is one body and the home is another body."

Then on pages 214 and 215 of *Annual Lesson Commentary*, 1946, "It was, therefore, 1. Not a community of goods, but a benevolence. 2. The goods were not in a common fund." End of that quotation. Another quotation: "This was not a universal disbursement but only for those who were actually in need." Yet, in the *Cogdill-Woods Debate*, on page 55, he said this: "He cites us to the example of Acts 6 which is not a case of benevolence in the true sense at all because, actually, there was a common matter out of which they all lived."

He even said last evening that every member of the church participated in that thing, and yet he said here, that it was only for those who were in need, not universal disbursement. We notice also in *Gospel Advocate*, 10/28/54 issue, "The fatherless orphans are to be cared for by the church." but in the *Cogdill-Woods Debate* on page 183, he said, "You can't put orphans in the care of the church." You brethren can see that. He talks about me not believing in caring for the orphans. That's not the proposition, but he says you can't put them in the care of the church, anyway.

Now, I just simply said that to say this. This shows you, brethren, who is confused in the matter. Now, he may talk about this thing and that thing and something else. He may talk about the fact that I may be dry behind the ears, and I may be confused, and I may be this thing and that thing, but the fact remains that we see quotation against quotation. This isn't brother Woods against somebody else. This is brother Woods against brother Woods. I don't know which time he told the truth in some of these instances. I do in some of them. In every instance where he stood for what the Bible said, that's right, but when he spoke against that which the Bible says, that's wrong. Now, keep this in mind. The proposition says, "It is not in harmony with the scriptures for churches of Christ to build and maintain benevolent organizations that they in turn might do the work of caring for the needy. Such organizations as Tennessee Orphan Home, Boles Home, Home for the Aged, etc."

Now, we notice that brother Woods, last evening (with respect to chart number 24 that's entitled WHICH INSTITUTION?) had this to say: "You don't mean here by the private home here the house,

200

because you already got the building there. Is this private home an institution?" No, it isn't an institution when used in chart number 24 because it came under the place. Places aren't institutions. We notice also that he said concerning the pig, last evening, he wanted to know, "Now, who is the pig killer? Was it elders or the preacher?" Brother Woods, that's your problem. It's not mine because you're the one who said the church could send the money to the organization to buy the pig. He wanted to know if I was the pig killer. He's the one who's got the pig to kill. He's the one who sent the pig down. That's not my problem, that's his. No, I'm not the pig killer.

Then he said last evening concerning Tipton Orphan Home, he says, "The elders of the congregation may operate a home but they're not operating it as elders." Yet in 1939 [Wall chart on page 236], he showed how the thing that made Tipton right was because it was managed by the elders of the church. Thank you.

TOTTY: Moderators, brethren, and sisters. I'd like to make a statement just here. That is, that brother Sutton will not answer those questions because he knows it would incriminate him and his proposition. He'd like to hide behind the Fifth Amendment to keep from answering those questions. Now, those questions are on the subject. We are debating how to care for orphan children, and he knows that. I want you people, of course, all the people that are holding to the truth that brother Woods is teaching, know why he doesn't, and I'm appealing to the better judgment of you people to think in your mind why he won't tell whether the church can help the orphan or not. Now, that's what we're debating, and we want that answered. The rule of honorable controversy says that you must weigh your opponent's argument with fairness and candor. Now, I'd like to have those questions answered because I am a moderator and that is the proposition. Everything that you debate isn't worded in so many words in the proposition. If you did, you'd have a book as big as a catalog. Now, he knows that. Is this over here in the proposition. I just want to show you the inconsistency. Now, we don't mind him reading that. All that brother Woods has said since he's been a little boy, if he wants to, but that isn't any more in the proposition than those questions. The orphan children are the question. That's the proposition.

Now, let him read those all he wants to, but I just want you people to see why he won't answer them. I'd be ashamed of brother Woods if he refused to answer a question. If he refuses like brother Sutton has, I'd go home. I wouldn't moderate for him. Now, I want you people to see that.

Another thing I want to call your attention is that brother Sutton gets somebody to turn these charts. We can't take up all of our time turning charts, so get somebody, brother Sutton, to turn the charts for you. We'll be glad to take care of it.

HOLT: As far as I'm concerned, I think the audience can weigh the evidence. So, I'll not pass judgment for you as far as that's concerned. I'm just willing for you to listen to what is being said and also to look at the proposition, and I believe that when we do that, then the discussion will do good.

Since you came here to hear brother Carrol Sutton and brother Guy N. Woods discuss, I don't believe that I need to have to do anything to bolster what brother Sutton says, and I don't believe that you're interested in hearing two, who are supposed to be moderating, discuss something else.

TOTTY: I'm sure that you would like for us to quit. I'm satisfied with that. And if you like to have truth, get him to answer those questions. All those scriptures we want truth and the truth shall make you free and all that comes with poor grace when a man proves he doesn't want the truth. He won't answer the question that would bring out the truth. Now, that's what we want. Brother Woods.

Guy N. Woods' Fifth Negative Speech

Brethren moderators, brother Sutton, and ladies and gentlemen:

If I were in a court of law and was dealing with a shyster lawyer, I would expect him to try to hide behind every possible technicality. I'm hardly prepared to find a gospel preacher who will

202

avoid and evade and dodge and quibble in an effort to meet the issue. Whether it is on the proposition, we all know we're debating the question of the right of churches to support orphans in orphan homes, but whether it is or not, we're Christians, and we ought to be what we claim to be. If somebody asked me my opinion of cremation, if I had any information on it, I'd try to give it. I wouldn't hide behind some technicality. I don't see why he is so afraid of this if he has the truth. He thinks he has it. What then is it to keep him from answering the question, except the fact that he knows that it would slit his theological throat? That's the reason. Well, I know it will. I know he can't answer it, and he knows he can't, and you know it. You'll remember this a long, long time.

He said the subject here is not orphan homes but benevolent organizations. Benevolent organizations are orphan homes and orphan homes are benevolent organizations. I defined the terms in the very first three minutes of the first night after I got into the proposition. But does he believe that orphan homes have a right to be supported by the church? Now, he says it's not a question of orphan homes; it's the question of benevolent organizations. All right, Sutton, can orphan homes, in harmony with your definition, be supported by the church? You put any kind of definition on it you want to and answer my question. Can the church support what you call an orphan home? Do you think he'll answer that? No more than these others.

He talks about brother Oler's position, and he'll answer that brother Oler's position is contrary to mine. Oler's position at the present time is the same as my position, and he knows it. He cites a statement that brother Oler made many years ago with reference to the matter, but what does that have to do with it? I'm not up here trying to prove Oler consistent or inconsistent, or right or wrong. My purpose is to show the error of brother Sutton.

Now, let's have chart number 7. You will observe here that he says, "Does visit the fatherless in James 1:27 authorize churches to make contributions to benevolent institutions such as Childhaven?" Well, it makes it obligatory upon somebody to support orphan children. I maintain that is done in a home, a family, and Childhaven is one of those families. You see, he wants to make me even use his own phraseology in the answer to his questions, but now, if that follows, "Does 'visit the sick' in Matthew 25:36 authorize churches to make contributions to hospitals?" I want you to see his dodge here. Here is what I said last night regarding that. He made no answer.

Now, I'd like an answer to this: If a congregation has one sick person, has 200 members and one sick person, one indigent sick person, can there be a room rented and a nurse employed and the services of a doctor obtained and medicine supplied, and that out of the church treasury? Suppose instead of having 200 members, you had 20,000 members, in which case suppose you had a hundred of these indigent sick people; you'd have a hundred rooms and a hundred nurses. What would that be? It would be a hospital. I say it would be right. If it's right to take care of one sick person, it would be right to take care of 100, under the same circumstances, but that's a far cry from saying that's the same things then as an organization like the Methodist Hospital that operates for profit. Of course, you can't set up something like that. We're talking about indigent sick people. You can't compare orphan children with people that are worth $100,000 and able to pay their own hospital bills.

Well then, what about feeding the hungry? "Does feeding the hungry in Romans 12:20 authorize churches to make contributions to grocery companies?" Now, that's as far down as he got in his comments on it. Now, I'll deal with as much as he presents. Now, watch. I suppose, at least in times past I know, that somewhere down here in the basement you must have had a storeroom in which you brought in goods. Well, what have you got down there? You've got a grocery store, and you made contributions to it in the form of groceries, but that's a far cry from saying that it would be all right then for the church to operate a grocery business. We're not talking about a business of that type or a hospital of that type. We're talking about taking care of needy people. Anybody that can't see that needs to have his head examined.

Let's have chart number 8. That's right, brother Holt, chart number 8. Now, observe here, friends, this again: If churches contribute to one, why not to all? He says you have here human organizations. I deny it. That doesn't represent my position at all,

204

because I don't claim that the church can contribute to a human organization to do the work of the family. I don't claim that. I deny that, and thus the very chart itself is a misrepresentation. His implication is that when you eliminate the human organization the church can support and care for orphans and relieve the aged. He doesn't believe a word of caring for orphans here, does he? I've shown you why it would be wrong to support the grocery company or a hospital operated, as I pointed out, for profit. The church is not in the profit-making business. There's the difference.

Let's have his chart number 11. Well now, I want to ask you another question. That's all right, go ahead. He said he didn't object to the church buying services. I wonder why it would buy services if it's able to do all it needs to do for itself. Sutton takes the position, when he gets in a tight spot, that the church can buy services of another organization. Well, if it needs those services, if it's an all-sufficient church, why can't it provide them? But if it can buy them and still be an all-sufficient church, then you've got an all-sufficient church using another organization. On what basis do you justify that, Sutton? I don't believe he'll even try.

Let's have chart number 11. That's it: MISSIONARY AND BEVEVOLENT SOCIETIES PARALLEL. Now, this is a Jim Dandy. Both originated in the mind of man. Well, maybe so. I'm not defending the kind of benevolent society that he justifies as in my proposition. I deny it, but now look. Here's his idea. Because there are a good many similarities here that, therefore, they are identical. You know what I can do with that kind of argument? I can prove that Sutton is a monkey. Sutton's got two eyes and a monkey's got two eyes. Sutton's got two ears and a monkey's got two ears. Sutton's got two feet and a monkey's got two feet. Sutton's got hair on his head and the monkey's got hair on his head (something I don't see any use for). Now, Sutton eats and a monkey eats. A monkey drinks water and Sutton drinks water. A monkey sleeps and Sutton sleeps. Therefore, they are the same. Therefore, I proved that Sutton is a monkey. Now, that's the kind of argument that he introduces. Nothing to it at all.

Let's have chart number 31. I might say before you leave this, though, this is the same argument that Sommer makes, or made, against the colleges. He maintained that they have no right to exist and used the same phraseology as far as it would be applicable to a school.

All right, now, chart number 31. Here we are, NO, THE "HOW" ISN'T, BUT THE "WHO" IS. They're great on talking about the "who" and telling us that the "how" is not involved. You know, it's not often that I do this because I don't think that there's any credit, especially in this debate, of showing up Sutton. But it happens here that I have a quotation from the ***Totty-Holt Debate***, and that was held in Indianapolis, and since he's so good about reading from other things, I'll just give him a little of his own medicine. Here's what Holt [that is, Charles] said (and that's not this Holt [that is, Alvin]). I'll distinguish between the Holts, but it was a Holt on the same side of this thing. I'd have a little difficulty in deciding which of them is deeper into it. Here's the quotation: "This issue in this debate has not been about what we should do. The 'what' hasn't been under consideration. The 'who' that should be helped is not the issue. The issue has been 'how' or the 'way.' The scriptural procedure by which the preaching of the gospel, for looking after orphans and widows, the needy and bloody man in the street, is to be done. That is the issue." Now, I'd suggest that you and Holt have a debate; that is, the other Holt [Charles]. Decide whether it's "how" or "who." It proves not a thing, but it has just as much to do as it does with all these quotations from me.

Now, look at it again. NO, THE "HOW" ISN'T, BUT THE "WHO" IS. Who? The church. What may the church do? It may provide a place, facilities, necessaries, and personnel for the care of the needy. It was right at that point that I came up on my feet, and I asked, "Now, does that include orphans?" I couldn't find out. I know it doesn't in his belief, but he wouldn't state it before this audience. He was trying to leave that impression with you that this would include orphans here, but it doesn't in his concept. Yet, he's taken the position here that the church can operate another facility, and that it can support it. Now, I ask him this question, not that I hope to get any answer, but Sutton, would you tell us, even if this is aged people and excludes orphans, is this a church or is it a home? Now, what is it? What is this thing right here where these people are living, that the church is supporting? There's a place, there's facilities, there's necessaries, there's personnel. There is nothing there. Now, what is that? If that was that, what's the address of this building here? Right quick, and there's no trick in it. I just don't know the address. [Someone in the audience says, "1509."] What is it?

All right, suppose that 1507, there was the place and the facilities are in that place and the necessaries are in that place and the personnel are in that place. Now, what is it that's operating over there, Sutton? What is that? Is it a church or home, and if you say it is not the church, is it another organization beside the church? Now, do you think we'll get an answer for that, friends? Oh, I know it's painful, but then, Sutton, answer that. Now, tell me what that is at 1507? If we're just assuming that's the place, and, again, if you have any respect for this audience and its intelligence, tell us whether there could be any orphan children provided for in that way? While you're at it, tell us about whether you can provide a kitchen in the basement for orphan children. Now, he hasn't answered that, friends. It isn't funny, Sutton. It isn't funny. It's pitiful. I feel sorry for you.

Yet, this now, this whole business here, is hypocritical. He doesn't believe a word of this regarding orphan children. He puts this up here and leads you to believe it. He was sailing along smoothly there. "I don't object to an orphan home," he said. "I object to your benevolent organizations. I'm going to show you the right way." All right, what is the right way? "The church supports this, not this. This is what's wrong," he says. "This is what you've got, but this is what I say is right. What have I got here? This is the way that we're taking care," he says, "of orphan children. That's wrong," he says. "This is the right way." Are orphans in that? Did you find out? Do you know? Not from what he said. Sutton, you are the biggest theological coward I ever debated with. I've had over 100 debates, and I never had a man that I couldn't, in some way or another, get him to answer a question. Never in my life. Yet he parades over this country as one of the most courageous men ever; afraid of nobody. Well, I think there are going to be some people who'll remember this tonight here. I tell you there will. I'm not mad at you. I love you. I appreciate you. I just wish you were a little more responsive to questions.

Now, I've charged, friends, that upon him. Now, if that's not

207

so, you know what I'd do? I'd come charging up from there, just, I'd have my say on that. I wouldn't let a fellow talk to me like that. I can't imagine you, Sutton, with the reputation you have over the country. I can't imagine you doing that. Oh, you may do it after I leave here next week, but you aren't doing it here tonight, I'll tell you that. You remember this, ladies and gentlemen. When these fellows crank up these mimeograph machines next week and start telling how Sutton laid it on Woods, you sure laid it on, didn't you? I tell you he sure did. Sutton, I feel sorry for you. I'll give you half a minute of my time to get up here and answer that question: Are there any orphans in that place? How much time have I got? [TOTTY: Well, you've got about seven minutes.]

All right, well now. Oh, the next one is a good one. Now, when I pointed out to him that what we have here is a restored home, he said, "Well, if you can restore the parents, then when you have a widows' home you'd have to restore their husbands. And he, I'm surprised at him, he sidetracked off on trying to be a little funny about some, a man having two wives. Now, it so happens that a widow doesn't have to have a husband in order to subsist, but it does happen that an orphan child has to have food to live. There's a vast difference. A husband is not an essential, but food and shelter, clothing, and so on are essentials for an orphan. But, Sutton, that's a deal that cuts both ways. You say that in James 1:27 it's exclusively individual. All right, then according to him if I argue that the church can do this and that, therefore, it must be supported by the church and that we must have a Board of Directors and that Board of Directors constitute husbands of the widows. What about the individuals? How many widows have you got in your home and how many husbands are you? According to that, the individual would have to become a husband of the widow before we could help the widow. It's strange that these fellows can't see one inch ahead of their noses. I want to know about that. How many husbands are you?

Chart number 9. Now, here's the one, friends. Chart number 9: SOME "HOWS" IN CARING FOR THE NEEDY. I'm looking again, friends. He said the church could do this. The divine organization could put the needy in the private home and pay for the upkeep there. Can it

208

put orphan children in a private home and pay for the upkeep, Sutton? Now, that's what he put that up there for. That was the implication. Friends, he doesn't believe that you can take a dime out of the church treasury to care for orphan children that way. That is, he doesn't think you can take money that way and do it. Be sure and let me know when I have five minutes.

I want to show you something here in answer to some questions. I want to show you the shape that this man is in here. [TOTTY: You have five minutes.]

Alright. I asked him these questions: Since you teach that the church cannot relieve sinners, would you forbid an alien sinner here tonight to: 1. have a drink of water from the fountain in the basement; 2. use the restroom; 3. wet a washcloth from the fountain; 4. provide shelter for accident victims; 5. use the telephone to call a doctor or ambulance; 6. permit use of the church building by homeless victims of a tornado; 7. allow a baby, not old enough to obey the gospel and not related to any member of the church, to use a crib in the nursery?

Now, let's take those one by one. Number 1. Since you teach the church cannot relieve sinners, would you forbid an alien sinner here tonight, number 1, to have a drink of water from the fountain in the basement? Answer: "No, but according to your teaching, that would make a home out of the church." Now, that doesn't have any remote connection with it, but you notice that he said, "no" that he wouldn't forbid it. Now, he believes then, that the church can supply the water for a sinner to drink but he thinks the church can't supply the food for the sinner to eat. He makes a distinction between the food and the drink.

Look at number 2. He believes that the sinner can use the restroom. I asked, "Do you forbid a sinner using the restroom?" No. I asked him, "Do you forbid the sinner to use a wet washcloth from the fountain?" No. "Would you forbid a sinner using the shelter, sinners who are accident victims?" No. "Would you permit the use of the church building for homeless victims of a tornado?" I don't see any, yes. No, he wouldn't forbid that. He would allow that. Number 6: "Would you allow a baby, not old enough to obey the gospel, not related to any member of the church, to use a crib in the nursery?" No, he wouldn't forbid that. Now, you listen. It's all right to supply the materials, buy the materials, and then supply them here for the sinner to use them, but it would be wrong to give them the money to buy the water to drink or the food to eat or the shelter to have. He thinks it would be all right for the church to supply that. Now, you know, friends, that he's preached all over this country that's sinful so to do. He does that. Now, Sutton.

Now, listen here. He's trying to leave the impression over here that I'm not correctly representing him. In every instance he's got the word *no* down here, so he's saying that the church can supply facilities for sinners. Now, get this. He may say, "Oh well, the crib back there in the nursery, that's just for a baby that's brought to church on Sunday." Now, you get this. He believes it's alright to furnish a baby a bed that doesn't need one, but if a baby hasn't got any bed at all, it's sinful to furnish it. That's the conclusion that would follow from that if you can put a crib back there for a baby, babies that have cribs at home, but you can't give a baby a crib who hasn't got one at home or anywhere else. Not any home to put it in. That's the position of this gentleman here tonight. Now, Sutton, you're going to have more than just a silly grin to deal with that tonight.

Now, let's take these so-called contradictions. Friends, anybody that is so disposed can take statements that a man makes who's written for more than a quarter of a century as I have, lift them out of their context, and make them to appear contradictory. I tell you that these are flagrant misrepresentations. Now, as fully as I can do so, I'll show you. "The church is the only charitable organization the Lord authorizes or that is needed to do the work the Lord expects its people to do today." Now, what was I talking about? I was talking about the work of the church. I've told you that it's not the work of the church to supply child care for orphans, that is, to actually engage in it. That's the work of the family, and yet he censors me for an additional organization or different body apart from the church to perform that function. What function? Child care. Now, that's his contradiction. He knew he was misrepresenting me when he did that, and yet, it has a lot to do with the proposition, doesn't it?

Number 2: "The early church operated a home for destitute

210

widows." Yes, I believe that. I believe they supplied the money. I think the word "operate" carries with it that suggestion, and that's the sense in which I mean it. "Well, but didn't the church in Jerusalem operate a needy home? No, sir. There was never a more absurd conclusion drawn than some draw from that." But, what was the context in which that appeared? I was showing that as a distinction between the church and the home. I was saying that a man gives his children an education. I later say that a man has no education at all and a college gave his children the education, and he comes up and says, "Well, you contradicted yourself." Yet, the man supplied the money, the child got the education in the college; those two statements are not contradictory. Honest people don't do things of that kind, friends. They don't array statements of that type.

Number 3: "When we come to the question of benevolence, we still have the same organization, the church." Well, we have the churches in 1 Timothy 5:16. I never questioned that.

Four: "Here are the essential items: the organization apart from the church and operating as a home." What? "Operating as a home." I'm distinguishing between the home and the church.

Number 4. "Stephen was one of the seven selected to dispense food to the Grecian widows. Apostles appointed the seven, not to supervise the feeding of the widows, but to administer the fund out of which their support was taken." Now, those two statements, one of them occurred in 1946 and the other one was made in the *Woods-Cogdill Debate*, are in two entirely different categories. Now, that shows it and that's enough.

Carrol R. Sutton's Sixth Affirmative Speech

Gentlemen moderators, brother Woods, ladies and gentlemen:

I'm glad to appear before you for the next 20 minutes in defense of the proposition as we've been discussing for the last two evenings, counting this evening.

I believe all of us can truly see that in the absence of any authority from the scriptures for these benevolent organizations being built and maintained by churches, that such would not be in harmony with the scriptures. I would like to suggest to you, in the very outset of our study this particular time, that brother Woods has begun playing on your emotions. He'll start suggesting this thing and that thing about matters that are not even pertinent at all to the proposition at hand and try to get your mind away from the proposition. Away from this thing that we're discussing as whether or not churches of Christ may build and maintain these benevolent organizations. You might look for that in the last speech, too.

WOODS: Sutton, if you want to make a speech, you better quit anticipating.

SUTTON: Brother Woods had quite a bit to say about having a lot of debates, and brother Sutton is the weakest, or something to that effect, that he's ever met. It just so happens that I've heard brother Woods, or read a number of debates that he's had, and in each one of them…

WOODS: Brother Sutton, you're misrepresenting me. I never said you were the weakest. I said that you were the most difficult to get to answer questions. I've met one or two that was even weaker than you are.

SUTTON: Alright, thank you.

WOODS: Well, now, why don't you tell the truth? There's a reason, friends. He's got a little statement that he wants to soften the effects of my next speech, and I know all the signs. Now, Sutton, get on the subject.

SUTTON: Alright, if you remember when I said that he said that I was the weakest, or I said something to that effect. I wasn't quoting him, but that's what if amounted to, because last evening he even suggested that when a person thought somebody else was confused that sometimes that the person who thought that was the only one that was confused, or something of that effect. That's why that I said what I did. You be the judge in the matter. I might mention, also, the fact that in nearly every debate he's ever had that I've read after him, that he says the man that he meets is the weakest he's ever met.

Time and time again, but, of course, you can see why.

Well then, concerning the Tipton Home, he says, and he said this several times about the elders of the congregation may operate a home, but he says they're not operating it as elders; that they're doing it as trustees and not as elders at all. And, of course, he specifically mentioned Tipton last evening. There's at least 10 or 11 of the orphanages or homes for the aged that are operated by churches under the oversight of the elders, and in each one of those cases that I'm going to mention, the elders say that they're doing that as elders. The Children's Home in Lubbock, the Maude Carpenter Children's Home, the Tipton Home, the Sunny Glen Home, Childhaven for Children, Turley Home, and so forth, there's about six or seven of them there. Notice, for example, that we have a booklet here from Maude Carpenter Children's Home, and it says this on page 11: "The home is owned and operated by the Riverside church of Christ. It is under the supervision of the elders and the property is held by the elders as trustees, the same as the church building and preacher's home." In the same category as the preacher's home. Now, that's what they said.

From the Children's Home of Lubbock, from the superintendent of it, John B. White, we have this: "The Children's Home is under the supervision of the elders of the Broadway church of Christ here. These elders supervise this work in the same way that they do works of edification and evangelism. The Children's Home of Lubbock is not a separate organization from the church to any greater extent than is our Sunday morning Bible classes." That's what they had to say about it.

The Tipton Home. We have this quotation from the letter from the superintendent. "The Tipton Home is under the local elders of the Tipton church of Christ. They're over it in the same sense as the Bible classes in that they are the overseers of all the religious activities of the church."

We have from the Sunny Glen Home this: "The Sunny Glen Home is under the elders of the San Bonita church of Christ. The elders are over this work in the same sense that they're over the Bible classes and other phases of the work of that congregation. This is one phase of their benevolent work. The Sunny Glen Home is not an institution that is separate and apart from the church but is one phase of the work of the church."

Then from *Childhaven for Children*, the superintendent wrote this, March 2, 1962: "The Home is the work of the Meadowbrook church of Christ under its elders."

From Turley Children's Home superintendent, October 2, 1961, that he says that "I feel that the elders as elders can oversee the work of the church and that it consists of providing for homeless children."

We could read statement after statement, but that suffices to show that he's not representing these men as they represent themselves, and they're the superintendents. He says, "It can't be done." They say they are doing it. You be the judge in the matter.

Then last evening, brother Woods says, "Now, these fellows condemn us for having fellowship kitchens, yet he admits such now." That isn't so, brother Woods. I haven't admitted that churches of Christ may operate kitchens for fun, frolic, and fellowship, so-called. I'm asking for proof of it when he comes up here. I'm asking him for the proof since he believes that churches of Christ may operate fellowship kitchens. For the proof in the word of God that such may be done. I don't believe they can do it, brother Woods.

WOODS: Is that in the proposition?

SUTTON: No, but you introduced it.

WOODS: You sure of that?

SUTTON: Yes, sir. The tape will show it.

Then also, last evening, brother Woods said that the church can't sell or convey property without trustees. You know, he contended the second evening that the church cannot own property without trustees after we produced two copies of the deeds of some congregations. Then, brother Woods, instead of admitting he was wrong about it, because here are some that do own it without trustees, he came back and said, "Well, they can't sell it." Now, brother Woods, we were discussing whether or not they could own it. The second night you said they couldn't own it, but now, he says they can own it, evidently, but he hasn't apologized for saying they can't. If he knew nearly as much about the law as he lets on like he does, he'd know they

214

can sell it, too. Produce the statute that shows they can't sell it, brother Woods.

Then, last evening, he said, "I despise and detest the doctrine of discrimination against sinners." Well, where is the passage of scripture, brother Woods, where God has promised to provide for sinners? Matthew 6:33 shows that God will provide for His children, those who seek Christ's kingdom first. I wonder if God is discriminating against sinners when he lets sinners get on the left hand in the judgment and the righteous on the right hand? Is that discrimination? Do you detest that?

Then he said, "Sutton said the widows in Acts 6 was just widows, and that's all that was receiving assistance. Widows were not homes." Now, "that shows how little the fellow knows about the text" himself. He said that last evening. He's going to prove that there were homes that were helped in Acts 6. He went to Acts 2, he went to Acts 4, and never did even consider Acts 6, and I'd said, "Acts 6." That's a classic example of misrepresentation. Acts 6 says neglected widows.

Also, brother Woods said he's paralleled the trustees of the church property, the benevolent organizations. I wonder if he's saying, by that, that these benevolent organizations hold in trust property for the church just like the trustees hold in trust property for the church. If not, he doesn't have a parallel in it. It isn't parallel at all because these trustees of church buildings simply hold in trust the property for the church. They have no control over any work of the church, but these benevolent organizations, the Board of Directors, has all of the oversight, all of the control over all the expenditures of the money, and all the work involved in it. There's a vast difference. All of us can see it. Now, I believe even brother Woods can.

Then brother Woods said this evening that, "We interrupt only when Sutton misrepresents." You notice, friends, in my first speech he didn't interrupt me a time, I don't believe. That means everything I said was right, according to brother Woods.

WOODS: Brother Sutton, that doesn't mean anything of the kind.

SUTTON: If not, why not?

WOODS: As long as you were making your affirmative speech, the audience knew that you were trying to set out proof of your proposition. When you started replying to me, you started telling them what I meant and what I said, and that's when you started misrepresenting me. Go ahead.

SUTTON: It still stands. He says that, "When he tells the truth, we don't interrupt but if he doesn't, we will interrupt." So, he didn't interrupt me, so it must have been the truth.

WOODS: If I did, I'd interrupt you every 30 seconds.

SUTTON: Well, if you don't, you falsified about it. You said you did.

TOTTY: Point of order, moderator. Saying he falsified it is pretty strong language. Now, brother Woods didn't say that. He said when you misrepresent him, he interrupted you. That's what he said, He didn't say when you were speaking the truth he doesn't interrupt you. He said when you misrepresent him, he does. That's what he said. Now, that's what he said.

SUTTON: Can I go ahead with it? Are you through?

WOODS: You mean may or can, which one?

SUTTON: Either one.

Now, with respect to the chart that I had on COMMANDS: GENERIC AND SPECIFIC, chart number 1, brother Woods didn't answer the argument I made on it. I showed how God specified the church to evangelize, edify, and relieve, and brother Woods came back and says, "Is the word 'relieve' specific?" You know, he says that's not a specific term but a generic term. Brother Woods, the church in 1 Timothy 5 is a specific term. That's what I said was specific, was the word 'church.' He tried to get you away, your thinking away, from the fact that God specified the church, a specific organization, by asking, "Is the word 'relieve' generic or specific?"

No, I'm not saying that the word relieve is specific, but I'm saying that the organization that is to do the relieving is specific, the church. So, he misrepresented that. Incidentally, that wasn't even the issue at all as far as the relieving itself but the organization. Can churches of Christ build and maintain benevolent organizations, even homes for the aged?

Then he had quite a bit to say, "Where is the bachelor on here?" Well, I could ask him, if I wanted to get off on all of that, where

216

is the old man on here? That wouldn't prove a thing, would it? That wouldn't prove a thing. I know what Paul said. Paul simply showed here in 1 Timothy 5, there were widows indeed. Acts 6 said neglected widows. 1 Corinthians 16:1 says the saints, "collection for the saints." Acts 11 shows brethren in need. There's a lot of passages that could be given.

Then he talked about there being hypocrisy on the chart. If it is, brother Woods, I wonder where it is. I've got scriptures for every one of these things here and right here, and I'm not contending for this. Where is the hypocrisy involved? Is it in the scriptures? That's what I read.

Then with respect to chart number 2: COMMANDS, AIDS, OR ADDITIONS, he says, "Show how it's to be done." Well, I've already shown that it's not a matter of 'how' but organization involved. Are his benevolent organizations, such as those homes for the aged are, additions to the word of God because they're another kind of organization? They're human organizations and the church being a divine organization.

Then chart number 3 about the Tennessee Orphan Home benevolent society. He read from the Kentucky minimum standards and he says, "Now, Sutton is right. Even if he's right or not right, you still have to have a Board there." Now, I asked brother Woods last evening, I believe, to produce the stature that required the church to set up a separate organization from the church to do its work. His minimum standards doesn't require that. He's just talking about minimum standards. He didn't quote any stature that shows that the church must set up a separate corporation or institution that it, in turn, might do the work of the church. But, if it does, and he's conformed to it like he said he did, then he does have a separate organization, a Board, that, in turn, provides the home. That's what I've been showing that he had all of the time. Thank you, brother Woods.

Then on chart number 20 ... chart number 4 first of all: IS "BOLES ORPHAN HOME" A BENEVOLENT SOCIETY?

He talked a little bit about it but didn't mention the question on the bottom of the chart. He says this isn't right. This isn't a benevolent society, and I say if it's not one, what would it take to make one? He didn't mention that. That is a benevolent organization, friends. A benevolent society. It's not a family, it's not a church, it's not a home. It's a Board of Directors separate and apart from the family, separate and apart from the church, to which churches send funds that it, in turn, might provide for the needy. He didn't answer the argument on that one, either.

Chart number 20. That says, PLEASE CONSIDER THESE PASSAGES VERY CAREFULLY. He said, "Did they give it to the family to spend?" He says, we say, "Yes, they gave it to the family here." But, you know, brother Woods said the other night that what was actually involved was that they gave it to the individual members of the family. I have the quotation here, directly from the tape. "I'm not going to allow brother Sutton to quibble over whether the contribution is to the family organization, let it be to the members of the family, that's all right with me. That's what it is actually." Yet, he says that's not what it is now. He says it was the homes or families, but the other night he said, the first night, that it really was individuals, and that's what I've said all of the time.

Then on chart number 15. He said that the church is not an adoption agency, but he missed the point entirely. These human organizations that brother Woods is defending, that I read off a while ago, which includes Tennessee Orphan Home, is an adoption agency. Do you deny that, brother Woods? If you do, I'll produce the proof of it. So then, here's one. In fact, here's five that are adoption agencies, and brother Woods says that even Christians, and he claims these are Christians that make up these boards, that even Christians, by support of the church, cannot serve as an adoption agency. No authority in the scriptures, yet he's defending that which he says there's no authority for. It stands untouched. I didn't say the church was serving as an adoption agency. I said these institutions he's defending are, and he says that they are comprised of Christians, and Christians, by support of the church, cannot serve as an adoption agency. That rules all of those out, yet he's defending in his proposition the Tennessee Orphan Home which is one of them. That is, an adoption agency. I'm asking him to give up that which he says is not authorized in the scriptures. That agrees with my proposition.

218

Then brother Woods says, "Why is Sutton afraid to answer: Can the church care for orphans?" If he thinks I'm very much afraid to, I said I'd be glad to sign up with him and discuss that particular phase of the question. We'll see whether or not he's anxious to. We might do that in Huntsville, Alabama if he'd like to, or even let him come back here or let him stay here a few nights and we'll do it.

Then he says, "Now, can the church support an orphan home, and he means by that a benevolent organization, and that's what we're discussing, brother Woods. Why, no. We've shown that isn't right. No authority for it, and yet, the very first night he said that the money in Acts 6 went to the individual members rather than the family itself. So, he agrees with me on that particular point.

Then on chart number 7: WHERE WILL MY OPPONENT DRAW THE LINE? He talked about the first two or three things. He didn't answer it at all. He just talked a little bit about it, and then he said, "Well now, talking about the hospital or this thing and that thing," he'd say. Talk about the first two or three here and he said, "Why, no. He's trying to get me supporting or defending these organizations that would involve in profit making and so forth." But he says, what about these that aren't profit making things? Well, brother Woods, these missionary societies aren't set up to make profits. They're non-profit corporations. Would you support them? They're non-profit corporations. Would you let the church build and maintain them?

Then he asked about this one individual widow or woman. I believe he said widow, at least a saint, and is cared for. "What if there's a hundred of them put in a room and nurses employed to care for them?" Well, brother Woods, you don't have benevolent organizations involved there such as Tennessee Orphan Home! According to him, we'd have to have this human organization here that provides this thing, and churches send to that to provide this. He doesn't have that pictured, though. We won't let him get away from it. He doesn't describe here what he is defending, not at all.

Then with respect to the restored home argument, he says, "Here's the family. It is broken down and then it's restored." It just happens that brother Woods says something about restoring the widow's home, too. He said tonight, of course, "She doesn't have to have a husband," and that "Sutton thinks she has to have a husband" and "is he the husband over some widows?" No, but if I believed what brother Woods said, I'd believe that. Here's what he had to say about it. In the ***Woods-Cogdill Debate***, on page 55: "In 1 Timothy 5:16, the apostle Paul makes obligatory upon the church to supply the needs of the destitute widow. Whatever that widow had before and lost must be restored." She lost her husband, and brother Woods says, "Whatever she lost must be restored." He's the one that does believe in the restoration of the husband. He can't get around that unless he apologizes for what he said on page 55 of the ***Woods-Cogdill Debate***. Thank you, brother Woods. That's not my problem, that's yours.

Incidentally, I want us to notice just a thing or two about the worth of this human organization that's called Boles Orphan Home. He tries to bring it under church support. We showed that the other night, and we even read a letter from the superintendent, that in 1955 the superintendent said that they had about 2,000 acres of land and fixed assets worth $706,000. Yet, brother Woods is saying they're needy, that churches ought to send contributions to the needy. $706,000. They've got oil wells operating. They've got gas wells. They've got dairies and farms and hospitals and schools. One organization, Boles Orphan Home, operates a farm, a dairy, gas well, oil wells, hospitals (one hospital to say the least), two homes, and then talks about destitute people being helped. No, I'm not, brother Woods. I'm opposing churches of Christ building and maintaining benevolent organizations such as Tennessee Orphan Home, Boles Home, etc.

Then with respect to the chart number 11: MISSIONARY AND BENEVOLENT SOCIETIES PARALLEL. He said, "According to brother Sutton's logic, that would prove that brother Sutton is a monkey." That isn't so, brother Woods. I may look like one, but that won't prove it. Now, here's the difference in it, friends. He said, "Brother Sutton's trying to claim identity." That isn't so. I said these things are parallel. I didn't say identical. If they were identical they wouldn't be benevolent and missionary societies. They'd just be the same thing, but they're parallel. They're alike in essential features and, therefore, they either stand or fall together. Now, let me show you, for example. Here's a big difference. Here's one line and here's another line. They're parallel lines. Are they identical? No, sir, but they're parallel, and the same thing that makes the missionary societies wrong would make these benevolent organizations wrong because they're alike in those essential features. He simply quibbled on that. He got a laugh out of it, but he's here for seriousness and for truth.

Then, brother Woods said concerning his contradiction chart [Chart Number 17]. He says, "You know those who are honest don't do things like that." Well, it just happens he's done the same thing in other debates he's had. For example, in the *Cogdill-Woods Debate* in Birmingham, he brought up about 16 or 17 things he said brother Cogdill was inconsistent in, and yet, people were following him in his inconsistencies. So, therefore, according to his logic, he's not honest. I'm just saying, according to his logic. But I want all of you to keep in mind that brother Woods for four nights now has contended that it is in harmony with the scriptures for churches of Christ to build and maintain benevolent organizations. Yet, he hasn't produced one scripture that shows that churches may do that in harmony with the scriptures. Think for yourselves, study your Bibles, and accept what's revealed therein. Thank you.

Guy N. Woods' Sixth Negative Speech

Gentlemen moderators, brother Sutton, ladies, and gentlemen:

I'm now before you for the final 20 minutes of this discussion, and I hope that this time will pass rapidly and pleasantly for you.

May I say first of all, and brother Sutton told us, that the problem of being a pig killer is not his. He asked me the other night if the care of orphans is not parallel, or the care of the needy is not parallel, to the matter of operating the Sunday school, Bible school. I pointed out that this difference would exist, that you couldn't give a child in the Bible school a pig scripturally just because he was a part of the Bible school. The implication being that you could give an orphan child a pig. I pointed out that according to his position, that since he says the church can perform every need of the needy, that then he'd have to have a pig killer. He tells me tonight that's not his problem, it's mine. I found that out. I've found out that he doesn't have any problems regarding pig killers for orphan children because he's not going to give any orphan children any pigs. So, since he's not going to give them any pigs, there won't be any pigs to be killed. That's very clear from what he said.

He told us that the orphan homes are not in the proposition, and yet, he spend five minutes of his time in the outset telling you about the homes at Wichita, and Tipton, Lubbock, and Sunny Glen, and Turley.

I said, a night or two ago, I had no objection to elders overseeing a home. In fact, they have to oversee their private homes. But that in so doing they were not performing the functions of elders. These various publications specify, even including Tipton and Sunny Glen and Turley, and I can produce then if he wants them, specify that the elders of the church are the trustees of the home. I accept that. I believe that to be scriptural. All of that, of course, according to him, not on the matter.

Now, he said that I was classifying what he said about the kitchen with fellowship kitchens. I haven't said a word about fellowship kitchens. Not a word. Never mentioned the word "fellowship" in connection with the kitchen. I have simply called attention to the fact that, according to his position, the church could operate a kitchen. Now, up until now, he's preached against all such, and especially in the meeting house. Even forbidding little girls who are attending a vacation Bible school eating their cookies in the basement. They had to go outside of the building to eat them. Now, I charged that, and he didn't deny it. Yet, he now, comes up when he gets in it tight and says, "Well, I believe that you could have a kitchen in the basement under some circumstances." Now, he doesn't believe that. The truth of the business is he doesn't believe the church could have a kitchen in the basement. How many of you—How many congregations in fellowship with you, have got kitchens in the basement? Name one

222

that's providing for the needy that way. Just name one. Now, he says that he thinks it's all right, but tell me one. Give me the address of one, Sutton. You don't know one, do you? No, you don't. You know you fellows would oppose it with all the strength you've got. You know that. Tell me the address of just one that's practicing it like you say it could be. He knows there isn't any, and he would oppose it, and he's already preached against it.

He said, "Show where God"—I think he miss—I think he didn't intend to say this, and I'm not going to charge it upon him unless he wishes to avow it. "Show where God ever provided for sinners." I feel sure he meant 'show scripture for the church providing.' I think that's what he must have meant, because surely he thinks that God provides for sinners since the text tells us that God "sends the rain on the just and the unjust." Now, if I were as unfair as you are, Sutton, I'd charge that upon you and tell you there's a good example of these.... Brethren, I don't do that. I don't have to. I'm thankful that I don't have to resort to such tactics. But if I followed your method, I would, because you said it. I don't think that's what you intended, and so I'm going to be more charitable than you are. One that has the truth can afford to be.

Now, he says, "If I had your position, I might do worse than you are." I suspect I would. Now, he says, "Woods is trying to parallel the trustees of the church and the trustees of an orphan home." No, I wasn't doing anything of the kind. I think there's a difference between a church and a home, but the parallel is in the fact inasmuch as there is this organization, which he alleges between the two, if he objects to trustees between the members and the church building or the church and the church building, but rejects the idea of trustees between the church and the home, now, wherein is the difference? I didn't say that they're the same. They're not the same. The church is not the same as the home and the home is not the same as the church. That wasn't my argument. Here is the argument. He accepts this, rejects this. He says this puts another organization between the church and the home, but this doesn't put another organization between the church and the preacher's home or the church building. Now, he's just as inconsistent on that as he is on 100 other things.

Now, let's have the first chart he introduced. Did you have a number? No, he didn't give me any number. He said, "Woods misapplied his argument here." And I had no intention of misapplying it. I just take it like he says he intended it. As a matter of fact, he didn't place any emphasis on that phase of it until in his last speech. Now, I have no desire to misrepresent him. He says, "What I mean is that the idea of the church is specific. The church, the local congregation, is specific. In doing what? In relieving the needy." Now, if that be true, if that has any merit al all, that is the argument? There isn't but one organization that can do 1 Timothy 5:16 and Acts 6:1-6. What is that? That's the church. Do what? Relieve. What is the only organization? The church. Therefore, the home, the family, can't relieve the needy. If it can and it's not the organization, it's the only organization that can relieve. If the family can do this, then this is not specific, it's generic. I believe that it's generic. I believe that the organization is generic. That in the relieving, that both the family and the church can do it.

All right, let's have his "AIDS AND ADDITIONS" chart now. Now again, friends, observe this. He hasn't at any time replied to anything that I said about this. Not at any time has he made any remote reference to what I said about this. I called your attention to the fact that our argument is that it's not an aid or an addition that we're defending. Why didn't he pay some attention to that? No reference to it at all.

You notice that he didn't reply either to my charge that he's hypocritical in making it appear that he believes that the way that children can be provide for is by the church. He doesn't believe that. He's let this debate go, so far as his part of it is concerned. He'll tell you next week on the radio about it. He'll crank up his mimeograph machine, and he'll put out sheet after sheet on the subject. He'll tell you all about it then, after Woods is gone, but he wouldn't tell it here tonight. Sutton, I'm disappointed and surprised in you. I had more confidence in the courage of your conviction than you've evidenced.

He's not interested in the law of the land. I thought it was quite symbolic in the fact that he threw it down on the floor. Well, sometimes people get in trouble when they flaunt the law, brother Sutton. I would suggest to you that there's some danger involved in doing that. Of course, you're not going to get in trouble having the church take care of orphans though, are you? Because you're not going to do any of it. There was something symbolic about it.

Now then, he says with reference to this adoption chart here. Brother Sutton is the fellow that needs to tell us if the church can serve as an adoption agency. As a matter of fact, Sutton, do you believe it can? Can the church serve as an adoption agency? I know a church that had some that tried to. You remember that article in the **Guardian** in which they had children they were trying to get off of the hands of the elders down at Blytheville? Do you remember that? Now, the only organization that's qualified and that's authorized to take care of children had them, but they made a pitiful appeal, too, regarding some family come and take these children off our hands, trying to get them out of God's organization into another. Now, that was one church that was willing to adopt them. I tell you that's a good way to let these brethren decide if they believe in adopting them. Just get some orphan children on their hands.

He wants to know about another debate. Sutton, if I didn't have anything else to do, I don't know of anything I'd enjoy more than tormenting you about every other week during the year. I don't. I tell you that so far as that's concerned, I ... just any time that the brethren want me to meet you and debate, I'll be delighted to do so. One place that's already indicated is over here in Indianapolis, and I'd be glad to negotiate with you as soon as you get some representation over there. Be delighted to do so. Just delighted. So far as that's concerned, I'm ready to debate any time my brethren want me to.

But, now, that chart that's got the "Ways," some of the "Hows" of doing it, let's have it up here, please. That's not up here, it's over here. [TOTTY: You have about ten minutes.]

Okay, thank you. It's the one, you know, where he says it would be all right to put them in a private home. I want to know about this address over here that I had, 1507. Now, Sutton, why didn't you say something about that? It's over here. You saw it on that side.

SUTTON: I believe it's over here, brother Woods.

WOODS: Over here, on this side. I know where it is. No, that isn't it. It's over here. These fellows are confused. They don't know their left from their right. That's not what I'm looking for; I'm looking for one over here the whole time. I know where the chart is. Let me tell you, it's the one—don't you know, I came over here and said, "Now, right over here. Suppose the address there is over here, 1507." I'm not trying to make fun of you, sir. I don't want you to think that at all. I just—it's on this side, though, brethren. It is. Well, I'm sorry. I don't know the number. What is it, brethren? What was the number of it?

TOTTY: I don't know the number, but it's the one that has the ...

WOODS: Let's help him find it. Let's help him find it. There it is. Isn't that it? Brother Sutton, it's the one that in which you said, "Now, I'll show you some of the 'hows' by which it can be done." Well, that isn't the one. Here it is, right here. That's not it. What about this? That's it. I told you it was over here. I don't make statements I can't prove. There it is. I knew which side it was on. All right, here it is.

I said, "Now, brother Sutton, tell me if this place right here had its address at 1507 over here, would it be a church or would it be a home?" Which would it be? Would you tell me now, brother Sutton? Sutton, aside from all the point involved, just tell us tonight, what would that be? Would that be a church or a home? Why don't you tell us? Brother Holt, I appeal to you as his moderator, tell him to answer my question. Now, you're not debating at all. You're the moderator. You ought to be able to think clear ahead of yourself.

TOTTY: Brother Woods, that's on the proposition, too.

WOODS: That's it. This is his chart here. He says this is the way it's being done here. That's the right way. That's one of the "hows." I've even got the address of it over here. I'm trying to find out what it is. Is it a church or is it a home? Sutton, what is it? Any of you fellows know? What about it? Don't you want to go to Heaven? Don't you want to go to Heaven? I don't see how you think you'll go to Heaven and deal with me like you are here tonight. Now, I tell you, ladies and gentlemen, the reason he won't answer that question is, he knows he will absolutely submerge himself in such an answer. Well, we all know that it's not the church because you already got the church. When you provide something else, when this provides this, obviously,

226

and this is already existing, and this hasn't existed until you provided it, that's surely not this. It surely isn't when you already got the church, and besides you don't have to have the church licensed. Besides that, the address of the church building is not 1507, it's 15-0-what, 9. I'm talking about 1507.

He said that I was dishonest with Roy Cogdill because I brought up contradictions. I didn't say you were dishonest in trying to show contradictions. If you can show contradictions, that's not dishonesty. The dishonesty was in misrepresenting the statements. There's where it was. Oh, show all you can, if you can. You'd have to do better than you've done.

He says the homes are rich institutions. He mentioned that Boles Home had over $706,000 assets. May I point out to you that they're got over 300, or approximately 300 children. It fluctuates, and that they keep ahead about supplies for about two months. That is, they're operating capital is usually about two months ahead. I'm glad to know that I have a little more than two months ahead to eat. I don't think that's unreasonable for people to have at least two months ahead. It costs approximately $60 a month per child to keep those children in Boles Home. I don't think that's an unreasonable amount of money, and it so happens that at least 10 or 15 of those dollars do not come out of church treasuries, either. They come as a result of contributions, in many instances, from people who are not even members of the church. I don't claim that those homes are perfect institutions. I don't think there's any institution that is comparable to the private Christian home, but we're not discussing that. We're talking about the places for children who have no home and for whom these homes are provided.

I might tell you, I've referred to it before, that there are some 25 of these homes today operating. I wish we had more than that. There are approximately 2500 children being provided for in these homes. These homes are not places where people can put their children and escape responsibility, as is sometimes claimed. They're simply places for children that have nowhere else to go. I could give you example after example along that line. Sometimes people say, "Well, why not adopt them? Aren't there lots of homes that would like to have these children?" I'm sure there are lots of homes that would like to have children, but, in most instances, not the children that are in these homes. As a matter of fact, most of them are children that come from delinquent homes. In most instances, they would not be available for adoption anyway. I just mention an example of a little boy whose father hired a man to put him in an automobile and drive him out into another state, 400 miles away, push him out of the car, and drive off and leave him. Now, that little fellow became a ward of the court. If there hadn't been a place like Tipton, then he would have been placed in a Catholic or denominational home. But as a result of the fact that somebody had sufficient interest in that little fellow, he was picked up, and through the direction and jurisdiction of the court, placed in Tipton Home where they'll raise him up as a fine young man and, perhaps, make a gospel preacher out of him.

Some time ago, brother Brock told me about a family that he picked up, who were living out on the dump of the city; that is, at the garbage dump and living off of the stuff hauled out there. He picked these children up and he carried them, started with them, down to Childhaven. One of the boys, on the way down there, was so vicious and mean that he had to stop the car and stop by the side of the road and give him a spanking. Yes, they have a system by which they can spank them. He stopped on the side of the road, taking them to Childhaven, and gave him a spanking. He said that, for a few days, this boy would curse his food instead of being willing to bow his head. He never saw a more vicious young fellow. But as a result of the influence that they wielded upon them, that young fellow is now developing into a gospel preacher. I heard him step up on a box, though he was this little fellow, and preach a remarkable sermon. I heard many others from similar homes do exactly the same thing. I rejoice in that. I'd like to tell you this: That the first gospel sermon that was preached over a nationwide hookup was preached by a boy from Boles Home. You'll be interested in knowing that the first gospel sermon that was preached in Germany after the war was preached by a boy from Boles Home.

I'd like to tell you this further. Of all the many thousands of children that have gone through the doors of Boles Home in its existence, of those who graduated from high school there, only three left there who were not members of the church when they left. And two of those went back and were baptized there. So, of all the thousands of children that have fallen under the influence of Boles Home, there has just been one that left there and did not obey the gospel of Christ.

I'm not offering that in proof of their scripturalness, I've already established that. I'm offering that in proof of the fact that they're doing a work that's remarkable in its nature, that deserves the support and encouragement of all good people, and even though a congregation cannot sent much, we ought to send what we can as an evidence of the fact that we believe in doing the Lord's work in the Lord's way.

Such men as Sutton, instead of supporting the Lord's way, are themselves seeking to destroy. You have evidence of it right here. This congregation is not more than half its former size. I can give you example after example all over the country. Take 10th and Francis in Oklahoma City. There is an example of a congregation that had, used to have, hundreds of people in its membership, who used to have perhaps 600 or 700 in Bible study. Their contribution was more than $1000 a Sunday. They espoused this doctrine. They're now having slightly more than 200 people in Bible study. I can give you case after case after case. I think it's tragic that young men who have obvious ability, as do brother Sutton and others, and who could mean much for the cause of Christ, have actually become church troublers and church dividers who are going over the country to the dedicated purpose of trying to destroy the Lord's work instead of helping it. I protest such. But as long as they do, they must be repudiated and opposed.

I think it's tragic that a man like brother Sutton, who went to Freed-Hardeman College and who got his ability largely from that school, has now turned upon it, and upon his former teachers, and upon his former friends, and now fights that which he formerly objected ... or accepted. Objects to that which he formerly accepted. I think that's tragic, but he's a grown man, and he'll answer for that in the judgment. But don't let him lead you, too, into the judgment unprepared by his false teaching. Before you retire tonight, and in your reflections upon this debate, you remember that Sutton dodged and evaded. That he resorted to hypocritical efforts and has made no attempt whatsoever to answer the questions that I have submitted to him. You know the reason. It's simply because he can't.

Now, let me appeal to you as Christians, as members of the body of Christ, to recognize the fact that we're all rapid passengers from time to eternity. We're all beating a rapid march to the eternal shore. One of these days, it'll be very soon for some, it can't be long for any, the things that now claim your attention will fade into insignificance. It'll not be very important what kind of house you lived in here or what kind of business or profession you followed or what kind of clothes you wore or automobile you drove. Such things will have faded into insignificance. But there will loom up with vast importance this question: Are you ready for judgment? That's a question that all of you will need to answer. I thank you.

TOTTY: I want to thank all these people in this—not in this congregation because they didn't do it—but all these good people around in Peoria who have invited me out and shown me such a good time here. I thank you every one for that. Then, to this congregation, who repeatedly threw it in our faces that they're furnishing the house and the parking lot for us and that, therefore, we'd have to do what they said. They didn't say that tonight, but before tonight. We've been repeatedly told that this was their house and that the parking lot was their lot. I hope they will present me a bill tonight, so I can pay for my car being parked on the lot and if any damages has been done the house. Now, I did take one drink of water out of the fountain, I'd be glad to pay for that. I just want a receipt after I pay it. That will be fair enough, won't it, brother Sutton? I do not want to impose upon anybody. I've never been treated like that by any other church, and I want to pay my way because I'm leaving immediately after it's over.

Now, concerning the debate. Brother Sutton has twice challenged for debate. We'll be glad to have him come to Garfield Heights in Indianapolis, or anybody else of his persuasion, who can get endorsement from one of the churches: Belmont or Lafayette Heights (and the preachers from both of them are here tonight). Or any other church of his persuasion in Marion County. Now, we'll have you over there, and we'll treat you nice. I'll even buy your lunch every day for you. We want you to come. Will you do that? Will you do that? This is an invitation. You challenged us. Brother Woods will meet you there. Now, will you do that? If you won't go there, will you go to Clearwater, Florida? We're invited there for debate if they can get somebody. If you won't go to Clearwater, will you go to Tampa? We're invited there. Now, you see how much his challenge meant. He won't go to either one of these places. The truth of the matter is that he can't get any endorsement in Indianapolis. If he hadn't put that in the proposition that brother Woods would have to have backing, we'd take him without any endorsement. Now, there's the invitation. Will you accept it? Any of you men? So, I can go home now. Don't say, "Well, you were doing that without the elders." No, the elders gave him a letter a year or more ago. He's had that letter for two years. He's welcome there any time one of you fellows want to debate. Now, what about it? Will you try to get some endorsement over there? Will you try it at Clearwater? Will you try it at Tampa? We're not afraid of you, brother Sutton. No, sir. This audience knows that.

Now, I just want to clear that up to show you that all that was so much water over the dam or under the fence, either one you want to put it. We'll meet him or any other man on earth at Garfield Heights. We'll furnish the lot to park his car. We'll furnish the house, and we'll not throw it into his face every time we get in the pulpit.

Again, let me thank you good people when you come to Indianapolis, and that includes those who have thrown it up to me parking my car out there, you come to my home at Indianapolis any time you want to. Don't all of you come at the same time. I'd be glad to be courteous to you and show you a good time if I can. To you, my brethren, who have been so courteous to me, I certainly am indebted to you.

HOLT: Brother Woods, do you want to make an announcement or anything?

WOODS: Just this word, now. Of course, the debate's over. I have nothing more to say with reference to that, at least, so far as the arguments and the matters stated along that line. Just to say again that I'm grateful to those who have backed me in this discussion. I've enjoyed my association with the Keplingers and am grateful to them for their hospitality. I've enjoyed the visits that I had in the homes of the people who invited me. I wish I could have accepted the others. I'm not mad at anybody. I feel very kindly toward all. I have no disposition whatever to carry rancor in my heart at all. If you're interested in my immediate plans, on this Lord's day I shall begin a meeting in Memphis with one of the congregations there. Then on to southern Alabama for another one, and then to a debate down there with a Baptist preacher, and then on and on for nearly 200 meetings that I have scheduled ahead at present. I thank you.

HOLT: You have sat and listened, and we have allowed, of course, as we listened, a statement. I think it ought to be clear because the congregation here is not in a position to speak before those who are visiting. Of course, knowing the congregation here, I preached in a meeting while in the basement. Since that time, I have been here on different occasions since the building's been put up. I have been in lots of places and preached with a lot of congregations and meetings, and I never have in one place been with a group of people who wanted to be fairer nor work harder, as I believe, for the cause of Christ. Oh, it was suggested that they made a decision before the discussion started, and since they were as in time past had been furnishing, when they did, the facilities for other discussions, they were not discriminating in this case anymore than in any other cases. That was their judgment. They don't want any pay for any parking of anybody's car and neither do they want any pay. In fact, they (I imagine) as individuals would be glad to have paid some more to come because they wanted everybody to come. I think that's only fair to say that on their behalf. I never have been here what I've been helped, from the first meeting that I preached in the basement to every time that I visited them.

Now, we're going to ask that maybe brother Sutton has some announcements, as brother Woods had a statement. Then I'll have just another thing or two to say.

SUTTON: I'd like to express my personal appreciation to brother Woods for his having come and been with us for these past four nights in these discussions. I'd like also to express my appreciation to each one of you who have come any or all of the times that you have. I thoroughly enjoyed the discussion, and I hope there can be more of them. I would like to say, first of all, before I mention the discussion further, the fact that in the morning there will be services here. Brother Earl Robertson from Indianapolis will be preaching at 10:00 a.m., and then tomorrow evening beginning, brother Holt will be preaching for a few nights and each morning at 10:00.

I would like to mention also the fact that brother Hiram Hutto was supposed to come and moderate for me during this debate. It had been planned for several months that he come, and also he'd been scheduled to hold a meeting here. Due to the fact that brother Hutto could not come, I learned only a little over a week ago that brother Hutto was sick and unable to come, and then at the last minute nearly we called brother Holt, and that's why that he's here. We do appreciate very much brother Holt's coming and doing such a good job in the capacity of moderator and is willing to preach for us for the next few evenings.

I would like to mention with respect to the discussions in the future that, if brother Totty would allow me to follow the procedure that he says that he follows, then I'll be glad to accommodate brother Woods in Garfield Heights building in Indianapolis or anywhere else in the country. Brother Totty says that he doesn't ask for endorsement. If people wants him to come, they ask him. If they don't ask him, he doesn't ask for endorsement. Therefore, if he doesn't require me to ask for endorsement, I'll be glad to come to Garfield Heights and meet brother Woods in debate beginning next Monday night, or three months from now, six months, twelve months, two years, three years, whatever it may be, if the Lord's willing to spare. But I would like to say this. If there should be a question over endorsement, I'd like to invite brother Woods, and I believe the congregation here will stand with me in this because of past decisions, to come back here and let us have at least another four-nights' discussion.

APPENDIX

Carrol Ray Sutton's Charts

- Several of brother Sutton's charts from 1962 were not located for inclusion in this Appendix. If any other charts are later found, they will be added in a future edition of this book.

- Brother Woods did not use the charts he had used in previous debates; therefore, none of his are included in this Appendix.

Wall Chart A

Guy N. Woods In 1939

"THE TENDENCY TOWARD INSTITUTIONALISM. The ship of Zion has floundered more than once on the sandbar of institutionalism. The tendency to organize is a characteristic of the age. On the theory that the end justifies the means, brethren have not scrupled to form organizations in the church to do work the church itself was designed to do. All such organizations usurp the work of the church, and are unnecessary and sinful....

This writer has ever been unable to appreciate the logic of those who affect to see grave danger in Missionary Societies, but scruple not to form a similar organization for the purpose of caring for orphans and teaching young men to be gospel preachers. Of course it is right for the church to care for the 'fatherless and widows in their affliction,' but this work should be done by and through the church, with the elders having the oversight thereof, and not through boards and conclaves unknown to the New Testament. In this connection it is a pleasure to recommend to the brotherhood Tipton Orphans Home, Tipton, Oklahoma. The work there is entirely Scriptural, being managed and conducted by the elders of the church in Tipton, Okla., aided by funds sent to them by the elders of other congregations round about. We here and now declare our protest against any other method or arrangement for accomplishing this work."

Abilene Christian College Bible Lectures, 1939, pp. 53-54.

Wall Chart B

Guy N. Woods In 1946

"For it hath been the good pleasure of Macedonia and Achaia to make a certain contribution for the poor among the saints that are at Jerusalem.' (Rom. 15:26.) ... When these brethren heard of the distress that was occasioned in Judea because of a famine in those parts, they determined to send relief. There were many poor saints in Jerusalem at this time. The brethren there had undergone many persecutions and had likely been spoiled of their goods. The Gentile churches had profited by the fact that the Jews had brought the gospel to them, and they determined to repay in part this obligation by sending to their needs in a financial way. Paul explains it thus: 'It hath been their good pleasure; and their debtors they are. For if the Gentiles have been made partakers of their spiritual things, they owe it to them also to minister unto them in carnal things.' (Rom. 15:27.) Concerning this contribution, see 1 Cor. 16:1,2; 2 Cor. 8:1 and 9:2. For another such contribution for the poor in Jerusalem, see Acts 11:27-30. It should be noted that there was no elaborate organization for the discharge of these charitable functions. The contributions were sent directly to the elders by the churches who raised the offering. This is the New Testament method of functioning. We should be highly suspicious of any scheme that requires the setting up of an organization independent of the church in order to accomplish its work."

Annual Lesson Commentary, Gospel Advocate Co., 1946, page 340.

Chart Number 1

Commands—Generic or Specific?

Commands	Generic	Specific
Build Ark – Genesis 6:14	Wood	Gopher
Wash – 2 Kings 5	Water	In Jordan
Offer – Leviticus 14:12-13	Animal	Lamb
Go Wash – John. 9:7	Water	Siloam
Preach – 1 Timothy 3:15; 1 Thessalonians 1:7-8	Organizations	Church (Local Cong.)
Edify – Ephesians 4:12-16	Organizations	Church (Local Cong.)
Relieve – 1 Timothy 5:16; Acts 6:1-6	Organizations	Church (Local Cong.)

When God Specifies A Thing, Others Are Eliminated!

Chart Number 2

Aids and Additions		
Commands	**Aids**	**Additions**
Baptize – Mt. 28:19; Rom. 6:14	Baptistry, Heater, Clothes, etc.	Sprinkling (another **kind** of action)
Eat Bread – 1 Cor. 11:23-29	Servants, Plates, etc.	Beef (another **kind** of food)
Sing – Eph. 5:19; Col. 3:16	Books, Pitch Pipe, Lights, etc.	Mech. Instr. Music (another **kind** of music)
Church Preach Gospel – Eph. 3:10; 1 Tim. 3:14-15	Pulpit, Literature, Radio, etc.	Missionary Society (another **kind** of organization)
Church Edify Self – Eph. 4:16	Place, Facilities, Teachers, etc.	Sunday School Society (another **kind** of organization)
Church Relieve the Destitute – 1 Tim. 5:16; Acts 2:44-45; 4:32-37; Acts 6	Building, Facilities, Personnel, etc.	Benevolent Society (another **kind** of organization)

Chart Number 3

Is "The Tennessee Orphan Home" A Benevolent Society?

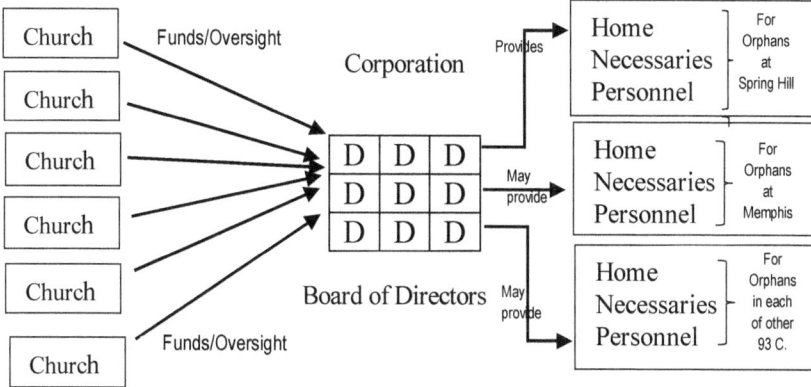

Church	Funds/Oversight →	Corporation	Provides →	Home Necessaries Personnel	For Orphans at Spring Hill

Church

Church

Church

Church

Church

Board of Directors

D D D
D D D
D D D

May provide → Home Necessaries Personnel — For Orphans at Memphis

May provide → Home Necessaries Personnel — For Orphans in each of other 93 C.

Funds/Oversight

Would This Be A Missionary Society?

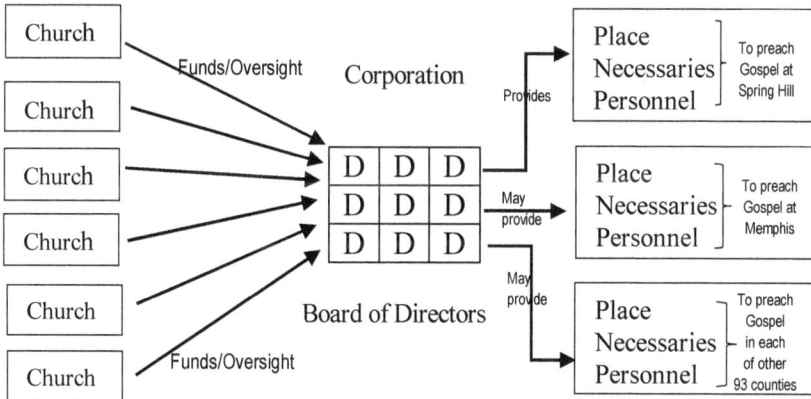

Church

Church

Church

Church

Church

Church

Funds/Oversight Corporation

D D D
D D D
D D D

Board of Directors

Funds/Oversight

Provides → Place Necessaries Personnel — To preach Gospel at Spring Hill

May provide → Place Necessaries Personnel — To preach Gospel at Memphis

May provide → Place Necessaries Personnel — To preach Gospel in each of other 93 counties

Question: If Churches Can Support One, Why Not the Other? Show Why!

Chart Number 4

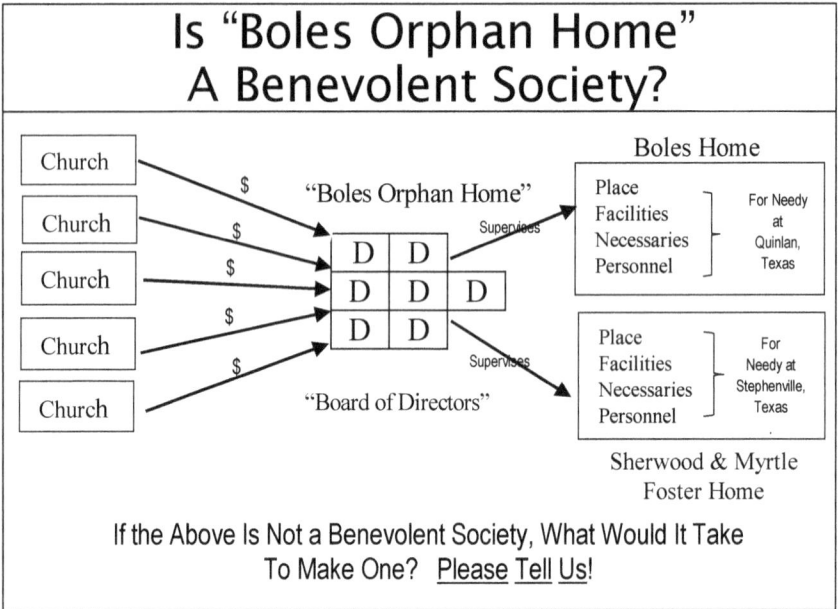

Is "Boles Orphan Home" A Benevolent Society?

Church

Church

Church

Church

Church

$

$

$

$

$

"Boles Orphan Home"

Supervises

D	D
D	D	D
D	D

"Board of Directors"

Supervises

Boles Home

Place
Facilities
Necessaries
Personnel

For Needy at Quinlan, Texas

Place
Facilities
Necessaries
Personnel

For Needy at Stephenville, Texas

Sherwood & Myrtle
Foster Home

If the Above Is Not a Benevolent Society, What Would It Take
To Make One? Please Tell Us!

240

Chart Number 5

God's Way Versus The Ways of Men

Which?

Elders

Local Cong.
(Divine)

Elders

Local Cong.
(Divine)

Elders

Local Cong.
(Sponsoring)

B
C

E
O

M
S

Preach
Gospel

Edify
Itself

Relieve
Afflicted

Preach
Gospel

Edify
Itself

Relieve
Afflicted

1 Tim. 3:15	Eph. 4:12-16	1 Tim. 5:16
1 Thess. 1:8	Acts 9:31	1 Cor. 16:1-6
		Acts 6:1-6

God's Wisdom
Divine — Sufficient!

Scripture Please For This Setup _____?

Man's Wisdom
Human — Not Needed!

241

Chart Number 7

Where Will Opponent Draw The Line?

1. Does "visit" the fatherless in Jas. 1:27 authorize churches to make contributions to benevolent institutions such as Childhaven?   Yes ☐   No ☐

2. Does "visit" the sick in Mt. 25:36 authorize churches to make contributions to Hospitals?   Yes ☐   No ☐

3. Does "feed" the hungry in Rom. 12:20 authorize churches to make contributions to Grocery companies?   Yes ☐   No ☐

4. Does "entertain" strangers in Heb. 13:2 authorize churches to make contributions to Hotels?   Yes ☐   No ☐

5. Does "clothe" the naked in Mt. 25:36 authorize churches to make contributions to Clothing companies?   Yes ☐   No ☐

If One Authorized, Why Not All?
Will My Opponent Tell Us? Wait and See!

Chart Number 8

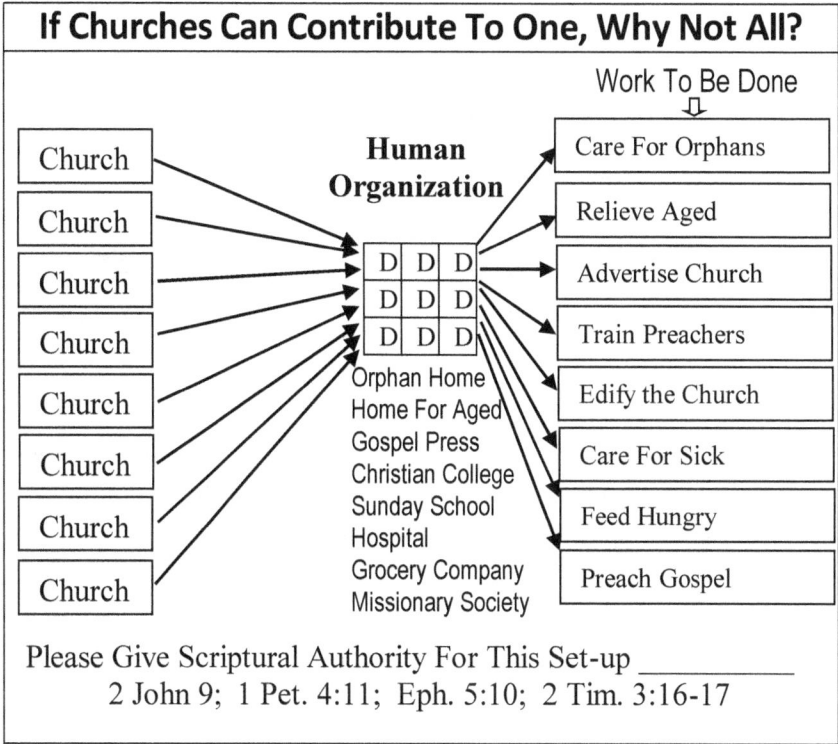

If Churches Can Contribute To One, Why Not All?

Work To Be Done
⇩

Church

Church

Church

Church

Church

Church

Church

Church

Human Organization

D	D	D
D	D	D
D	D	D

Orphan Home
Home For Aged
Gospel Press
Christian College
Sunday School
Hospital
Grocery Company
Missionary Society

Care For Orphans

Relieve Aged

Advertise Church

Train Preachers

Edify the Church

Care For Sick

Feed Hungry

Preach Gospel

Please Give Scriptural Authority For This Set-up _____
2 John 9; 1 Pet. 4:11; Eph. 5:10; 2 Tim. 3:16-17

Chart Number 9

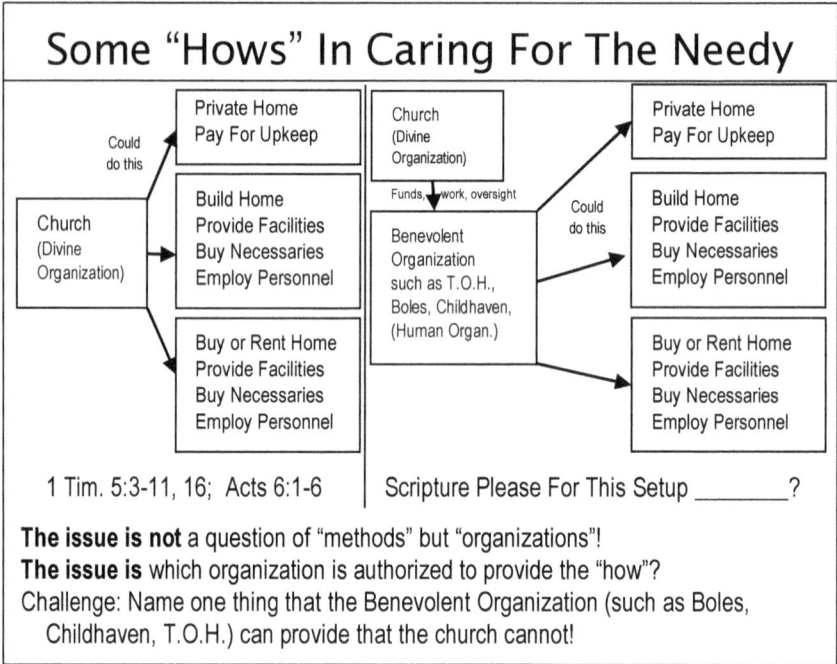

Some "Hows" In Caring For The Needy

Church (Divine Organization)	Could do this →	Private Home / Pay For Upkeep
		Build Home / Provide Facilities / Buy Necessaries / Employ Personnel
		Buy or Rent Home / Provide Facilities / Buy Necessaries / Employ Personnel

Church (Divine Organization)

Funds, work, oversight

Benevolent Organization such as T.O.H., Boles, Childhaven, (Human Organ.)

Could do this →

Private Home / Pay For Upkeep

Build Home / Provide Facilities / Buy Necessaries / Employ Personnel

Buy or Rent Home / Provide Facilities / Buy Necessaries / Employ Personnel

1 Tim. 5:3-11, 16; Acts 6:1-6 | Scripture Please For This Setup _____?

The issue is not a question of "methods" but "organizations"!

The issue is which organization is authorized to provide the "how"?

Challenge: Name one thing that the Benevolent Organization (such as Boles, Childhaven, T.O.H.) can provide that the church cannot!

Chart Number 10

What About Preacher's Home & Church Building?

Some say: "The same argument that justifies the preacher's home justifies the home for the aged. The same argument that justifies the church building ... justifies an orphan home." —Guy N. Woods (*Porter-Woods Debate*, p. 215).

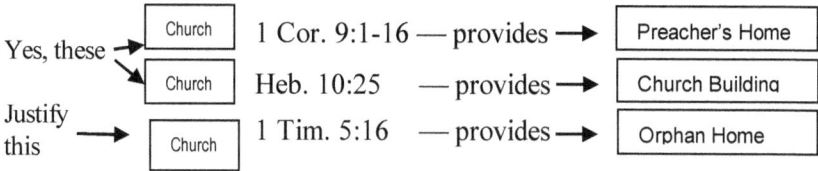

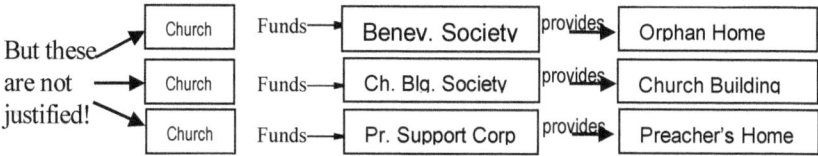

Yes, these → | Church | 1 Cor. 9:1-16 — provides → | Preacher's Home |

| Church | Heb. 10:25 — provides → | Church Building |

Justify this → | Church | 1 Tim. 5:16 — provides → | Orphan Home |

But these, are not → justified!

| Church | Funds → | Benev. Society | provides → | Orphan Home |

| Church | Funds → | Ch. Blg. Society | provides → | Church Building |

| Church | Funds → | Pr. Support Corp | provides → | Preacher's Home |

Chart Number 11

Missionary & Benevolent Societies Parallel!

1. **Both** originated in the mind of man.
2. **Both** are human organizations.
3. **Both** are designed to do the work of the church.
4. **Both** perform a work of the church.
5. **Both** have a Board of Directors.
6. **Both** have own constitution, by-laws, etc.
7. **Both** solicit contributions from churches.
8. **Both** accept contributions from churches.
9. **Both** are human organizations to activate universal church.
10. **Both** have to employ means and methods.
11. **Both** are operated by those who claim to be Christians.
12. **Both** are "justified" by some as "an expedient."
13. **Both** are doing a "good work."
14. **Both** cause division in the church.
15. **Neither** exist by <u>divine</u> <u>authority</u> to do work of church!

How Can We Reject One and Accept The Other?

Chart Number 13

Bro. Woods Has Held These Positions!

Which Is Right?

Under the oversight of elders ...
Church only charitable organization ...
Any other method sinful!
---- 1939-1946

Orphanages & homes for aged were "simply means by way of which the church accomplishes its work." ...
Early church operated a home for destitute widows.
---- 1954-1956

Orphanages & homes for aged must be apart from the church.
---- 1957-1962

Bro. Woods STILL Holds These Positions, He Says!

247

Chart Number 15

BRO. WOODS SAYS: "NO AUTHORITY"!

"And besides that, there isn't any authority in the Scriptures for the church to serve, or even Christians by support of the church, to serve as an adoption agency. No authority." -- Huntsville Alabama, 9/28/58 (2nd session, 2nd speech)

The following institutions serve as adoption agencies:
1. The Tennessee Orphan Home, Spring Hill, Tennessee
2. Potter Orphan Home & School, Bowling Green, Kentucky
3. Turley Children's Home, Tulsa, Oklahoma
4. Christ's Haven For Children, Keller, Texas
5. The Children's Home, Lubbock, Texas

According to Bro. Woods, churches have no scriptural authority to support the above institutions! Yet he is defending them!

Will He Be Honest Enough To Stop Defending That Which He Says Is Not Authorized?

Additional Notes:
1. Tenn. O. Home – (*Gospel Advocate*, 1/4/62, back page) Also Annual Financial Report of T.O.H.
2. Potter O. Home & School – (*Gospel Advocate*, 7/14/55) Also *Potter Messenger*, Oct. 1961.
3. Turley Children's Home – ("The Why, What, Where, & How – Children's Homes," p. 6, by Lloyd Connel, Supt.) – Also letter to me from Lloyd Connel, 9/19/61.
4. Christ's Haven for Children – *Christ's Haven Messenger*, March 1961.
5. The Children's Home – (*The Children's Home Bulletin*, April 1961.)

248

Chart Number 20

PLEASE CONSIDER THESE PASSAGES VERY CAREFULLY!

1. Acts 2:44-45 "... Parted them ... as every man had need."
2. Acts 4:34-35 "... Distribution was made ... according as he had need."
3. Acts 6:1-6 "... Daily ministration ... serve tables ... look ye out among you."
4. Acts 11:27-30 "... Send relief unto the brethren ... sent it to the elders...."
5. Rom. 15:25-26 "... To make a certain contribution for the poor saints ...."
6. 1 Cor. 16:1-4 "... The collection for the saints...."
7. 2 Cor. 8 & 9 "... The ministering to the saints...."
8. 1 Tim. 5:16 "... That it may relieve them that are widows indeed."

NOTE: There Is Not the Slightest Hint of a Benevolent Organization Thru Which the Church Functioned in Any of These or Other Passages!
QUESTION: Are the Scriptures Sufficient To Guide Us?

Chart Number 21

What Does Opponent Mean By "Home"?

Definition No. 1	Definition No. 2	Definition No. 3
"House" (Dwelling Place)	"Family Relationship" (Unit of Society Formed By Family living together)	"Organization" (Benevolent Institution such as T.O.H., Childhaven, etc.)

I Am Asking My Opponent to Tell Me What He Means When He Says "Home"! Will He Do It?

Chart Number 22

The State of Alabama Recognizes Childhaven As A Benevolent Society!

Proof: *Title 10, Chapter 7, Article 3, Section 124* of the 1940 Code of Alabama, under which Childhaven Is Incorporated, Provides For the Incorporation of <u>Churches</u>, <u>Educational</u> or <u>Benevolent</u> <u>Societies</u>.

Note: Since Childhaven is not a Church or an Educational Society, It Must Be A <u>Benevolent</u> <u>Society</u>!

Yes, My Opponent Is Defending A Benevolent Society!

Chart Number 23

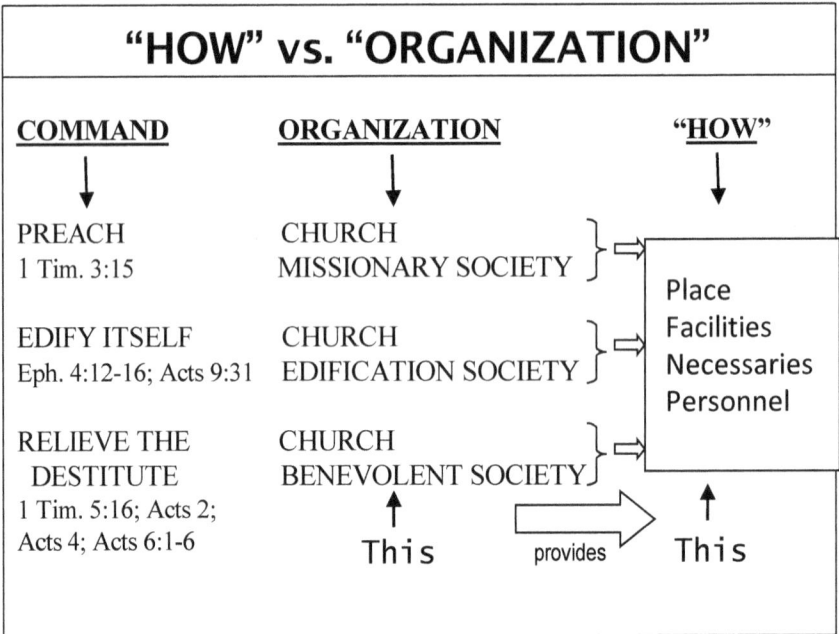

"HOW" vs. "ORGANIZATION"

COMMAND	ORGANIZATION	"HOW"
↓	↓	↓

PREACH   CHURCH
1 Tim. 3:15   MISSIONARY SOCIETY }⇒

EDIFY ITSELF   CHURCH
Eph. 4:12-16; Acts 9:31 EDIFICATION SOCIETY }⇒

RELIEVE THE   CHURCH
 DESTITUTE   BENEVOLENT SOCIETY }⇒
1 Tim. 5:16; Acts 2;
Acts 4; Acts 6:1-6

Place
Facilities
Necessaries
Personnel

This → provides → This

Chart Number 24

Which Institution?

CHURCH (Divine)	Board of Directors (Human)
1 Timothy 5:16	? ? ?
↓	↓
Care For Needy	Care For Needy
↓	↓

HOW?

1. Place (buy, build, rent, private home)

2. Necessaries (food, clothing, etc.)

3. Supervision, etc.

HOW?

1. Place (buy, build, rent, private home)

2. Necessaries (food, clothing, etc.)

3. Supervision, etc.

Chart Number 25

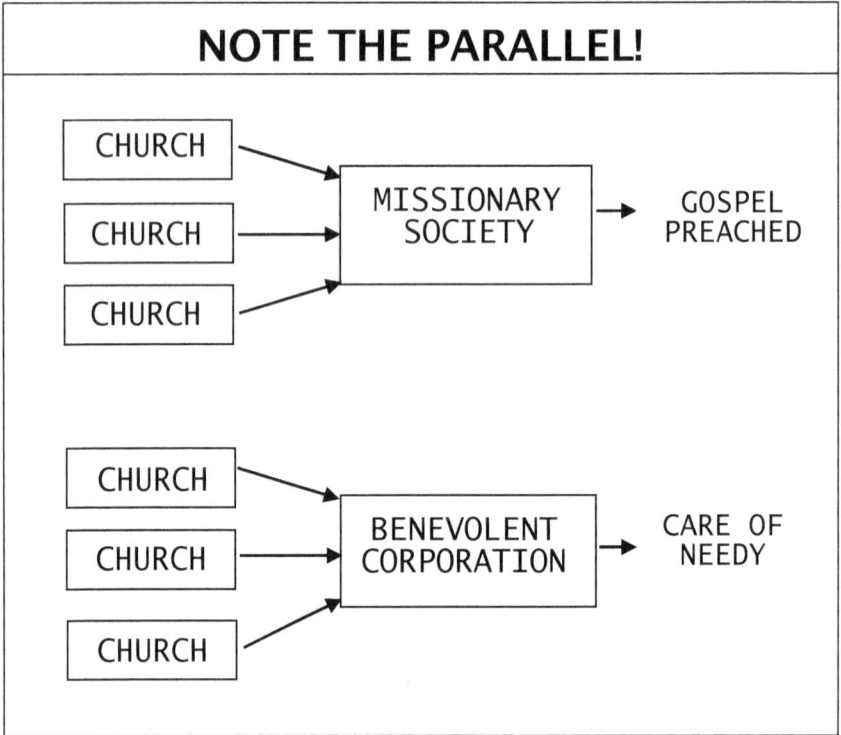

NOTE THE PARALLEL!

CHURCH →
CHURCH →   MISSIONARY SOCIETY → GOSPEL PREACHED
CHURCH →

CHURCH →
CHURCH →   BENEVOLENT CORPORATION → CARE OF NEEDY
CHURCH →

Chart Number 26

YES, THE CHURCH CAN "RELIEVE"!

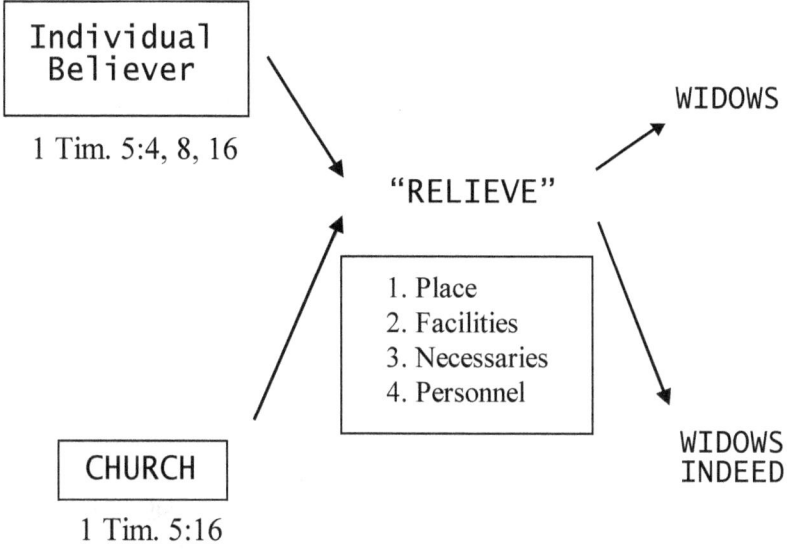

Individual Believer

1 Tim. 5:4, 8, 16

"RELIEVE"

WIDOWS

1. Place
2. Facilities
3. Necessaries
4. Personnel

CHURCH

1 Tim. 5:16

WIDOWS INDEED

Chart Number 28

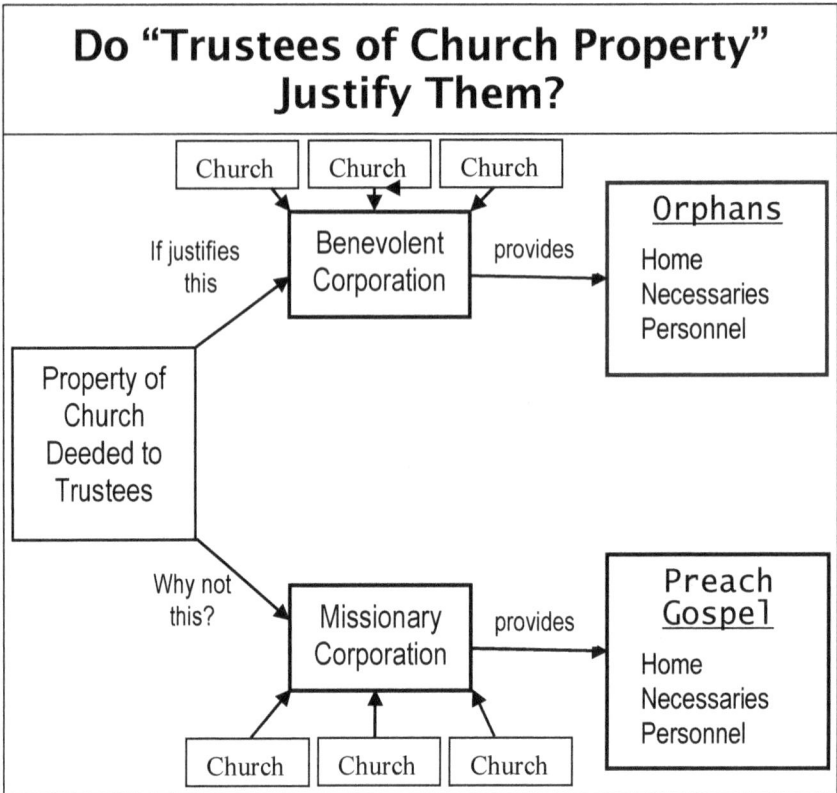

Do "Trustees of Church Property" Justify Them?

Church   Church   Church

If justifies this →

Benevolent Corporation

provides →

Orphans
Home
Necessaries
Personnel

Property of Church Deeded to Trustees

Why not this? →

Missionary Corporation

provides →

Preach Gospel
Home
Necessaries
Personnel

Church   Church   Church

Chart Number 30

Consider the Word "Visit" In James 1:27

Does It Authorize Churches To Build & Support <u>Benevolent</u> <u>Societies</u> As Childhaven, T.O.H., etc.?

If So:

The word "visited" in Matt. 25:43, 36 authorizes churches to build & support "Sick & Prison Visiting Societies" such as hospitals, etc. IF NOT, WHY NOT?

Same Word In Both Passages!

How Can We Reject One And Accept the Other?

Chart Number 31

No, the "How" Isn't, But the "Who" Is!

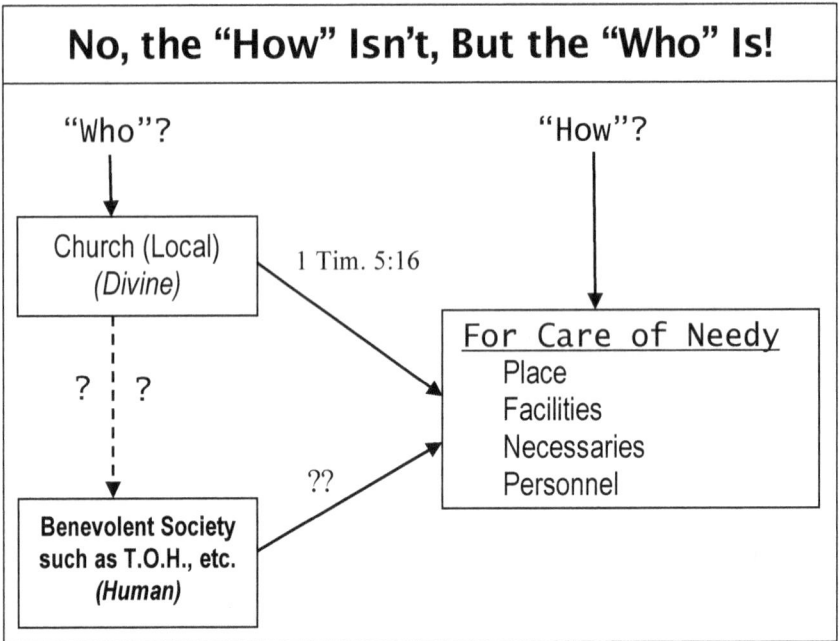

"Who"?

"How"?

Church (Local)
(Divine)

1 Tim. 5:16

? ┊ ?

??

Benevolent Society
such as T.O.H., etc.
(Human)

For Care of Needy
Place
Facilities
Necessaries
Personnel

Chart Number 32

Authority For Buildings And Organizations

Divine Authority For These:	Human Authority For These:
1. Preach (Eph. 3:10) - Place to preach	1. Missionary Society
2. Baptize (Mt. 28:19) - Place to baptize	2. Baptismal Association
3. Teach (Mt. 28:20) - Place to teach	3. Sunday School Organization
4. Assemble (Heb. 10:25) - Place to assemble	4. Church Building Society
5. Support Preacher (1 Cor. 9:1-16) - Place to live	5. Preacher Supporting Corp.
6. Relieve (1 Tim. 5:16) – Place for needy	6. Benevolent Corporation

God authorizes the use of anything that is **necessary** in order to carry out His commands or that aids in so doing as long as some scriptural principle is not violated.

QUESTION: Are human organizations NECESSARY? They violate the principle of the "all-sufficiency of the church."

Chart Number 36

Notice the Simplicity Involved!

I. God has commanded the church to relieve widows indeed.
   1 Tim. 5:16
II. Elders oversee the work of the church.
   Acts 14:23; 20:28; 1 Pet. 5:2
III. *Therefore: The church is to relieve widows indeed under the oversight of elders!*

But Consider This:

Some say that the church is obligated to care for the needy (W. & O.), but that it cannot do so under its elders. *Therefore, some do not believe that elders oversee the work of the church!*

Will You Accept God Or Man?

Chart Number 37

What I Believe	What I Do Not Believe
1. I believe that needy people should be cared for (Eph. 4:28; Jas. 2:14-17; Rom. 12:13) 2. I believe that individuals have an obligation to the needy (Jas. 1:27; 1 Jno. 3:17; Lk. 10) 3. I believe that churches have an obligation to the needy (1 Tim. 5:16; Acts 6:1-6; 1 Cor. 16:1-4) 4. Individuals and churches should do so!	1. I do not believe that churches are scripturally authorized to build & maintain benevolent organizations such as T.O.H., Childhaven, Boles O.H., Schults-Lewis Children's H. & S. for the care of the needy. 2. Nor that individuals may contribute to such as "church institutions."

Question: Is It Possible For Anyone Here to Think that I Do Not Believe In Caring For the Needy? Is It?

Chart Number 39

WHAT'S WRONG WITH THE MISSIONARY SOCIETY?

1. A human organization that rivals the church (Eph. 4:4; 1 Tim. 3:15)
2. Operates by human authority—charter, by-laws (Mt. 15:9; Col. 3:17
3. Has boards and officers that are unknown to the New Testament (1 Cor. 4:6; 1 Pet. 4:11; Eph. 5:10)
4. Has oversight of a portion of the Lord's treasury (1 Cor. 16:1-2)
5. Exercises authority belonging to many elderships (Acts 20:28; 1 Pet. 5:1-3)
6. A centralized agency for universal church action (Acts 14:23; Phil. 1:1; 1 Pet. 5:1-3; 1 Thess. 1:7-8; Phil. 4:15-16; 2 Cor. 11:7-8)
7. Denies the all-sufficiency of the church (Acts 14:23; Phil. 1:1; Eph. 3:10; 1 Tim. 3:15; 2 Tim. 3:16-17; 2 Pet. 1:3)
8. Reflects on the wisdom and power of God (Eph. 3:10; 1 Cor. 1)
9. It becomes a "machine" over the churches!

Chart Number 40

SHOULD WE DO EVIL THAT GOOD MAY COME? (Romans 3:8)

1. Should we <u>kill</u> our enemies that we may <u>live</u> in peace?
2. Should we <u>buy liquor</u> that schools may <u>have revenue</u>?
3. Should we <u>steal</u> that we may <u>clothe the naked</u>?
4. Should we <u>lie</u> that we may <u>profit financially</u>?
5. Should we <u>rob</u> the rich that we may <u>feed the poor</u>?
6. Should we <u>support women preachers</u> that the <u>gospel may be preached</u>?
7. Should we support missionary societies that the <u>gospel may be preached</u>?
8. Should we <u>support unscriptural church cooperation</u> such as in "Herald of Truth" that the <u>gospel may be preached</u>?
9. Should we <u>support denominational orphanages</u> that <u>orphans may be cared for</u>?
10. Should we <u>support benevolent societies</u> such as "the orphan home" that <u>orphans may be cared for</u>?

WE MUST OBEY GOD REGARDLESS OF THE CONSEQUENCES! (Gal. 1:8-9; 1:10; Lk. 6:46; Mt. 7:21; 7:28; 28:18; Rev. 22:14; Acts 5:29; 2 Tim. 3:16-17)

IS CHILDHAVEN (or T.O.H., etc.) A "CHURCH of CHRIST ORPHANAGE"?

IF SO:

1. Is it because one or more churches built it?
   Yes ☐   No ☐
2. Is it because one or more churches hold title to its property?
   Yes ☐   No ☐
3. Is it because one or more churches have control over it, operate it, and direct its affairs?
   Yes ☐   No ☐
4. Is it because it is doing a "good work"?
   Yes ☐   No ☐
5. Is it because its "Board of Directors" are members of the church?
   Yes ☐   No ☐
6. Is it because churches contribute to it?
   Yes ☐   No ☐

Apply the last three questions (if answered "yes") to Schools, Hospitals, Drug Companies, Grocery Companies, Missionary Societies, etc.

Chart Number 43

HOW TO ESTABLISH SCRIPTURAL AUTHORITY

I. PRECEPT (Command or Statement).   *ILLUSTRATED*
II. APPROVED EXAMPLE.   *IN THE*
III. NECESSARY IMPLICATION (Inference). *LORD'S SUPPER*

I. Its <u>Observance</u> (Precept): "... This do in remembrance of me."
  (1 Cor. 11:24).

II. <u>Time</u> <u>of Observance</u> (Approved Example): "And upon the first day
  of the week, when the disciples came together to break bread..."
  (Acts 20:7) — only way to establish time of observance.

III. <u>Frequency</u> <u>of Observance</u> (Necessary Implication): "And upon the
  first day of the week, when the disciples came together to break
  bread..." (Acts 20:7) — We necessarily infer its observance as
  regularly as "the first day of the week" comes.
  Compare: "Remember the Sabbath day..." (Exo. 20:8) — Only
  way to establish frequency of observance.